W9-BOA-919

SACRED MATTERS

ALSO BY GARY LADERMAN

*The Sacred Remains: American Attitudes Toward Death,
1799–1883*

*Rest in Peace: A Cultural History of Death and the
Funeral Home in Twentieth-Century America*

SACRED MATTERS

Celebrity Worship, Sexual Ecstasies, the Living Dead, and Other Signs of Religious Life in the United States

Gary Laderman

THE NEW PRESS

NEW YORK
LONDON

© 2009 by Gary Laderman
All rights reserved.
No part of this book may be reproduced, in any form, without written permission from
the publisher.

Requests for permission to reproduce selections from this book should be mailed to:
Permissions Department, The New Press, 38 Greene Street, New York, NY 10013.

Published in the United States by The New Press, New York, 2009
Distributed by Perseus Distribution

LIBRARY OF CONGRESS CATALOGING-IN-PUBLICATION DATA

Laderman, Gary, 1962–
    Sacred matters : celebrity worship, sexual ecstasies, the living dead, and other signs of re-
ligious life in the United States / Gary Laderman.
        p. cm.
    Includes bibliographical references (p.) and index.
    ISBN 978-1-59558-437-3 (hc.)
    1. United States—Religious life and customs.   2. Religion and culture—United
States.   3. Implicit religion—United States.   I. Title.
    BL2525.L34 2009
    200.973—dc22   2008053215

The New Press was established in 1990 as a not-for-profit alternative to the large,
commercial publishing houses currently dominating the book publishing industry.
The New Press operates in the public interest rather than for private gain, and is
committed to publishing, in innovative ways, works of educational, cultural, and
community value that are often deemed insufficiently profitable.

www.thenewpress.com

Composition by dix!
This book was set in Bembo

Printed in the United States of America

10   9   8   7   6   5   4   3   2   1

To all the teachers and students
I have met along the way.

CONTENTS

Acknowledgments   ix

Introduction   xiii

1. Film   1

2. Music   23

3. Sports   43

4. Celebrity   63

5. Science   85

6. Medicine   103

7. Violence   123

8. Sexuality   141

9. Death   161

Notes   181

Index   197

ACKNOWLEDGMENTS

This book came to life on November 2, 2004, the day after George W. Bush won the presidential election, and in the post-victory media cacophony about the role of religion and values in American politics. My own despair in the wake of that victory was only compounded by the incessant public clamoring about the power and influence of evangelical Protestants and conservative Catholics in the election. The media's narrow preoccupation with these faith communities and the ridiculous polls identifying faith-based political attitudes was particularly infuriating to me, as they glossed over a deeper, more nuanced, and fascinating religious complexity by framing the discussion about religion in simplistic, dualistic, naïve terms like conservative versus liberal, or believer versus nonbeliever, or red state versus blue state.

From the moment of its conception to the moment of its completion, this book, I have come to realize, may be tied to this particular historical moment, but it is not defined by it. The more I think about the content of the book, the more I see it as a natural, organic outgrowth of my professional life teaching students, collaborating with others, editing encyclopedias, writing books about death, and reflecting on religion and culture in American life. So in a very real sense this book is my attempt to express an alternative vision of religious life in America and challenge commonly held presuppositions and paradigms—goals that I have brought to my research projects and classroom strategies over the course of roughly fifteen years in the field.

While I take full responsibility for the content of this book, I also must identify friends and colleagues who have had a hand in its generation and execution, either directly or indirectly. First, I came to understand after writing the first draft that Catherine Albanese's brilliant book *Nature Religion in America: From the Algonkian Indians to the New Age* (University of Chicago Press, 1990) serves as a critical model for *Sacred Matters*. Her full-length monograph explores Nature as a deep-rooted, central source of sacred life outside of conventional religious settings in American history. My book looks at nine different themes that, like Nature in her work, anchor the sacred in American culture. Cathy was my dissertation advisor, along with Richard Hecht, in religious studies at the University of California, Santa Barbara, and though life as a graduate student there is a dim, distant memory, I continue to be grateful to all my teachers from those years and see how their creativity, intelligence, and generosity made a strong, long-lasting impression on me.

Next, close friend Jill Robbins, professor of comparative literature and religion here at Emory University, got the book rolling by encouraging me to "let the dog run" after I began to toy with the idea of writing in the wake of the election debacle. Our frequent coffee breaks were a refreshing pause from hectic Emory days, and whether we were discussing Durkheim and Hertz on the sacred, or reminiscing about Dead shows or old Woody Guthrie songs, those Starbucks conversations helped stir the pot and got me motivated to write.

Other good friends around Emory—including Arri Eisen in biology and the Institute of Liberal Arts; Paul Courtright and Bobbi Patterson in religion; Jeffrey Lesser in Jewish studies, history, and Latin American studies; and Howard Kushner, who is hard to pin down in any one field—all provided a great deal of intellectual stimulation, comic relief, and valued friendship, so contributed not so directly but in less material ways to this book. A couple of other Atlanta-based comrades, Louis Ruprecht from Georgia State University and Jack Fitzmier from the American Academy of Religion, are also worth acknowledging as culprits in this endeavor.

Beyond Emory, my professional life over the last few years has been entangled with a new online web magazine, Religion Dispatches.org, and my excellent friends and conspirators in this project have known about and are, therefore, by osmosis involved with the book. Editorial partners Evan Derkacz and Lisa Webster in San Francisco and Linell Cady in religious studies at Arizona State University are wonderful, creative, stimulating colleagues who make me want to quit my day job. The creative force behind ReligionDispatches was Sheila Davaney, professor at Iliff School of Theology and currently at the Ford Foundation, and working with her on this project, as well as other collaborative ventures, has undoubtedly made a difference in much of my professional life over the last decade. I have always valued her intellect, critical edge, and scholarly commitments but now value her most for her friendship.

More materially and concretely, this book would not be seeing the light of day without Marc Favreau, editor at The New Press and now a personal savior of mine. His interest and editorial input was in many ways quite literally liberating, and the depth of my gratitude for Marc and others at The New Press with a hand in this book cannot fully be captured in words. Perhaps if I pump my fist in the air a few times and jump up and down you will understand my appreciation. I would also like to express my deepest gratitude to the Centre for Studies in Religion and Society, University of Victoria, where I was a visiting fellow in fall 2006. The Centre and the setting were ideal for me to put the final finishing touches on the first draft of this book.

On the home front, Liz read through chapters and always offered encouragement and support. The boys, Graham and Miles, did not read through this manuscript and will not be allowed to read the book until they are at least eighteen years old. But they are the best and bring unbelievable amounts of joy to my life, which contributes to everything I do. Finally, at home and in the office, music makes my world go round, and the musical output of Jeff Tweedy of Wilco, Uncle Tupelo, Golden Smog, and Loose Fur dominated the playlist while I was "working" on the book.

INTRODUCTION

No doubt the United States is a deeply religious country, with vast numbers who believe in God and the afterlife, pray to God, and engage in other forms of divine worship at home and at church, synagogue, and mosque. Signs of monotheism of one sort or the other dominate the public square and are constantly in the media—the death and funeral for Pope John Paul II, for example, the evangelical presence in the 2004 presidential election, or the post–9/11 surge in attention to Islam. Surveys and polls consistently show Americans outpacing most other developed nations in rates of belief in God—according to some estimates, close to 90 percent of the population. Religion also permeates the rhetoric of our politicians, whose references to God are as normal as proclaiming love of country, support for the military, or security for the nation's children. But there is more to religion than what first meets the monotheistic eye.

Sacred Matters proposes that there is more to religious life in America than belief in God, many more holy possibilities than what is offered in the so-called "Great Religions of the Book"— Judaism, Christianity, and Islam—or from other sacred texts with religious authority like the Upanishads in Hinduism or the Tibetan Book of the Dead in Buddhism. Religion is instead a ubiquitous feature of cultural life, assuming many expressions though tied to and inspired by basic, universal facts of life and fundamentally biological phenomena in human experience: suffering and ecstasy, reproduction and aging, family and conflict, health and death.

Religious thoughts, actions, behaviors, impulses, sensibilities, and communities are not all necessarily about God, or about being a good Jew, Catholic, Muslim, or Hindu. They are instead grounded by perceptions and experiences of the sacred, a word like religion without a fixed universal meaning or reference that everyone will agree on, but nonetheless a word signifying religious cultures or communities tied together emotionally and cognitively, but also spiritually and materially by vital rituals, living myths, indescribable experiences, moral values, shared memories, and other commonly recognized features of religious life.[1]

Even though perceptions about the essence of the sacred are not consistent across cultures and do not harmoniously converge within them, signs of religious life associated with these perceptions often revolve around a constellation of questions that resonate throughout human history and around the globe: What gives life meaning to individuals? Why is there life, as well as death and suffering? How do we live the good life, find happiness, purpose, and fulfillment? Where can we locate truth, or some kind of ultimate source of values and morality that is worth our spiritual and material investments? Who deserves our friendship and support and who is the enemy that must be destroyed? The answers to these questions, and therefore the shape and content of the sacred, are derived from physical acts and social engagements embedded in everyday life as much as formal religious teaching handed down from authorities in an institutional setting.

The sacred participates in common forms of expression and shared social experiences tied to myths and symbols, rituals and ceremonies, power and order. What is considered sacred becomes a vital source of empowerment and ultimate investments, and is connected to human inspirations and desires, meaningful actions and attitudes, and social identities and community affiliations. The sacred explains what cannot be explained, it accounts for the incomprehensible, and it communicates the inexpressible. Communities have a lot invested in the sacred—everything is at stake, so individuals will give their lives to preserve and protect it, or in other instances, to profane and plunder what is most sacred to the outsider. In various cultures, the religious life may be anchored in totems or natural phenomena, in shamanic experiences or astrological signs, in oracles or amulets. In contemporary American society, religious life without God and beyond the reach of religious traditions is anchored in a range of social phenomena that provide people with order, meaning, and purpose—critical ingredients that mix together in the pursuit and experience of the sacred.

Today, religious practices and commitments emanate from unlikely sources: science and the pursuit of truth; music and the social effervescence at concerts; violence and the glorification of warfare; celebrity worship and technological wonders; heroic doctors and evil villains; funeral spectacles and sexual compulsions; the Super Bowl and sacrificed soldiers; Elvis and drugs, both legal and illegal. These and other areas of fascination and fixation, often intermingled with fear and trembling, awe and faith, speak to the breadth and depth of religious cultures in America. But unhinged from religious traditions generally and monotheistic traditions especially, spiritual anchors so profoundly important in the lives of Americans—anchors that ground ultimate concerns, establish moral communities, transform personal identities, and make lives meaningful—are left unspoken, or worse, evaluated as false religion, or still worse, as signs of the apocalypse.

So *Sacred Matters* is about robust, thriving forms of religious life, experience, and community that are less about theology and more about anthropology; less focused on the narrow category of monotheism, emphasizing God or one divine reality, and more focused on the sacred as the defining mark of gods and religious life generally, but also as a fundamental and fundamentally human characteristic of social life; less constrained by religious traditions as the only source of access to the sacred and more attentive to the flexibility, fluidity and, indeed, the true messiness of religious life.

And religious life is often very, very messy. Today more than ever we have become aware of an important fact: religion can no longer be understood as a separate sphere of social life, neatly compartmentalized and privatized, set apart from economics, entertainment, education, or politics. Religious sensibilities seep deeply into and permeate everything about who we are and how we live, driving personal, community, and national attempts to create order out of disorder, meaning in the face of suffering, and hope when all seems lost. The sacred, in other words, is a force to be reckoned with in almost any social situation, even though it cannot be reduced to one essence, like God, or identified by one standard of measurement, like adherence to the Bible.

The sacred is a robust, dynamic, shape-shifting force that now more than ever is free-floating and disconnected from conventional anchors, such as specific texts like the Koran or particular institutions like the church, cut loose in the cultural sea of rock stars and casinos, virtual memorials and Viagra. It can be confusing as well, because individuals can exhibit, indeed embody, contradictory forms of sacred life: the prominent evangelical risking it all for secret, consecrated encounters with hookers; the liberal Jew openly devoted to the *Star Wars* saga; the Hindu doctor who performs miracles with modern healing technologies. Simplistic and clean divisions separating sacred and secular no longer hold up in this complex cultural arena of interpenetrations and cross-fertilizations.

Put another way, ostensibly secular aspects of social life, like sports, music, science, violence, or sexuality, can have meaningful religious dimensions in practice and experience that have nothing to do with God or religious traditions. Additionally, religious encounters and exchanges often, but not always, draw from and are informed by concepts and rituals from religious traditions. For example, devoted fans who make a pilgrimage to Graceland because of their love for Elvis are enacting a well-known ritual pattern toward saints in the history of Christianity. Likewise, modern-day physicists wanting to understand and explain subatomic mysteries that elude standard forms of measurement look to Eastern mysticism.

If you take God and religious traditions out of the picture, what is left of religious life?

- Multiple forms of cultural activity that do not simply appear to be *like* religion, but are in fact dynamic expressions of genuine religious sensibilities and sentiments underlining many of our everyday, seemingly mundane experiences as well as those extraordinary experiences that defy explanation;
- Wide-ranging rituals and myths that are not quite functional equivalents to similar behaviors and stories in "real" religions, but instead provide profound yet practical fulfillment and order in an often chaotic, confusing, unfulfilling world;
- Communities bound together not by institutional ties and affiliation with conventional sites of worship, but by more diffuse sacred bonds that shape identity, provide orientation in a larger cosmic frame, and infuse moral sentiments and sensibilities in a larger group;
- Rich sources for inspiring the religious imagination, anchored by the shifting though ever-present encounters with the sacred in body and soul, or whatever word is used to account for more than the body.

This book takes a fairly radical position in the current politicized climate surrounding the role of religion in society: God does not have to be a factor in the religious lives of many Americans. From this starting point, *Sacred Matters* traverses social terrain that is not spiritually desolate but instead abundantly religious and blooming with sacred icons, popular devotions, deep-rooted mythologies, and other sure signs of spiritual vivacity. It argues that people can inhabit multiple religious cultures at one time, and be in contact and interact meaningfully with diverse sacred anchors in their lives. These multiple sacred worlds can be in harmony, or in conflict; they may be contradictory or supplementary, but they all point to powerful forces in social life that provide real-life sources for meaning, order, and transformation in daily life. Channels of communication and expression in this environment are virtually limitless, with virtual reality, popular culture, and the streets in towns and cities throughout the nation providing the playing field—a field leveled by a slew of historical forces tied to the guarantee of religious freedom and democratization as well as technological innovations in printing, photography, film, television, and most recently computers—on which religious dreams and desires, reflections and meaningful practices, infuse life with values to live by.

Much public attention about signs of religious life in America is directed to God, front and center throughout, and increasingly to the realities of religious diversity. But this narrow theological and tradition-based view leaves buried and undetected a variety of alternative but just as powerful sacred sources and forces that play a crucial role in American religious life. *Sacred Matters* excavates this spiritual ground and brings some of these forces and sources to the light of public consciousness. Its overriding premise is that Americans are even more, not less, religious than they think, and materials from a wide-ranging historical and cultural survey of the twentieth century and early years of the twenty-first century will prove that God and religious traditions are not necessary to see the truth of this premise.

1

FILM

The history of film is a religious history.

In the beginning, or close enough to it, Hannibal W. Goodwin, a clergyman at the House of Prayer Episcopal Church in Newark, New Jersey, experimented with a chemical mixture of gun cotton and gum camphor to create celluloid photographic roll film. He filed a patent in 1887 for the revolutionary transparent, flexible film that could roll instead of remaining flat, only to become embroiled in a series of legal battles over the process with George Eastman, who was just introducing the Kodak camera, a "roll holder breast camera," to the world. Unfortunately, the Reverend Goodwin did not live to see his ultimate legal vindication when the courts ruled that Eastman had infringed on Goodwin's patent. He died in a traffic accident on December 31, 1900, before he was able to start his own company manufacturing supple, transportable film. Goodwin's primary motivation in this endeavor was to create a medium that could make the Bible more accessible to children.[1] He had no idea that the new medium he helped develop would acquire its own sacred powers.

The movies contribute to a culture in which the Bible is no longer the sole foundation on which to build religious truth and spiritual order. In the past and in the present, this sacred text dominates the religious worlds of many Americans, who access their God through the words and stories in the text, and the rituals and experiences associated with its reading. But since the very beginnings of United States history, competing cultural forces have appealed to Americans' religious sensibilities, drawing them away from biblical authority and toward alternative sources for sacred authority and meaning in their lives. Despite the desperate efforts by many Christians to place the Bible, and by proxy, God, at the center of national life, America is now more than ever a country without a sacred center.

There's no question that monotheistic sacred texts enliven, enlighten, and encapsulate religious life for many Americans. The words and stories in the Hebrew Bible, New Testament, and Koran—when heard or read, imagined or memorized—spark peculiar attachments and commitments that transform lifestyles and personal identity, ground perceptions of order and meaning in the universe, and embody social values that are understood to emanate from the text and give life direction and purpose. Religious life with these texts inspires but also requires Americans to take something away from them and, most significantly, to give something up and over to them—transactions that have real-world social implications. The "something" in both transactions varies radically—on the one hand, multiple, often contentious interpretations taken from the sacred texts in Judaism, Christianity, and Islam shape very different communities in each; on the other, investments by community members in the sacred texts are not limited to tithes and donations, but range far and wide, encompassing such diverse activities as putting time and effort into ritual life with the text, ensuring the safety and protection of the inviolable text, and living a life that can be easily measured and sanctioned by the precepts in the text.

In the past, the rituals associated with these sacred texts were generally restricted to institutional spaces like churches or synagogues, domestic spaces like bedrooms or parlors, or certain public spaces like revival tents and camp meetings. The individual engagement with and experience of the Word of God, particularly with respect to the Old and New Testaments in the dominant Protestant culture, significantly shaped the religious landscape in the United States from the Puritans of the eighteenth century to the Pentecostals in the twenty-first. But despite the centrality of all of these texts and the monotheistic God that is behind, within, and above them, religious Americans have also increasingly drawn from other culturally rich resources to imagine and engage with the sacred in their lives.

From the early years of the twentieth century, social transformations in America tied to industrialization and urban growth, immigration and social diversity, corporatization and consumer markets, and other familiar modernizing forces and trends at work led to seismic shifts in the religious terrain to be discovered and staked out in American culture, popular or elite, high and low. Protestants, Catholics, and Jews underwent their own radical transformations in the early decades of the century, with European immigration having an impact on the composition and community structures of Catholics and Jews, and political and theological differences reconfiguring the community boundaries for Protestants.[2] In the tumult of these times, with wars small and large raging over the years, economic instability challenging industrial growth and labor rights, and technological innovations in transportation and communications, modern Americans increasingly found outlets and inlets for their religious life in sacred activities beyond the Word of God, outside churches and synagogues.

By the early twentieth century, watching movies in the darkened theater had become one such activity. The history of film illuminates the shifting sands of sacred life in twentieth-century America, a century obsessed with glitz, glamour, and the grace of cinematic escape. It is religious history as much as a history of entertainment, a story that opens up new vistas into primary spiritual investments Americans made in new, though hardly profane, sources of sacred authority.

After the death of Goodwin, George Eastman had to pay Ansco Company, the owners of the patent for the new kind of film, five million dollars cash and then went on to make a deal with Thomas

Edison, who bought rolls of Kodak film for his studio—truly the beginnings of the movie industry as we know it. But there is more to the religious story of film in these very early years of movie-making than the tragic story of an inventive clergyman's role in the technological evolution of cinema. Goodwin would have been proud of the ubiquity of biblical stories that appeared on celluloid soon after his discovery—*The Life of Moses* (1909), *The Deluge* (1911), *From the Manger to the Cross* (1912)—even if other images appearing on screens across the country were less biblically in-spired, depicting stories that included the frightening return of the dead, exhilarating encounters with the law, sidesplitting antics by master comedians, and titillating romantic entanglements, to name a few popular themes.

The range and diversity of Christian views on Hollywood pro-ductions in the first half of the century, however, belie any easy generalizations. From volatile public debates and collective anxiety about what to make of movies by religious leaders to coordinated forms of collaboration between Hollywood producers and reli-gious institutions, Christians in the darkened movie houses and in the pews were saturated with multiple, sometimes contradictory, impulses and teachings about the new and radical visual medium.[3] Despite these conflicts, the Bible remained a vital source for the filmic imagination and drew millions of moviegoers to theaters around the country in the early decades of Hollywood film pro-duction. The career of Cecil B. DeMille and particularly his more well-known biblical epics come immediately to mind. Without a doubt, God has played a leading role in making films popular.

The historical connections between films and institutionalized religion, whether in the form of mass protests from outraged be-lievers, creative inspiration from foundational sacred texts, or cal-culated collaboration among filmmakers and religious leaders, are an abiding feature of American cultural life. The potential rewards that can accrue from these intersections are as material as they are spiritual. Just ask Mel Gibson, whose recent movie phenomenon,

The Passion of the Christ (2004), is now one of the highest grossing films in history, in a league with such other otherworldly blockbusters as *Star Wars* (1977), *ET: The Extraterrestrial* (1982), and *The Lord of the Rings: The Return of the King* (2003).

But the religious story does not end with how much money Mel Gibson has made, nor does it end with God. The first movie picture house, opened in Pittsburgh by Harry Davis in 1905 with the premiere of *The Great Train Robbery*, was eventually called a "nickelodeon," combining the cost of admission with the Greek word, "odeon," a moderately sized theater for public performances in ancient Greece. In a relatively short time, thousands of "movie palaces" and other modern theaters catering to more middle-class tastes opened around the country, transforming the external, urban landscapes of America but also the interior, spiritual landscapes of Americans through a popular, unprecedented form of ritual activity—going to the movies.

Religious impulses often find expression in response to unusual physical experiences: the corporeal isolation of the person on the vision quest, the mystical possibilities of self-flagellation, the collective effervescence at a roadside revival. When Americans in the early decades of the twentieth century entered the space of the movie house, sat down next to others in a darkened hall, and watched a film on the screen—sometimes accompanied by music, sometimes by lectures, sometimes by moments of pandemonium in the audience—many experienced physical sensations that were far outside their normal, everyday realities. In short, they discovered religious ritual and lived according to a common characteristic of most ritual action that draws participants back for more and soon becomes a routine for meaningful, repeatable action.

On any day of the week in the first half of the century, Americans experienced close, physical intimacy with strangers, or in the case of some patrons, with a first date, a distant spouse, an aging parent, or a rebellious son. They were deeply impressed by captivating visual representations of compelling images and stories that often had a profound emotional impact, and they enjoyed the pleasure, pure and simple, of escaping from one world and entering, in effect, another one that promised a range of visceral and vicarious enjoyments, often associated with moral anger and righteousness, dramatic conflicts and resolutions, mind-boggling fantasy, and even sexual arousal. Taken together, these physical experiences and sensations occurring in the theater, so novel and fantastic for audiences in the early years of movie-going, and so valuable and reliable to theater owners, studio heads, and others in the burgeoning industry, were publicly and personally framed in distinctly religious terms.

The evolution of theater architecture is brimming with religious motifs, icons, imagery, and statuary, impressing the patrons and creating an ethos that was truly out of this world. Stylistic details ranged far and wide from Loews 72nd Street Theater in New York City with Buddhas and magic lanterns to the KiMo in Albuquerque, New Mexico, which had distinctive chandeliers made in the shape of Indian farewell canoes. From the popular "orientalist" leanings of the time that included fascination with ancient Egyptian themes after the discovery of King Tutankhamen's tomb to the transparent imitations of Gothic cathedrals, movie houses were confusing spaces that often combined crass commercialism, kitsch aesthetics, leisure entertainment, social interactions, historical settings, and religious exoticism.[4]

When the Roxy Theater, the new picture palace in New York City, opened for business in 1927, the owners billed it as the "Cathedral of the Motion Picture." With frankincense emanating from air ducts, over 6,000 seats, a symphony orchestra, three magnificent golden organ consoles, and other spectacular elements, this new, modern temple of popular culture was made even more explicitly religious in the opening ceremonies after ushers had guided audience members to their seats. As the lights dimmed, a spotlight fixed on a robed monk who read from a scroll: "Ye portals bright, high and majestic, open to our gaze the path to Wonderland, and show us the realm where fantasy reigns, where romance, where adventure flourish. Let ev'ry day's toil be forgotten under thy sheltering roof—O Glorious, mighty hall—thy magic and thy charm unite us all to worship at beauty's throne."[5] When the monk called out, "Let there be light," the lights came on for the patrons to see the "Glorious, mighty hall" and the musicians rise from the orchestra pit.[6]

The blatant borrowing of religious symbols, architecture, and rhetoric in building, advertising, and running movie theaters may appear to be only external trappings that do not correspond with real experiences of patrons. But, in fact, many viewers have relied on religious language to characterize their inner experiences when frequenting movie theaters. One popular history and picture book on movie theaters, the aptly titled *Ticket to Paradise*, includes reminiscences from a range of folks, including writer Deborah Larsen, who confesses that the Grandview Theater in St. Paul, Minnesota, in the 1940s and 1950s was "a kind of alternate cathedral"; Thomas Adamson, who spent many Saturdays—"the Shangri-la of seven days of anxiety, anticipation, and planning"— in his youth at the West Theater in Cedartown, Georgia, a place that he describes as "the real chapel of hope, prayers, worship"; and Jerome Franks, who, growing up in New York, remembers that "by the time we were ten we went to the neighborhood theaters. . . . Like all the rest of the kids of that time, we had a Saturday afternoon matinee that practically all of our friends, and, of course, all of my brothers and sisters, went to religiously."[7]

Even scholars of film allude to a distinctly sacred quality to film-going. At the beginning of his article "Cinema, Religion, and Popular Culture," Professor M. Darrol Bryant describes his experiences of going to the movies as a youngster in a small North Dakota town in the 1950s: "I regularly participated in the weekly Saturday ritual of going to the movies. This event was one I shared with a wide variety of folk. . . . For two hours the cares and demands of every day were set aside as we entered the magical world of the cinema. Seated in the darkened theater we allowed our private fantasies, fears, and aspirations to meet the drama enacted on the screen. . . . Filtered through our own particular feelings, the drama on the screen moved us, and shaped us."[8] It is certainly not the case that every American who entered a movie theater in the first half of the twentieth century had a reverential or mystical experience—far from it. As many social and film historians have demonstrated, a wide range of emotions and activities could emerge from the diverse crowds inside theaters who are, after all, seeking modern forms of entertainment. But while historians rightly argue about the integral role movies played in the creation of new cultural forms of life tied to mass media, leisure time, and consumer society, dynamic signs of religious cultural life spilling out of theaters have been too long overlooked.[9]

It has long been said that Hollywood is a "dream factory." But it can produce more than entertaining dreams. The movie business is rather a time-tested source for sacred stories that captivate Americans, drawing on mythic qualities found in more familiar religious stories like Adam and Eve, or the death and resurrection of Christ, or the life and awakening of Buddha. These qualities include providing the audience with moral visions and practices to live by that can uphold or revolutionize existing social orders controlling life, with inspiration to transcend troubling obstacles and transform life, and with haunting stories that get lodged in personal memories and mark the journey through life. Indeed, certain Hollywood movies are not merely projections of wishful thinking or playful fantasy, though they certainly may give expression to these; some films are received by viewers as revelations in the most religious sense of the term—"dreams" offering a new, if momentary, view of reality that some might claim is the world of illusion but which in fact has extraordinary gravitas and power.

More than any other medium, film can generate religious values, images, and sensibilities that leave an imprint on, if not dramatically alter the lives of, communities of viewers.[10] As forceful and integral in the lives of individuals as any other collection of sacred stories found in, for example, the Bhagavad Gita or Black Elk Speaks or the Hebrew Bible, certain Hollywood films provide myths that frame and make sense of basic, universal dilemmas faced by finite, mortal humans and serve as touchstones for making sense in a cruel, painful world full of suffering, injustice, and chaos. Like the sacred texts so central in the lives of devout practitioners of the world's religions, films offer sacred stories that do not simply remain stuck in the collective imagination of momentarily entertained viewers. Instead, some movies, whether they were adapted from another source or written originally for the screen, make a mark on individual viewers, larger communities of fans, and in some instances, American society as a whole. The marks some films make have physical, material aftereffects on individual bodies and the social body that translate into a religious idiom—from the chill running up and down the spine of an individual moviegoer in the theater, to the annual conventions for some films that draw thousands of enthusiasts, to the cultural transformations that follow in the wake of a particularly popular Hollywood production.

A good example of sacred Hollywood stories—iconic in every sense of the word—is family films associated with children, containing narratives that address a universal rite of passage and a particularly key moment in the inculcation of fundamental values in most societies: the transition from youth to adulthood. The obvious place to begin a discussion involving Hollywood, family, and kids is with the man most intimately associated with the imagination of children in twentieth-century America: Walt Disney. Disney's cultural productions, including films, television shows, and amusement parks, have left an indelible impression on the life of the nation. In many ways, Disney helped usher in the emerging value systems that transformed the United States in the first part of the century, becoming a celebrity icon by the end of his life and an embodiment of a new, modern American way of life based on an ethic of mass consumption, leisure, and self-fulfillment.[11] A spokesman, yes, but Disney like no one else was the premier mythmaker of the century. The mythic worlds animated and brought to life in Disney's work provide Americans with both an escape from reality and effective interpretive tools to make sense of reality—in other words, his cultural legacy has as much to do with religious expression as it has to do with mass entertainment.

Disney was both pioneer and prophet in American society, a storyteller who expressed a range of celebrated American doctrines in a form that any child could understand. His animated films—*Snow White and the Seven Dwarfs* (1937), *Pinocchio* (1940), *Bambi* (1942), *Cinderella* (1950), *Sleeping Beauty* (1959), to name only a few—are myths disguised as modern fairy tales, primarily but not exclusively created for consumption by children, and conveying distinctive religious messages about life and meaning in the twentieth century. These messages can be characterized as religious because they teach about order, meaning, transcendence, and orientation. In addition, like many religious expressions, they arouse a great deal of interest and sentiment because they are so intimately tied to a desire to triumph over death.[12] The popularity of Disney films is fueled by religious sensibilities not contained within the bounds of any particular religious tradition but freefloating and diffuse, enlivened by entertainment that strikes a chord and resonates with some of the most profound yearnings in human life, yearnings made stronger because they are often not met in real life: justice will prevail, evil forces will fail, redemption can be achieved in this life, and death can be overcome—palatable themes for middle-class, Americanized tastes that could, at least in consumer culture, easily transcend divisions between Protestants, Catholics, and Jews.

After the Great Depression and a world war, and riding a wave of popularity that followed the introduction of Mickey Mouse to the world, Disney released his first feature-length, animated film,

Snow White. We all know this adaptation of a Grimm's fairy tale telling the harrowing story of an evil queen's attempts to kill a young girl, "the fairest in the land." After befriending lovable dwarfs who try to protect her, and falling prey to the queen's poison, the girl lives happily ever after in a castle in the sky with the prince who resurrects her from "sleeping death." In this film, like so many to follow, the young, vulnerable protagonist—vulnerable because parents are either missing or dead—must confront some maleficent figure who embodies evil and wants to harm the young and defenseless. The young survive, sometimes by their own wits, oftentimes through miraculous, extraordinary interventions by forces of good in the cosmos that overcome our darkest fears about abandonment, disintegration, and chaos: the power of romantic love in that kiss; the supernatural powers of the fairy who brings the dead wooden puppet-boy, Pinocchio, back to life as a real child; the cloud-spirit of Mufasa, the *Lion King* father who inspires little Simba, the orphaned lion cub.

When *Snow White* originally came out, it was a cultural sensation because of both the technological innovations in this groundbreaking film and the story itself. Critics raved, with even the Russian film director, and critical voice in the early years of cinema, Sergei Eisenstein purportedly calling it the greatest movie ever made. The public clamored to witness it in theaters with family, friends, and lots of strangers. They still do: *Snow White* is one of the most popular animated films ever released. These are not "just" movies that entertain children, though they certainly do that. They are also myths, weighty and evocative stories ritually retold for children and adults that draw the religious imagination to fundamental sacred values for many in American culture: happiness is attainable in this life even with the reality of death; the moral order of good over evil, though temporarily threatened, is reestablished; individual initiative is critical for salvation in this life even if other forces may be at work as well.

But the myth does not begin and end with the individual alone in the world, especially in the narrative details of this journey out of childhood. Disney films generally end with the promise of domestic bliss, a reinvigoration of family relations in spite of fragmentations and ruptures, a ray of hope of meaningful bonds with others in an uncertain, wicked world. Over the span of Disney's life, his films were released during a period in which American society as a whole was struggling with both national and international conflicts—World War II, Korea, civil rights, Vietnam—and relied on a variety of domestic symbols and images to make consequential stories that resonated with audience members who may have gone to church and synagogue but who also sat enraptured in movie theaters, receiving spiritual instruction of a different sort from those institutions. The idealized domestic order presented and represented in Disney's mythic, modern fairy tales transmits moral teachings about the centrality of the family in terms of gender roles, the relation of the individual to the family, the fragility of these relations, the transition out of childhood, and the idea that God the Father does not play any role in this moral system.

These themes, so firmly enmeshed in Disney films, are prominent in other sacred American movie myths narrating the plight of a vulnerable youngster as well. Louis B. Mayer, like other early Hollywood moguls, was inspired by the enormous success of *Snow White* and two years later, MGM released the innovative film *The Wizard of Oz*, another Hollywood production that achieved a cultural apotheosis like few others and has near-universal recognition to this day—some even believe it is one of the most popular, though not necessarily highest grossing, films ever. Everyone you know has seen it. The story of Dorothy's visit to the land of Oz and her long, treacherous, enlightening journey to get back home to the farm in Kansas is a fixture in the American imagination; it has more, though, than just iconic value, an immediate nostalgic air of familiarity and sentimentality captured in the words "somewhere over the rainbow," or by the sight of those ruby slippers, or simply when conjuring up images of a young Judy Garland holding Toto. *The Wizard of Oz* is a part of our cultural landscape like only a few entertainment phenomena—closest in many ways to Elvis, who will appear later in these pages—and freighted with religious meanings, reminiscences, and longings.

This religious freight is surely odd, considering the original source for the film is L. Frank Baum's populist-inflected children's story first published in 1900, *The Wonderful Wizard of Oz*. The book also ends with a rather unequivocal indictment of religion: Dorothy and friends unmask the all-powerful Wizard—the God of Oz—and expose a fraud: " 'I thought Oz was a great Head,' said Dorothy. . . . 'And I thought Oz was a terrible Beast,' said the Tin Woodman. 'And I thought Oz was a Ball of Fire,' exclaimed the Lion. 'No; you are all wrong,' said the little man meekly. 'I have been making believe.' " [13] Also, although in the book Dorothy's "silver shoes" magically transport her physically back to Kansas, in the sacred text of the film, she wakes up from a *dream*, with all the Technicolor glory of her journey evaporating upon coming back to consciousness, and to the gray, dusty squalor of the Kansas farm and her adopted family, but with a new appreciation of "home." In the end of the film, it was all only a dream, a common psychoanalytic charge against religion itself.

How can a film based on a novel some conservative folks see as a socialist-inspired attack on institutional religion—leading many to call for a ban on it in public school—be a vibrant fount of religious creativity and inspiration? Myths are powerful because the sacred stories they tell are open to multiple interpretations by the audience, interpretations framed with religious language and addressing familiar religious themes. [14] The power of myth is also based on the fact that the story it relates does not require any correspondence to material reality, and its point of origin, or how the story came to be, is not relevant in understanding its popularity and efficacy. Myths may arise from visions and ecstatic trances offering a glimpse of other worlds; from communications from God or the gods about human origins and purpose; from dramatic human experiences or deep thoughts that are enfolded in stories that strike a chord and get passed down through the generations. When they resonate with communities by providing compelling, illuminating, meaningful stories that address the big questions and mysteries of life, their cultural value adds up to a great deal more than can be answered by such simple questions as whether the story is true or false, fantasy or reality, entertaining or edifying.

Testimonials to the extraordinary attraction of *The Wizard of Oz* abound in books, in communities of like-minded fans, and in chat rooms and websites across cyberspace. They speak of its "magic," the "values" it imparts, the "rituals" of watching it, how it touches the "soul." Sappy to some, many comments emote nostalgia for childhood—a time long past yet somehow still meaningful, brought to life by watching this film—and, for millions of baby boomers, the accompanying hallowed memories of the family gathering around the television set when the film had its annual broadcast in the middle decades of the century, a time when viewing choices were much more limited than today and the film truly made its cultural mark. A few samples from the Internet Movie Database's, "user reviews" of the film include a fan from El Paso, Texas, who writes: "The story of 'The Wizard of Oz' has always appealed to me because of it's [sic] story that is attached with many kinds a values that we as humans treasure"; or the fan in Clearwater, Florida, who writes that "From the earliest scenes in the film . . . there is a magic that accompanies the film"; or finally the fan from North Carolina, who is especially offended by those interpretations that reduce the story to a political allegory: "Movies like this bring the world together. A story of love, friendship and bravery. In a way all of Dorothy's problems must be faced by us too . . . with friends to guide you and the brightness of your soul, nothing can stop you. My childhood began and ended watching this film and its power still touches me deeply." [15]

The power this film has over people is truly startling, a power that is not limited to sentimental emotions triggered by watching the movie and tied to the loss of childhood. Take the ruby slippers, for example. After filming ended, the shoes that were used on the set eventually took on a life of their own. Not simply artifacts left over from the movie production, these are now holy relics with one pair enshrined in the Smithsonian and still others that have acquired a value that cannot be adequately reduced to simply the enormous price they will cost in the open market: a pair recently sold at auction for over $600,000. These ruby slippers have more than monetary value—though the astronomical price combines with, but does not work against, this something extra. This surfeit value is obviously associated with the film in which they made an appearance and, perhaps even more important, with the young girl who wore them, Judy Garland.

Garland is a cult figure herself, with a community of dedicated fans in straight, gay, cineophile, and other subcultures. Her young feet helped transform mundane costume accessories into powerful objects worth far more than any price paid at auction. On a recent 2008 episode of *The Oprah Winfrey Show* featuring "Classic Americana," Brent Glass, the director of the Smithsonian Institution's National Museum of American History, brought the shoes, which were closely protected by two armed guards on the journey to Chicago, out on live television and explained why they are so sacred: "There's the value to the American public and really to the whole world because people treasure the memory of seeing *The Wizard of Oz*," he said. "The value, I think, is really important because they are a treasure of our youth. They're a treasure of the story of *The Wizard of Oz* and Dorothy's quest to find her way home." [16] A separate website devoted to the shoes, the Ruby Slipper Fan Club, includes the host describing his surprise at the large number of visitors from around the world who also share what he labels "Slipper Fever." [17] Even beyond "Slipper Fever," adoration by fans has led to the creation of numerous other websites containing trivia, merchandise, movie and audio clips, photographs, and other popular materials from the film. Fans attend conventions that take place throughout the year and around the country, including the Ozmopolitan Convention, the Winkie Convention, the Munchkin Convention, and the ever-popular annual Chesterton Wizard of Oz Festival, which has been running for twenty-four years in Indiana. These activities, combined with the highly charged memories for many people of ritually watching the film, signal an investment and devotion that is truly rare but an unequivocal sign of how deeply *The Wizard of Oz* is embedded in American culture.

Is it "just" a film? Are these activities and reminiscences trivial, purely secular sentiments of emotional attachment to *The Wizard of Oz*? No, these are signs of religious cultures and identity not replacing Christian, Jewish, Hindu, or any other traditional markers of identity, but harmoniously coexisting with them, generating sensibilities and practices signaling that, for many, the film is a hierophany, a profound rupture in ordinary existence suggesting the presence of the sacred. *The Wizard of Oz* is a sacred text, with multiple interpretations, a host of meaningful, fulfilling practices connected with it, and an audience that considers it timeless and a vital source of inspiration. One of the people the film inspired is world-famous author Salman Rushdie, who claims in an excellent essay on *The Wizard of Oz,* "A Short Text about Magic," that the movie "made a writer of me." [18] In this essay, which is paired with a fictional short story, "At the Auction of the Ruby Slippers," in which Rushdie describes attending an auction where, in his words, "around the—let us say—shrine of the ruby-sequined slippers, pools of saliva have been forming," Rushdie offers his memories of the film, its similarity to Bollywood films, and its impact on him as a child and as an adult viewing it again. He clearly understands that a startling aspect of the movie is that it "is breezily godless," but is incorrect when he suggests that the worldview is completely secular. [19]

Rather, it is abundantly religious as a myth for so many fans who are fixated on, if not utterly attached to, this Hollywood movie. Rushdie does identify a key feature of this religious attraction: the film is pulled in two directions that are embodied in Dorothy's journey—the desire to return home, the home of childhood and family, but also "the human dream of *leaving*, a dream at least as powerful as its countervailing dream of roots." [20] It is this contradiction that adds to the moral force of the film for many, that self-knowledge and understanding emerge in the liminal, colorful, memorable space between this world and the worlds of imagination and altered experiences that are so critical for any religious journey of self-discovery and cosmic insight.

Finally, another filmic phenomenon has mythic, sacred standing in American culture but is godless to the core. The *Star Wars* saga, conceived and executed by filmmaker George Lucas, also depicts a rite of passage from youth to adulthood, from the dull, drab though precarious innocence of childhood to the difficult though enlightening but sobering experiences of adulthood. This film series, like so many other movies, creates a universe without God in which the transition to adulthood occurs—the "force" is not God the Father, the Son, or the Holy Spirit, at least according to the characters themselves. The force is an "energy field" of some sort that penetrates and binds together everything in the galaxy, to paraphrase an early speech by Obi-Wan Kenobi. Even though a godless universe is presented and elaborated on in each of the six films that constitute the saga, the tale as a whole—its structure, plot, characters, references—is religious through and through. From the opening in 1977 of the first film (though ultimately fourth in the series) to the release in 2005 of the final film (third in the series), the popular reception of audience members has transformed the religious story of the film into a religious myth overflowing from the theater and seeping into—and inspiring the creation of new forms of—American culture.

God is not required for the complex, deeply ingrained religious cultures spawned by the *Star Wars* films. Yes, Lucas seems to be carrying on in the spirit of old Reverend Goodwin at the beginning of this story—these films have a religious purpose, especially for children. Over the years, in interview after interview following the release of each episode, Lucas is clear about the moral dimension of these films: they offer a mythology that can be especially valuable in the spiritual lives of children and adolescents on their way to adulthood. The first three films released tell the story of young farm boy Luke Skywalker's initiation into Jedi manhood; the last three (called the "prequels") focus on Luke's father, Anakin, also a Jedi initiate, though one who turns to the dark side of the force and eventually is transformed into Luke's arch nemesis, Darth Vader. At the end of *Return of the Jedi*, released in 1983 but the chronological culmination of the entire six-part series, Luke and father are ultimately reconciled in a temporary, we assume, victorious moment when the spirits of the dead commune and celebrate with the living heroes, who can see their familiar physical features in spiritual form.

From the moment "A long time ago, in a galaxy far, far away . . ." first scrolled across movie screens, the *Star Wars* phenomenon has grown larger than life, though now deeply saturated in the American cultural landscape. The six-part film series has not only generated billions of dollars in ticket sales and merchandising, it has inspired the religious imagination of fans who see something more in the film than a commercially entertaining story. On the one hand, the narrative itself provides viewers with a mythology that is vivid and gripping, while at the same time covering well-trodden, mythically familiar territory—good battling evil, revealed mysteries about the true order of the cosmos, innocence lost, self-discovery, and transcendence of death and ultimate reconciliations.

Indeed, so much about the films is formulaic, drawn from a hodgepodge of ancient and modern mythological ingredients strung together in the form of "the hero's journey" as outlined by the famous Jungian analyst and popular writer on myths Joseph

Campbell, in his groundbreaking book *The Hero with a Thousand Faces* (1949). Building on science fiction and western films in an earlier era, Lucas layered his futuristic fantasy with allusions to various religious traditions of the world. He also made sure the story remained true to its singular vision, exploring the existence of evil, sometimes referred to as theodicy when the question is asked in a God-filled universe. In the standard mythical structure found in Campbell's book and identified as a "monomyth," the basic plot covers the journey of the hero, replete with adventures in different worlds, separation from loved ones, and initiation into new forms of knowledge and power.[21]

On the other hand, over the years the series has made a dramatic impact on the lives of devoted fans: personal identities have been transformed; tight-knit communities have been formed; complex and meaningful ritual systems have emerged in cyberspace, at conventions, with video games, and in other non-theater settings.[22] Seeing the films is simply not enough for many who seek to bring the *Star Wars* mythology to life and into their own lives. A quick glance at the publishing industry is one way to capture the wide-ranging, even contradictory, sacred resources that can be accessed through the films and embodied in the life of the reader and communities of fans. Like the books written about *The Wizard of Oz*, such publications as *The Dharma of Star Wars* (2005), *Christian Wisdom of the Jedi Masters* (2005), and *The Tao of Star Wars* (2003), to name only a few recent examples, illustrate how rich the films can be for spiritual instruction in the ways of familiar religious cultures.

Christianity, Taoism, New Age, Buddhism, and other sacred sources of wisdom are reimagined, and sometimes mixed together, in evocative and effective ways at least for these writers and their readers who latch on to these sci-fi fantasies and find spiritual nourishment in them. On the other hand, most religious traditions can likely find relevant wisdom in this well-concocted mythology that keeps all traces of God out of the story—again leading many

conservative Christians especially to recognize a particularly ne-
farious danger in the films. Many fans, affiliated or not with religious institutions, also participate in highly ritualized games that
bring the myth to life in peculiar, even extraordinary ways. On the
back of the elaborate *Revised Core Rulebook* for the popular *Star
Wars Roleplaying Game,* the stakes of this particular activity are
summed up in the following commandment: "Take control of
your destiny and become one of the greatest heroes of the
galaxy." [23]

An astounding number of communities—communities of
feeling, to play off the apt phrase of cultural studies scholar Raymond Williams, "structures of feeling," but also communities that
act out—have been formed in one way or another around *Star
Wars* in America and throughout the world, a cultural phenomenon of epic proportions best compared to communities of faith
surrounding other sacred texts with myths that come to life in the
imaginations and actions of followers. Some speak of the films and
memories of viewing them in terms of spiritual sustenance and
awakening, as filling something meaningful in their lives; friends
and fans are bound together in close-knit, often secret communities through shared viewing pleasures; individuals resist Lucas's vision and create their own versions of the story, sometimes by
creating rebel films that, for example, excise the existence of a
hated character from *The Phantom Menace,* Jar-Jar Binks, or sometimes by writing subgenre fan fiction, including the genre known
as "slash fiction," which introduces a homoerotic edge to the
mythology by imagining same-sex relationships among characters.
Internet communities endlessly debate what to include in the *Star
Wars* canon, a historically common controversy when it comes to
many sacred myths from traditional religions.

Again, the question presents itself: should this phenomenon be
treated as pure fantasy and play, or can these very characteristics be
signs of religious life and culture? *Star Wars* reproduces religious
forms of discourse, action, and community in the lives of fans be-

cause of the emotional impact of the films, the imaginative worlds they offer, the moral certainties they espouse, and the creative possibilities they leave with viewers. The reception of fans suggests that, more than reproducing religious forms empty of content, these films provide sacred content that can be used by audience members for play and serious reflection, as a way to escape from daily drudgery but also as a means of spiritual fulfillment. The explicitly religious understanding of this kind of serious play is easy to find in cyberspace.

For example, consider the welcome page for Sith Chicks Fanfiction Archive, a portal on the website of Star Wars Chicks, a female-run fan site "dedicated to every little girl who grew up wanting to fly an X-wing or be Princess Leia," that brings adult visitors to R-rated, sexually explicit fiction, "with both slash and heterosexual pairings," housed at the site. The introduction welcomes the visitor to "the realm of the Sith Chicks, and our sacred archives that house the power of both Light and Dark."[24] God may not be present in the story itself, in the interpretations of many fans, in the proliferation of products and stories based on the series and pervading American culture, or in solitary or communal activities of devoted fans, but the impact of the *Star Wars* mythology must be characterized as a religious phenomenon of the highest order, engrained in everyday life, language, reflections, and interactive communities.

The culturally productive mythology around these and other Hollywood movies, in terms of fandom, publications, storytelling, and all other manner of energized, devotional investment in them and interpretation of their significant meanings, attests to the sacred power of certain films in contemporary society. Now a century-old medium for mythmaking, movie-making magic will surely remain a dynamic, viable source for making sense of universal human experiences, like love and death, good and evil, individual and social transformation, which can compete with the Bible and other religious texts in the imaginative and practical lives of

Americans. Film, like other entertaining pursuits of the twentieth century, cannot be carelessly dismissed as only an expression of secular culture, but should be understood as containing sacred potential to become something much more religiously valuable in the hearts and minds of modern men and women, creating meaningful moral systems and new forms of religious community.

2

MUSIC

"This is my Sabbath, this is where my family is."
The young man attending a rave party expresses this religious sentiment, and he is not alone. "It's about being free and being spiritual," clarifies a young woman, also striving for the right words to capture her experience dancing to the music with a throng of other revelers. A DJ who goes by the name X-tastyle preaches, "There is not hate. It's all love. The party reflects what the world should be more like." An eighteen-year-old waxes enthusiastically about his experience: "There's a zone you go into where everything disappears. . . . It's just you and the music. There's nothing like it." And Sunshine, which is not this nineteen-year-old's birth name, innocently proclaims (while wearing a Catholic schoolgirl outfit and pigtails): "I've never seen somebody leave a party mad. That's why we're here, isn't it? To love each other and feel good." [1]

On the surface, this apparent lovefest is easy to dismiss as youthful, naïve, misguided expressions of what is really only secular fun—music and parties. But the true story may be more troubling for Americans who assume that religious rituals take place only in a church or mosque, and that genuine encounters with the sacred must bring an individual into contact with God. Spirituality tied to experiences of absolute freedom, love as an ideal to strive for in this life, feelings so extraordinary they defy rational as well as theological explanations—surely the sentiments communicated above reveal a deeper meaning. Below the surface pleasures aroused by listening to music are hints of religious possibilities that are subtle but powerful in the lives of these revelers.

Americans young and old, rich and poor, atheist and faithful, have turned to music as a sacred source of religious life, discovering in the rhythms and beats, lyrics and sentiments a valuable way to escape, if only momentarily, the mundane realities of this world and find a higher ground. But the sacred does not only offer otherworldly escape from this world. Music can be religious in every sense of the word, a meaningful alternative to traditional religion that generates moral perspectives, special communities, and life-altering transformations in tune with divine energies.

Music is much more than what you hear. In other words, music for the listener and the performer has a much fuller corporeal impact than sounds coming through the ear.[2] It inhabits and alters the body but at the same time has the potential to create disembodied, nonmaterial bonds among individuals that tie them together in memorable, often ritually appealing ways. It is a definitively social experience as well as somatosensory, and can in some cases bind American communities together through a shared sense of the sacred achieved during extraordinary moments of transcendence and regeneration often reported by participants in the revival-like, religious atmosphere of momentary collective musical communities—jazz clubs, rock shows, and raves, to name only a few.

The connection between music and religion is deep-rooted in human history and widespread across the cultural spectrum, with many theories suggesting integral links between the two in the formation of human societies. British psychologist Anthony Storr writes in his book *Music and the Mind*, "The origins of music may be lost in obscurity but, from its earliest beginnings, it seems to have played an essential part in social interaction. Music habitually accompanies religious and other ceremonies. Some anthropologists have speculated that vocal music may have begun as a special way of communicating with the supernatural."[3] Music plays a special role in human evolution and no doubt operates as a prime mover in the formation of communities, societies, and cultures through time and in the present.[4] Any investigation of the American religious landscape must take music into account as a biological and sociological force of solidarity and group identity, along with its pervasive, long-standing role as a source for sacred life—crucial ingredients in the mix of dynamic, sometimes politically powerful, religious cultures.

The presence of music on the North American continent predates the arrival of hymn-singing European Christians spreading the Gospel and wreaking death and destruction on the original inhabitants they found in the New World. Although archaeological evidence demonstrates the production of musical instruments, such as rattles, flutes, and drums, from roughly 3000 BCE in South American and Mesoamerican cultures, most musical expression throughout the hemisphere was based on vocalization and singing. And in most cases, in most places, music had a vital role in the religious life of native cultures—and still does in traditional ceremonies, profitable performances for tourists, and, since the arrival of the Christians, innovative hymnody and other adopted and embraced musical forms.[5]

The musical landscape in early American history was dominated by Christian, and particularly Protestant, sensibilities. Especially prominent were sacred songs in the form of hymnody, psalms, and eventually gospel. Sometimes these songs circulated through communities and were passed on to subsequent generations orally; sometimes they were written down and disseminated to congregations who incorporated them into their ritual rhythms, and sometimes they were adopted by non-Christians at the margins of society but under the dominant presence of Protestant American culture. Hymns were especially crucial in the musical economy of the New World, ameliorating the often abrasive relations between different ethnic groups. Protestant modes of singing their praises to God had a wide, deep cultural influence that shaped, in part, the musical styles of other non-Christians upon their voluntary or forced arrival to these shores, including Africans, Jews, and, later, Buddhists and Hindus.[6]

In the beginning is music for the sacred worlds of X-tastyle, Sunshine, and the other congregants at the rave church where this chapter began. Rave culture is a musical subcultural phenomenon that has captured the media's and the public's attention in recent years, including a *Time* cover story entitled "Rave New World."[7] It also ignited the legislative fires of Congress, which sees raves— basically parties that last through the night with loud, pulsating techno-based electronic music and masterful DJs—as a hotbed of drug use, especially the appropriately named Ecstasy, and temptation for young, vulnerable teenagers who would be better off if they would just stay home. Although suspect in the eyes of many old folks, participants who groove their bodies to the beat in the intimate midst of other moving, sweating bodies in this energetic music community often claim they experience something unusual, extraordinary, and liberating, if not downright transcendent.

A global youth movement not only limited to the young, raves create an alternative space from the everyday, a sacred time and place that is marked by the convergence of music, ritual, and religious experience, a historically familiar combination of social ingredients which can alter moods, expand minds, and bind communities together. In the case of raves, explicit moral systems take shape and grab hold of community members swept away in the collective effervescence elemental to this religious culture, including one summed up in the acronym PLUR, which stands for peace, love, unity, and respect. One Atlanta newspaper article covering raves in the South stated in terms everyone could understand: "For ravers, PLUR is gospel."[8] The undeniable religious dimensions of rave culture are not only articulated by participants themselves in interviews, they are also analyzed in an increasing number of serious, scholarly studies in anthropology, cultural studies, theology, and religious studies.

For many, the physical exertions, the visual sensations, the close contact with others, and especially the hypnotic, powerful music that permeates the scene is a sacred mix that has the power to transform identity, offer revelation, and provide liberation. Accounts from participants are deeply embedded in religious cosmologies that borrow words and images from familiar religious cultures like Christianity or Native American traditions but also highlight experiences of a completely different order, experiences powerful and radical enough in their own right to lead some to speak of healing transformation and spiritual rebirth—close to the common evangelical refrain of being born again, though in this setting not necessarily with Jesus in mind. Altered states of consciousness do play a crucial role, induced not by drugs only but by the music and the shamanistic ritual specialists—DJs—doctoring the crowds with fabulous musical mixes and inspired mesmerizing loops. Music is the magical potion that can weaken inhibitions and soothe the soul in individual listeners. But it also draws people together and ties them into larger communities and social networks, as well as arousing a state of collective life and energy characterized by anti-structure, radical democracy, and indeterminate, ambiguous, liminal experiences that are usually interpreted with religious language and categories.[9]

The spiritual content of this encounter with the sacred at raves is often, though not always, devoid of God. Many statements by ravers allude to a different supernatural order when seeking to explain these remarkable engagements with music. One self-described "non-drug-taking, middle age raver" wrote a letter to *USA Today* protesting the previously mentioned attempt to criminalize raves. His defense of raves combined scientific knowledge about biological process with a celebration of primitivism and its healing religious power, both common themes in insider and outsider attempts to better understand this subculture: "Ravers have inherited the spirit of people who have danced around bonfires to drumbeats since ancient times. By boosting my serotonin levels naturally through dancing, raving has relieved my chronic clinical depression." [10]

Many descriptions of raves tend to rely on ancient spirits and spiritual unity to capture the essence of the experience. In the words of one informant, when a rave is successful it all "melds into one cosmic soup and everything is one and you can't separate the music or the moves or which came first." [11] This common experience of entering a "cosmic soup" is easily framed by comparable mystical expressions in Buddhism, Taoism, Hinduism, and even Christianity and Judaism in some rave circles. It is often perceived as being rooted in indigenous religious communities such as the aboriginal cultures of Australia, Native America, precolonial Africa, and other societies that offer moderns a taste of the imagined primitive past. It can also be dressed in the language of human rights, with the international phenomenon understood as building a new global community. [12] As a hotly contested cultural movement that some see as the devil's work, others as fun entertainment, and still others as a spiritually viable channel for meaningful religious experiences, the raving subculture points to music as an unusually promising font of sacred wisdom and practice for many Americans. Music intersects with the sacred for millions of Americans who make sense of their lives with a musical soundtrack rather than the written word.

Most Americans are familiar with the legendary myth of the birth of the blues: Mississippi bluesman Robert Johnson sells his soul to the devil at the crossroads and revolutionizes guitar playing, and music itself, before dying tragically in 1938. Read any book or article on the blues and it is likely to refer to this common mythological refrain. Documentaries will add an air of mystery through old photographs, chilling music, and dramatic narration. Rooted in African history from the chains of slavery to the chains of racism in freedom, the blues offer one form of cultural expression that documents the social and existential realities of an oppressed people, sung by the likes of early figures such as Blind Lemon Jefferson, Mamie Smith, and Charlie Patton. It is a musical style and experience that is difficult to label as purely secular, though how it can be understood as religious is also a challenging exercise. Part of the problem with deciphering the religious culture animated by blues music was alluded to in the crossroads myth: the overbearing theological presence of one figure commonly associated with this element of black culture. Not God, but the Devil.

The history of blues music is rife with theological implications, as theologians will quickly assert. But it is not the entire story behind the religious vitality energizing, inspiring, and empowering musicians and communities of fans, a vitality and musical form that was associated with sexuality and, as usual when conjuring up sex in American history, perceived as a mortal threat to the moral life of the nation by many whites in the middle decades of the twentieth century. The "devil's music" is a designation that emerged out of long-standing fears about the presence of evil in the black body and bodies of blacks congregated together after Reconstruction, especially from the perspective of the church—both black and white—with the church being one of the few acceptable places for black bodies to assemble in intimate, highly powerful collectivities.

Local authorities and many in surrounding communities identified the "juke" joints and other clubs where blues musicians first performed and audiences clapped, sang, and danced to the music as hazardous to public health and safety; the visceral power of the music, combined with the collective, physical energy of the crowd served the wanton desires of the Devil, they feared, not the spiritual truths of the one true God. The phrase "devil's music" also gained stature and a certain social legitimacy in the writings of Paul Oliver, a white blues scholar in the early 1960s who took the music seriously as an object of study but also remained fixated on familiar themes for those who feared evil lurking in the pleasures and temptations of musical expressions linked to Africa: sexuality, devilry, and primitivism.[13] It also stems from a limited, and intolerant, religious imagination pervading dominant American culture that tends to see the world only in black and white, and sacred and profane.

God and the Devil do not have to figure into the religious equation for the blues to be understood as a source of identity, resistance, transcendence, and community. Black theologian James Cone wrote about the emergence of the blues as an alternate to the dominance of Christianity in African American history: "Not all Blacks could accept the divine promises of the Bible as a satisfactory answer to the contradictions of Black existence. They refused to adopt a God-centered perspective as the solution to the problem of Black suffering. Instead, they sang, 'Got the blues, and too dam' mean to cry.' "[14] In a more explicit passage making a critical distinction between the God-focused spirituals and the godless, but still religious, so-called "secular" blues, and echoing the perspective of this book, Cone states that "the blues people . . . sing as if God is irrelevant, and their task is to deal with trouble without special reference to Jesus Christ. This is not atheism; rather, it is believing that *transcendence* will only be meaningful when it is made real in and through the limits of historical experience."[15]

Rather than rely on the Devil or God to make sense of the music, many authors emphasize the instrumental and still flourishing presence of West African cultural forms such as conjure, hoodoo, and spirit possession in popular music that do not conform to western cultural logics about the place of religion, and music for that matter, in society.[16] Blues music became a sacred source of meaning thanks not to God or the Devil, but instead as a result of other religious forces that coalesced in the communities taking shape around early bluesmen and women, in and around the Mississippi Delta but soon across the urban landscapes of the South and North. African musical inspirations and forms did more than survive in the highjacked cultures and enslaved bodies of men and women forcibly taken from their families and communities across the Atlantic; they in many ways propelled communities into the future and actively shaped larger cultural movements by providing an immaterial tie that strengthened, indeed revitalized, collective bonds and a sense of identity.

Blues music can be understood as a resource of revitalization in black communities in early twentieth-century America, a culturally innovative way for self-reflection and collectively imagining and making sense of everyday realities tied to sickness and the search for health, or to dreams and the cruelty of social conditions.[17] The task of making meaning in and finding liberation from a world of suffering and chaos, injustice and violence, is a pivotal collective enterprise in the production and regeneration of religious cultures and a familiar trait through human history when communities are besieged, embattled, and severely disempowered—in enslaved communities in the southeastern United States at the birth of the nation or, to cite another example close to home, in ravaged, disenfranchised Native American communities with members who established the Peyote Church, or to give yet another example, further away in time but more relevant than ever, in persecuted Jewish communities around 33 CE.

In addition to the power and presence of the African past, many performers were quite charismatic, and their music could enliven a crowd, inspiring people to let go in body and spirit, an experience not uncommon in the black church, but here transported by the spirit of music and not the Holy Spirit. The spirit came through lyrically too. Sometimes sobering, sometimes playful reflections on embodied, real-life experiences in this world resonated with listeners who may not have lived through the stories communicated by song but who surely shared common frames of reference and angles of vision—love and heartbreak, alcohol and evil, powerlessness and sex—everyday realities that through the lyrics and performances do not simply speak to the mundane, wallow in misery, or titillate as crass entertainment, but instead transform the ordinary into something extraordinary. How does this transformation take place? Not by reliance on the "Lord, Lord, Lord," even though this word and others borrowed from the church are frequently invoked for lyrical punctuations rather than theological proclamations in the blues. Perhaps it is the power of the blues as a reconstructed cultural repository for African American supernatural perspectives and practices, such as conjuring, which leads to transformation, transcendence, and other signs of empowerment that can affect physical, material circumstances as well as modify the life of the individual soul and a larger spiritual community.[18] Perhaps it is just the music itself, the singing, the instruments, the relationships between performer and audience, along with the specific cultural and historical roots beginning in Africa but altered on the American shores thanks to slavery, Christianization, resistance, emancipation, and discrimination, that gives blues the power to create religious cultures.

Either way, the blues entertained as well and quickly became a commodified, commercialized form of entertainment—lucrative primarily for whites in the music industry rather than the musicians themselves. Clubs could get rowdy, too, with fights and drinking taking place inside. Yet these places also frequently created an atmosphere conducive to a kind of physical freedom—to sing and dance and groove with others—that was simply impossible in any other public, communal space, except in the church, of course.

The dynamic, complex forces at work in blues are fraught with a potent mixture of social energies that cannot be reduced to conventional theological ideas or one single essence with an irreducible core. Its transformative power emerges in the impressive physical sensations and powerful emotional impact of communities of listeners participating in highly ritualized, shared musical moments of collective vitality. It also flows, sometimes but not always, through one particularly compelling, charismatic figure. Many observers and analysts of the blues have made these kinds of arguments, drawing parallels between preachers and blues performers, between preaching the Gospel and "preaching the blues," and between religious rituals and musical performance. But the point remains: even though blues music is not gospel music and the house of blues is not the body of Christ, traces of religious life and meaning are interlaced with the generation and consumption of the music.

It may seem like a long way from blues to hip-hop, but the religious continuities are striking: grappling with oppression and disempowerment in lyrical content, challenging traditional musical forms in innovative ways, drawing on African cultural repertoires of meaning and action, and embodying musical rhythms as a form of personal expression and social bonding. No longer explicitly referred to as "devil's music," hip-hop, rap, and other kinds of popular music associated with black culture are nonetheless identified by culture warriors on the right, black and white, as doing the devil's work—a dangerous source for immorality, spiritual decline, and criminal activity in society generally, but especially in the younger generation. Although eventually crossing over and being embraced by white consumers and cultural producers, from imitative suburban kids to top-level executives in multinational entertainment corporations, this expression of black culture has attained phenomenal economic success and global reach despite or, probably more accurately, because of these charges.

But there is something more to the music than scandal and scintillation, something irreducible to any one factor yet potentially spiritually explosive and liberating. When the constellation of social ingredients are added up, including vigorous public debates over the merits and effects of the music, boisterous and effervescent concert settings, and lyrical content that meaningfully addresses and effectively reimagines the realities blacks face in white America, the presence of this "something" extra, the sacred, becomes crystal clear. As highly contested musical forms that graphically depict sexual themes and experiences, violent communities and police brutalities, capitalist excesses and social inequities, hip-hop and rap not only generate robust religious experiences and rituals but also carve out a significant space in the public arena to question and subvert putative American religious values tied to equality, democracy, and justice—hinting at a persistent, deep-rooted prophetic voice that has been an integral element of black culture in monotheistic America from slavery to civil rights.

Inspired not by the God of the Israelites as was the case for Martin Luther King Jr., nor by the prophet Mohammed in the case of Malcolm X in his later years, religious sensibilities in hip-hop cultures emerge from playful and poetic reflection on the here and now, embodied experience in an unjust, chaotic world, and this-worldly liberation through social action and the power of the imagination. God is not absent in this cultural milieu—indeed rapping for Jesus and other kinds of spiritual investments in this music by individuals who follow one of the Abrahamic faiths is now quite common. At the moment a Hasidic rapper from New York, Matisyahu, who merges African beats with Jewish mysticism, is all the rage in some hip-hop quarters.

Gangsta rappers consistently invoke God, or the Lord, or Jesus, and incorporate familiar religious imagery into their music, personas, and everyday language, effortlessly mixing sacred and profane in ways that completely subvert the meanings of each. DMX's first album in 1998, *It's Dark and Hell Is Hot*, gives props to a very special figure in the making of the album: "I am thanking my top dog, my Lord first," a popular "dog" for many in the religious cultures of sports and celebrities generally. Hip-hop mogul Kanye West released the immensely popular hit "Jesus Walks" from his 2004 album, *The College Dropout*. It was initially embraced by gospel music fans, who were so confused by its theology that the Stellar Committee, which oversees the popular gospel-focused

Stellar Awards, revoked a decision to include West on the nomination ballots for the year's competition.[19] To round out the monotheistic traditions, a strong Islamic presence is also a part of the picture, with Muslim rappers happily and creatively blending Koranic theology with the politics of the street.

But the point here, as throughout this book, is that hip-hop musical cultures reflect more than just God-flavored theological celebration and light or street-level degradation and darkness; there is more here that cannot be easily dismissed as misguided spirituality that ultimately serves the Lord or inspires his wrath. In media coverage of the popularity of crunk music, a new form of hip-hop pioneered by Lil John and the East Side Boyz, religious language is often used to capture and convey the impact of the music on fans. An Associated Press story on their 2004 release, *Crunk Juice*, the follow-up to the wildly successful *King of Crunk*, introduces the sacred to get to the heart of the story in the first sentence, stating that "crunk music incites a fervor in fans that's reminiscent of a religious experience." Then rapper David Banner is quoted: "I would define crunk as more of a spirit. Have you been to a Baptist church in the South? It's similar to that. . . . It's that feeling in the club that gets you through life."[20]

On the other hand, religious content emanating from hip-hop worlds of music can emerge out of mournful realities as well as celebratory club-cultures. After describing gang life on the streets in a barrage of violent, gripping images, including "Peace is a dream, reality is a knife," Ice T instructs those with the most liberal intentions in the early gangsta rap hit from 1995, "Colors," "Give me a break, what world do you live in? / Death is my sect, guess my religion." The source for this godless strand of religious identity and meaning-making is, as many artists and scholars have said, the reality of the streets, where encounters with violence and death and sexuality can generate the sacred and bring to life a religious imagination that is not always theological.

Like the blues, hip-hop ignites and incites religious cultures that do not depend on the written words of a sacred book for inspiration but instead create new worlds of sacred meaning through words, music, community, and movement, often improvised and therefore closest to the truth of the moment, but also choreographed and quite thoughtful, even philosophical to many. It is a spirituality of a different sort, one that works against the grain of conventional views that limit it to purely personal experience or to solitary and mystical practices of the individual; instead it is robustly social, emanating from spaces—such as street corners, house and block parties, and concert arenas—set apart by participants who ritually gather together and share in collective energies that emerge and bind both through the music, but also, after the music ends, through other channels, including merchandise, cyberspace, and celebrity watching.

Elvis Presley was not black. But the black roots of the music he helped popularize—and the popular, material, fulfilling, religious cultures that blossomed for millions of Americans at the end of the 1950s and still flourish today because of the music—is difficult to deny. For this very reason, Elvis is also an inflammatory icon of real-life white racism and cultural exploitation to some rappers. As Chuck D from Public Enemy sings provocatively in "Fight the Power" on the soundtrack for Spike Lee's 1989 cinematic meditation on racism in America, *Do the Right Thing*: "Elvis didn't mean shit to me." But Elvis did not cause a cultural revolution solely because of his partial formation by and exposure to African American cultures, particularly through gospel and the blues, during his early years growing up in Tupelo, Mississippi, and then Memphis, Tennessee. Instead, Elvis was something of a musical sponge, absorbing a wide range of musical influences including hillbilly, country, rockabilly, and blues, along with the gospel that was filtered through Pentecostal sensibilities when he sang with his parents as a child.[21]

But the notion of organic assimilation or natural influence

does not quite get at the more active power, truly mysterious and inexplicable, that follows Elvis's music, emanating from that young, energetic body playing the guitar, singing a tune, and moving above and below the hips to the undeniable rhythms—sexually suggestive, as is commonly stated, but sacred, too. More like a trickster or conjurer, to apply African categories, at the dawn of his long, ultimately tragic career, Elvis made music that combined available musical repertoires in entirely new, creative, transformative ways. The world is a different place after Elvis.

Elvis's performances in the late 1950s captured, and continue to capture, the public's attention enough to establish and maintain the myth that rock and roll began with him, now a permanent origin point in the sacred story of rock music. Especially relevant is the legendary effort to emasculate the sexual energy of the music—as always a destructive source of great concern to many in mainstream America—by filming Elvis on *The Ed Sullivan Show* in 1956 only from the waist up. The energy deriving from the music, filtered through his body, and radiating to communities of fans in his physical or mediated presence, could ultimately not be shut down or controlled. Denying this, even for one fateful moment, only fueled the popular fires then and now burning for more Elvis. The numerous other television shows and performances of the period in the mid- to late 1950s had already given the people what they most wanted, and what some most feared, and that was a full-bodied Elvis possessed by a musical attitude and spirit that was quite different than anything white, mainstream America had ever seen.

Legendary singer Roy Orbison, for example, states in a 1989 interview that he "first saw Elvis live in '54. It was at the Big D Jamboree in Dallas and first thing, he came out and spit on the stage. . . . I didn't know what to make of it. There was just no reference point in the culture to compare it."[22] In the immortal words of Butch Hancock, a singer and songwriter from Texas who commented on Elvis in the 1950s and is quoted in Michael Ventura's essay on the voodoo origins of rock and roll: "Yeah, that was the dance that everybody forgot. It was the dance that was so strong it took an entire civilization to forget. And ten seconds to remember it."[23] Perhaps African Americans recognized something familiar in the physical freedom and spontaneity of the dance they never forgot, and the defiant act of spitting on stage. But for many others, the musical energy, physical abandon, and liberatory potential of participating in this emergent cultural form of expression—that might include spitting, sweating, and gyrating—was infectious but until that moment in history unthinkable, engendering a social movement that had and still has political muscle on the streets, commercial value in the markets, and sacred power to inspire activities in each milieu for multiple communities of devoted fans.

Rock and roll culture, like hip-hop to some degree, spins out a variety of musical forms and styles that make it supremely difficult to establish one all-encompassing definition or fundamental characteristic. Folk, heavy metal, experimental, punk, psychedelic, alt-country, and many other labels can be bandied about in the rock music world and each one can generate its own version of a religious culture. On the other hand, religious cultures do not emerge from just any rocker; the sacred does not adhere in and exude forth from the likes of Steppenwolf or REO Speedwagon or Peter Frampton or Blink 182, no matter how momentarily popular they might be at any given time. The sacred, however, is an integral element of certain phenomena in the history of rock, found in its origins with Elvis (whose association with the sacred and American religious cultures is even more pronounced after his death as a living ghost haunting imaginative and commercial landscapes) and others who contributed to revolutionary musical transformations, including the Beatles, The Who, The Clash, Uncle Tupelo, and Nirvana.

What are the signs of religious life in rock and roll cultures? How do the music and lyrics contribute to popular religious experiences that reimagine and reconstruct the world (in this case not as grounded in real-life suffering and disenfranchisement as experienced by black Americans), invigorate and reinvigorate social bonds, and stimulate and liberate the body first, and then the soul? The God who gave Moses and the ancient Hebrews the Ten Commandments does not figure in the answers to these questions. Some songs acknowledge the entirely secondary nature of this figure in any form when it comes to more urgent matters that take precedence over Him, while still conveying a basic spiritual longing and search for meaning. Listen to Jay Farrar sing in "Whiskey Bottle" on Uncle Tupelo's masterful 1990 debut album, *No Depression*— "Whiskey Bottle, over Jesus, not forever, just for now"—as one example of how ultimate concerns and sacral relations are reconfigured as the singer struggles to "find something to believe."

Religion lives in ultimate concerns—what matters most, and cuts the deepest—and sacral relations between people, living and dead, two characteristics that have been prominent in rock and roll religious cultures from the 1960s to the present. One obvious setting to consider, identified by scholars and fans themselves as containing these and other religious characteristics, is a typical Grateful Dead concert, a setting that is highly charged with sacred meanings and compelling ritual, in the material world but not quite fully a part of it. Baptized by the countercultural fires of acid trips and Altamont, free love and painful deaths, the Grateful Dead flourished over roughly three short decades in part because they invested so much in touring and playing in front of a live audience.

Concerts are a prime site for collecting data about religious life in rock culture: pilgrimage, spirituality, mysticism, shamanism, identity, transformation, unity, sacraments, and other familiar characteristics signal the presence of the sacred, of supernatural actions, of the possibility for fulfillment and transcendence individually and with others. Whether drawing from obscure phenomenological theories on the numinous or from transparent self-descriptions in ethnographic data, scholars come to the same conclusion: Dead shows are not "like" a religion, they *are* religious, through and through, promoting religious experiences in pilgrims, religious community among fans, and religious values out of both. Some of the narrative themes that recur when Deadheads themselves describe music-inspired concert experiences include "loss of self and expansion of consciousness," "profound mystical union with the whole universe," "experience of disintegration, death, and rebirth," and "powerful emotional healing experiences."[24]

These snippets from Deadhead life and language reaffirm a persistent theme: there is more to music than what passes through the eardrum. The physical vibrations at the root of musical expression can penetrate and liberate bodies individually and collectively, creating personal and social experiences that are interpreted as religious, sacred, spiritual, and, for many Deadheads and rock fans generally, the source for extraordinary transformations and insights that do not end when the lights in the arena are turned back on. Rather, they are powerful and lingering experiences that spill out of the concert and remain meaningful—as memories of what took place in the past or an impetus for what shall take place in the future—in the lives of fans.

The Grateful Dead phenomenon, starting in the mid-sixties in the Haight-Ashbury district of San Francisco, is better characterized as a short, familiar story rather than a long, strange trip in the larger scheme of this book. The group's reign as one of the more eclectic, psychedelic, and popular bands to emerge in the vibrant though somewhat disordered and unpredictable musical landscape of the late 1960s and early 1970s lasted until the mid-1990s, when Jerry Garcia's ashes were scattered in the Ganges. A few band members still survive today, but soon they will be no more, and the spirit of the Dead will depend on the memories of their aging fans and whether future generations of Deadheads can endure without access to the sacred possibilities aroused by live music, and without being in the presence of the band at concerts, where devotees were ritually rejuvenated again and again, where old worlds were shattered and new worlds ordered, and where bodies easily experienced both drug-induced and drug-free ecstasies brought to life by the power of the music and community.

Is there a future in this religious culture now that Jerry is dead and the band is no more? Tupac Shakur, a lucrative ghost from the gangsta rap world, is one of many examples of musical life resurrected and sustained by communities—with purchasing power but also devotional commitments—in the face of the biological fact of physical death. Death and the disappearance of once present bodies, particularly flesh and blood celebrity bodies, will not kill musical religious cultures. On the contrary, religious cultures draw strength from biological truths, and the end becomes a means to solidify, and ritually revivify, still-living bodies bound together by the death of certain historical figures who become immortal gods of a sort—not God, but staying with Christian imagery, perhaps closer to "cultural saints," a topic to reappear soon. The Grateful Dead still live—in the hearts of fans, in films and documentaries, in scholarship, in cyberspace, in eternal recordings and new packaging, in ritual gatherings still focused on the music, either recorded or by a cover band, in rock and roll mythology, in holy relics and sacred texts: a religious culture in full bloom.

The Dead also live on and are accessible thanks to the sacred institution that is yet another expression of rock and roll religious culture: the Rock and Roll Hall of Fame. This shrine located in Cleveland, Ohio, contains the permanent Hall of Fame exhibit as well as other traveling shows, and is also available to the world on the web. The Grateful Dead were inducted into the hall in 1994 at the ninth annual ceremony, a year before the death of Jerry Garcia at age fifty-three. They are now a permanent part of the collection—an achievement that does not in and of itself signify the sacred but in this and many cases only enriches and solidifies it for many devotees. The textual tribute to the band on the web reads in part, "Deadheads and critics alike contended that the best way to experience the group was in concert, where the mystical band-fan bonding ritual drove the music to improvisational peaks."[25] The mystical bonding ritual may have led to creative musical expression, but the concerts themselves were rock and roll religious revivals with the music a vital source for cultural and personal transformation and fulfillment. Deadheads did indeed reach a higher ground at concerts and in the process transformed ordinary spaces like auditoriums and sports arenas into extraordinary settings experienced as sacred ground.

3

SPORTS

"Sacred Ground."

This is the name of an exhibit, dedicated to baseball stadiums and the fans they attract, that opened at the Baseball Hall of Fame, in Cooperstown, New York, the mythic birthplace of the sport, in May 2005. It includes hundreds of artifacts from baseball history and baseball lore—holy relics touched in some way at some time by baseball icons and teams. An ancient ticket booth from Yankee Stadium, an on-deck circle from Forbes Field in Pittsburgh, a turnstile from the ill-fated Polo Grounds (a Manhattan stadium that burned to the ground in 1911), a scoreboard pinwheel from Comiskey Park in Chicago—all objects that are sanctified by the presence of legendary teams and heroic men, containing magical residue that can produce awe, fascination, a chill, pleasure, or respect from the faithful fans who make the pilgrimage to the remote enclave in Cooperstown.

As this exhibit and the activities surrounding it suggest, baseball is much more than a national pastime, more spiritually potent than a competitive game with bats and balls would seem at first glance. In fact "Sacred Ground" at Cooperstown is just one of many examples that demonstrate how the world of sports is infused with religious frames of reference and meaning, and how sports energize legions of fans who ritually and mythically transform the secular into the sacrosanct. A careful examination of baseball, or any number of sports-related phenomena, points to a strange, but strangely familiar, confluence of religious sensibilities with competitive play. Over the course of the twentieth century, this confluence has produced flourishing religious cultures dedicated to specific teams, athletes, and moments in time that have ultimate value in the lives of many Americans and billions of dollars in material value to athletes, owners, and corporations.

Sacred spaces and moral dilemmas, rites and superstitions, legends and lore—these and other unequivocally religious dimensions of sports today remind us that there is more at stake in this social activity than winners and losers, endorsements and contracts, entertainment and leisure time. There is also more to the religious dimensions of sports than how often athletes pray to God before competition or, to take a more specific theological question, what role "Touchdown Jesus," a famous mural overlooking the Notre Dame football field, plays in the team's wins, or losses for that matter. Americans turn to sports in times of crisis and celebration; they mark the passage of time with signposts from memorable moments in sports history; they even draw moral sustenance from sports-related activities on and off the field.

Professionals and amateurs, casual fans and true fanatics expend a great deal of energy to be a part of the game—energy tied to economic activity associated with training for, participating in, and attending sporting events, but also energy drawing from something more fundamental and less material than the financial output that accounts for the commodification of sports: play. Playing games, physically interacting with others, playfully stepping outside of ordinary, routine social conventions provides humans with time-consuming, satisfying activity, but play also has a deeper impact on the quality of human life. It is a behavior humans share with many animals, suggesting that play may be an inherited trait embedded in our evolutionary past and tied to instincts deeply rooted in biology. But even if a "play" gene can be identified, or the exact location of experiences of pleasure derived from play can be imaged in the brain, this common characteristic of human societies ultimately creates its own unusual, socially powerful energies

that defy any rational, reductionistic explanations as to their purpose or reality.

In the fascinating and still-relevant 1944 study *Homo Ludens: A Study of the Play-Element in Culture*, cultural historian Johan Huizinga argues that play is rich with meanings and is highly significant activity. Starting out with the obvious physiological and psychological functions, Huizinga understands play as intimately tied to the emergence of ritual in archaic societies, allowing for unusual but vital social interactions explainable by neither individual biological drives nor social material needs. Contrary to the everyday worlds of work, domestic life, and ordinary consciousness, "play is a voluntary action or occupation executed within certain fixed limits of time and place, according to rules freely accepted but absolutely binding, having its aim in itself and accompanied by a feeling of tension, joy, and consciousness that is 'different' from 'ordinary life.' "[1] For Huizinga, play is a "life function" contributing to individual well-being and the health of the social body.[2]

The history of organized play is replete with examples of sports activity and structured competitions that have sacred significance. Native American ball games, Nigerian wrestling matches, ancient Chinese contests at fertility feasts, and—a mythic touchstone for contemporary sports events—the early Greek Olympics all demonstrate not only the close connections between religion and competition, ritual and play, but also the promotion of social order, inculcation of cultural values, and expenditure of consequential and highly valued energy for the individual and the group. They all also depend on one crucial, fundamental condition: physical exertions that bring bodies, often of the same sex and usually males, in contact with each other in peculiar, extraordinary ways.

In the modern era, sports and sporting events have often inspired quite conflicting interpretations about their social worth, let alone sacred values. George Orwell, the British essayist and novelist, was highly suspicious about the volatile mix of large crowds, aroused passions, and group (particularly nationalistic) identities in competitive, physical struggles. In his view, organized play had been transformed into violent spectacles that resembled cultic activity instead of good-natured sports matches: "Serious sport has nothing to do with fair play. It is bound up with hatred, jealousy, boastfulness, disregard of all rules and sadistic pleasure in witnessing violence: in other words it is war minus the shooting. Instead of blah-blahing about the clean, healthy rivalry of the football field and the great part played by the Olympics in bringing the nations together, it is more useful to inquire how and why this modern cult of sport arose." [3] The modern cult dates back to ancient origins, Orwell goes on to say, and then from the Roman Empire to the nineteenth century, it remained dormant, out of the public eye for the most part. In the twentieth century, social conditions in England and the United States were ripe for the birth of what Orwell calls an "infection"—modern sports—that spreads throughout the world thanks to the right combination of capital, nationalism, and, bubbling in the crowds of spectators, "rousing savage passions." [4]

Other commentators identify a distinctly more benevolent religious component in modern sports that invigorates and bodes well for the health of the social body. In the popular celebration of religion in sports, to take one well-known, often cited example, *The Joy of Sports*—a book that playfully apes the title of *The Joy of Sex*—theologian Michael Novak writes "sports flow outward from a deep natural impulse that is radically religious: an impulse of freedom, respect for ritual limits, a zest for symbolic meaning, and a longing for perfection." [5] What is so peculiar for Novak and so many other observers, fans, athletes, scholars, and others is that sports is a religious culture that permeates civil society and coexists with, rather the supplants, organized religion. Bonding with others; encountering powers outside the norm; engaging in fulfilling rituals and with meaningful symbols; overcoming suffering and defeat, even death; venerating unforgettable, morally exemplary heroes—these and other sacred signs suggest to Novak the spiritually generative, nontheistic but ultimately nationalistic possibilities of religious play in American society.

Michael Mandelbaum tackled the subject of sports in *The Meaning of Sports: Why Americans Watch Baseball, Football and Basketball and What They See When They Do.*[6] In the first chapter, tellingly entitled "A Variety of Religious Experience," Mandelbaum suggests that along with social changes in the mid-nineteenth century tied to education, urbanization, and transportation, a key factor in the emergence and popularity of team sports was longer childhoods, where learning to play these sports initiates a lifelong nostalgia for time past that is fulfilled in large part by watching others play. Sports and religion have crucial similarities with this view, including satisfying the needs of the spirit, participating in worlds beyond the working world, and providing what twenty-first-century Americans seek most in this world: enjoyable diversions from daily routines, a model of order and coherence, and heroes to look up to and follow.[7] Organized sports are not an organized religion, yet many identify something familiarly religious in this particular arena of social life.

Modern sports have been variously labeled as a popular religion, folk religion, secular religion, cultural religion, quasi religion, surrogate religion, and false religion. As a peculiar, highly ritualized, and emotional (not to mention immensely lucrative) social activity fixated on bodies in physically and mentally demanding competitions, sports has acquired multiple, conflicting meanings in contemporary culture. In contrast to the divine presence at the ancient Olympic Games in Greece, when athletes and spectators, slaves and elites participated in festivals dedicated to gods like Zeus and Apollo, religious devotions and sacred practices are less clear-cut in today's sporting events. Buick and Budweiser provide some of the dominant iconography in contemporary sports culture; beer drinking and the wave are two examples of ritual commonly observed at stadiums and arenas around the country. Regardless of

the particular cultural trappings and details of how play is organized and displayed for others, this ritual activity inspires behaviors
and motivations that express prevailing values and ideals as well as
less ennobling, more notorious acts that subvert those very principles and demonstrate just what is at stake in play. Even though
play is foundational in modern sports, the stakes are, as in war,
supremely high and ultimate investments in teams and athletes
make for some of the most serious moments in a person's life. Why
is there so much at stake in sports?

Baseball fields become "sacred ground" with or without God to
sanctify the space, as the popular 1989 film *Field of Dreams* suggests
in its mythic depictions of the game and its potential to blur the
boundaries between the living and the dead, dreams and reality,
fans and their heroes. At the opening ceremonies for the "Sacred
Ground" exhibit, current Hall of Fame president Dale Petroskey
put the special kinship between fans and the game in a distinctly
religious light: "Growing up in Detroit, Tiger Stadium was like a
second home to me. It was where we built memories. . . . This exhibit captures that magical connection that forms between fans
and their ballpark. These places will never be forgotten, and
through 'Sacred Ground,' they never will be."[8] The magic that
bonds fans and players or teams should not be discounted as a relic
itself, a suspicious, somehow inferior—evolutionarily but also
morally—category signaling "primitive" modes of thinking distinct from enlightened "religion." On the contrary, the magic experienced in stadiums by Petroskey and millions of other baseball
fans from the earliest games in the nineteenth century is effica-
cious in its ability to transform a mere game into a sacred source
for religious life.

    The exhibit is divided into six themes, including "Fans," "Ball-
park Business," "Evolution of the Ballpark," and "Reverence."
"Reverence" is a space dedicated to those extraordinary places that
arouse particularly intense feelings of attachment and value among

hometown fans, such as Tiger Stadium and Wrigley Field, and photos of statues from stadiums around the country of immortal players, dead and still living, such as Babe Ruth and Henry Aaron. Various interactive displays throughout the exhibit can bring the glory days of the past to virtual life in the present, providing visitors with a glimpse of the South End Grounds in Boston, another famous early ballpark lost to a fire; or a chance to sit in a pair of authentic seats from Philadelphia's Veterans Stadium; or a chance to hear the familiar, uplifting strains of "Take Me Out to the Ball Game" with a push of a button. The exhibit makes its case well that baseball stadiums are "sacred ground"—the sacred is grounded in this game, yet it also flows from these sights and sounds, objects and visions, artificially but substantially recreating realities that infuse lives with special meanings, feelings, communities, and memories.

"Sacred Ground" is part of a $20-million renovation finished at the Hall of Fame. Rededication ceremonies for this American institution, which first opened in 1939, took place during the annual induction weekend ritual in July 2005. In addition to honoring the featured inductions of Wade Boggs and Ryne Sandburg, the ceremonies also celebrated the extra ten thousand square feet for the building, the opening of new exhibits and galleries, and the refurbished interiors that are not only more accessible for visitors with disabilities but also very kid-friendly for pilgrims who are young or old and who are usually making the sacred journey with families. But from the beginning, the hallowed grounds of the hall have been more than a special tourist attraction in upstate New York; it is, to use one of the common words applied to this unique space, a shrine on the religious landscape that has unusual power in the lives of fans and athletes themselves. One newspaper article covering the ceremonies in 2005, entitled "New Look Puts Shine on Shrine," ends with the words of Hall of Famer Brooks Robinson: "There's something mystical about this place. . . . You look at those plaques and a shiver goes down your spine."[9]

These religious sentiments are echoed throughout the game's history by Americans who find the appropriate language to capture their feelings about it. At the opening of the Hall of Fame in 1939, which included induction ceremonies for such early legends as Cy Young, Babe Ruth, and Walter Johnson, NBC radio announcer Tom Manning describes the setting of the Hall of Fame and says that "inside . . . are priceless relics from one thousand memorable games"; Master of Ceremonies Charles Doyle sermonizes that the crowd attending the event "gather in reverence to baseball's immortals, living and dead"; and federal judge and baseball's first commissioner Kennesaw Mountain Landis makes the official dedication to open the doors of the Hall of Fame, what he calls "this shrine to sportsmanship." [10] The draw is strong for pilgrims, who go for more than secular reasons, driven to worship the game by a mixture of motives that are at one and the same time emotional, psychological, rational, irrational, and spiritual—perhaps even theological for some Jews and Christians who imagine God's presence at the hall. A newspaper article before the 2005 ceremonies notes that roughly 350,000 visitors a year make their way to Cooperstown before offering up a more personal story of pilgrims who "bond with baseball." In this case, an old grandfather tells of his birthday wish to bring his grandson to the hall. The wish is granted and the two travel from Houston to New York where, the article reports, the grandfather "had the bearing of a man shaking hands with a dream." The grandfather has his own words to describe the experience: "I feel like I'm in a chapel, or something." [11]

This shrine, also referred to as a sports "mecca," is something else indeed; it is not quite a chapel or a church, yet what takes place inside is so similar to worship—really, worship of another sort— that even awkwardly employed traditional religious vocabulary, words like "pilgrimage," "reverence," or "devotion," is simply for many the best way to communicate what it means to be there. The Hall of Fame itself is sacred ground, cultivated from the spiritual energies tied to planning and making the family journey, encountering the extraordinary items and virtual and real-life experiences offered inside, and sharing the effervescent space with others who are devoted to the game like everyone else there.

Many people who visit and experience the hall as a shrine bring God with them through the doors, no doubt; they also leave with their religious identity intact, secure in the durability of religious traditions to withstand encounters with a different kind of sacred source, one that is clearly accessible to pilgrims of all stripes, Christian or Jew, Hindu or Buddhist, pagan or unaffiliated. The Baseball Hall of Fame is an institutionalized expression of a much deeper, more pervasive religious sensibility surrounding baseball from its mythic origins with Abner Doubleday to the popular fascination with the infamous "Bambino curse" during the 2004 World Series between the Boston Red Sox and the New York Yankees. In Ken Burns's popular documentary on the game, which includes scandals and triumphs, heroes and villains, history and lore, one obvious conclusion is reached about the game: there is something uncannily religious about it, with a great deal at stake.

When Janet Jackson's exposed breast and starburst-covered nipple flashed for seconds during the halftime celebration at Super Bowl XXXIX in 2004, the sacred dimensions of sports and the high stakes involved in play, in this case professional football, were put into high relief in the uproar that followed. This championship battle between the AFC division winner New England Patriots and NFC leader Carolina Panthers was overshadowed by a bare female breast, a decidedly unusual sight even at the big game for viewers who are repeatedly exposed to female cleavage, bouncing breasts, camera shots angled from the ground looking up skirts, and other images associated with the female cheerleaders who are a staple of the game. Although male nudity was a common feature of the ancient Greek games, where bodily control, self-discipline, and military ideals reigned supreme, female nudity was not. Women watched the competition from the stands and participated in the surrounding religious and civic festivities. The male athletic body, nude in ancient Greece, fully clad with extra padding and a helmet in contemporary American football, dominates the field in sports and, though competition may verge on the erotic for some, it is generally framed in militaristic rather than sexual terms.[12]

The breast crossed a line for many viewers and spectators at the stadium, who were stunned at what many perceived to be intentionally provocative. Not crossing lines, playing by the rules, maintaining boundaries that ensure order—these are essential preconditions for sports play, as well as military and religious institutions for that matter. For each of these highly disciplined, body-monitoring activities, lines, rules, and boundaries are established around bodies in part because of the human propensity to cross, break, and transgress them. These transgressions create moments that contravene expectations of order and stability, structure and control, but that are also scandalous and thrilling breakdowns captivating, often enrapturing, a public routinely salivating for people who go too far.

Violence breaking out between players on the field or between fans in the stands, the growing scourge of steroids and other performance-enhancing drugs by athletes as well as gambling scandals and policy violations by coaches or management—these and other kinds of ignominious sports stories have moral import, as entertaining or as tragic as they may be, for larger social communities with members whose ethical formation and principles are shaped as much by play on the field as by words in a church. Indeed, morals are tested on these playing fields, where the temptations to transgress, deceive, and cheat are so compelling for players and sensational for fans that every game is a ritual reminder and reaffirmation of rules and laws, boundaries and prohibitions that will, of necessity, break down. The well-regulated male body in competition is a morally charged, ethically challenged body that is, however, only one piece in the larger religious complex of sports.

No doubt the moral outrage that erupted upon seeing Jackson's breast reverberated across all kinds of communities: Christian, Jew, and Muslim; Hindu and Buddhist as well; even atheists and pagans (well, maybe not pagans) vigorously complained about such an offensive act, especially because the halftime show is considered to be a shared, family viewing experience with vulnerable children present who can easily be led morally astray. Their fury may have derived from a New Testament understanding of a woman's place; or it might have emerged from a strong political commitment to family values; or it may simply have been based on a less tolerant limit on the line between decency and indecency. The range of people who complained and the impact of the collective crisis and debate about the nipple also point to a deeper significance, one that is especially pronounced during this event. The breast was clearly matter out of place. For a brief moment this particular part of Janet Jackson's anatomy illustrated the very inviolability of the Super Bowl, an event as sacred and ritually fulfilling as any holy day marked off on religious calendars from around the world.

The Super Bowl is certainly a media circus and an advertising godsend, but it is also a religious festival, as many observers and participants have claimed—a momentous event embedded in a religious culture tied to sports generally and, in this case, football specifically, with a litany of remembered moments like Joe Namath's famous prediction of a Jets victory over the Colts, or memorable icons like Vince Lombardi, who stands as a ghostly beacon in football lore. But in addition to the money and glory associated with the game, symbolic and ritual orders are also reaffirmed at the Super Bowl festival, one of the most popular television events in the country, and most especially at the very center of the festivities, the middle of the field, and in the middle of the game, as well as at the very end of a long season of conflict and strife, risk-taking and chance for the teams involved.

Flags flying, fans behaving, time passing, authorities presiding, athletes competing—the game is predicated on familiar sights and sounds, movements and interactions, a predictable order of things, in sports perhaps more so than in the daily world outside of sports. Yet the very nature of play is inherently unpredictable and volatile, and therefore ripe for emotionally driven, spiritually hungry humans waiting for something memorable and meaningful to happen in this game especially. Although some see it as simply a national, secular holiday, the Super Bowl plays out in American culture year after year as a religious event, sacrosanct and celebratory in the lives of millions of fans from all faith traditions and philosophical schools, including believers and nonbelievers, God-fearing fundamentalists and free-spirited lefties.

Although worlds away from Balinese cockfighting, the Super Bowl and football games generally are just as revealing social texts that express a story that Americans like to "tell themselves about themselves." Famous anthropologist Clifford Geertz sees at least this interpretive function in the social activities and symbolic systems surrounding the popular Balinese sport, which cannot be characterized simply as a rite or a pastime. Geertz's analysis of cockfighting can be applied to how one might "read" the Super Bowl: "What the cockfight [or Super Bowl] says it says in a vocabulary of sentiment—the thrill of risk, the despair of loss, the pleasure of triumph. Yet what it says is not merely that risk is exciting, loss depressing, or triumph gratifying, banal tautologies of affect, but that it is of these emotions, thus exampled, that society is built and individuals are put together." [13]

This "sentimental education," to continue with Geertz's insightful language, communicated through the emotionally and cognitively engaging story being told every year in January is both revelatory of culture and instructive to members of culture. But it is a distinctively religious story as well, with or without God in the action, that encompasses and resolves—however temporarily and precariously—a variety of social realities that are less clear, more chaotic, in the world outside of the field of play, such as the persistence of violence and group conflict, confusion around gender divisions and sexual expression, and hypocrisy and double standards in traditional religions where winners and losers do not always represent a just, moral order.

A time for carousing and partying, praying and gambling, the Super Bowl and the festivities surrounding the game arouse passions and behaviors that demonstrate intensive life investments and ultimately valuable stakes. Janet Jackson flashing her breast is one way to identify how much is at stake, but the somber, solemn halftime show in January 2002, only a few months after the extraordinary 9/11 terrorist attacks, also captures and reinforces the stakes of the game as well as the centrality of this ritual event in American lives. With the names of the dead scrolling behind them, the band U2 performed on a heart-shaped stage surrounded by patriotic symbols of the American nation, a poignant, heartbreaking image in a night full of ritual acts for the dead and social solidarity, including the raising of a World Trade Center flag by a group of New York City firemen.

According to some reports, the resumption of life and especially accepted forms of play like professional sports after that fatal and fateful day had healing power and religious meaning. In one *USA Today* article in September 2002 that included an image of the flag-raising at the Super Bowl, journalist Erik Brady writes that "ballparks and stadiums became town squares where much of the ritual of public healing took place. . . . Ballparks became home to sacramental ceremony," places that he later refers to as "miniature gardens of Eden."[14] An Eden, though, that does not require the creation of God but instead has sacred vitality on its own terms, a meaningful space where the religious values and valences spring from the play on, and rituals surrounding, the field itself.

The Super Bowl is a holy day as much as it is a sports event, holy as a sacred carnival dedicated to, and undergirded by, consumerism and masculinity, nationalism and play. But at bottom, as popular culture scholar Jack Santino has proposed, the game is really about the desire for power and empowerment.[15] Physical power of athletes competing on the field, strategic power among coaches, corporate power in the expensive stadium suites and celebrated advertisements, iconic power for performers at halftime, and fan empowerment for individuals who identify with teams and have awe-inspiring experiences watching them play—taken together, these sacred powers exuded by the Super Bowl cannot be reduced to purely material forms tied to physical strength, financial might, or alcoholic inebriation; nor can this power be allied only with God, a familiar force called upon by athletes in the will to overpower opponents and by fans in search of a saving grace before the final seconds tick off the game clock.

Instead, the big game has empowering, memorable, ritual vitality in the lives of participants and spectators whether they bring God with them to the game or not; it possesses value-laden drama in the game itself but also in the pre- and postgame activities, all teaching moral lessons relevant to life outside the game; and it assumes mythological status in the popular imagination where whole teams but especially players can enter the pantheon of immortal heroes remembered and idolized as not quite God but more than men, as superhuman exemplars engaged in consequential defining moments that will live on in memory and NFL Films.

Basketball star Michael Jordan has been mistaken for God. After Jordan scored sixty-three points in a particularly memorable playoff game against the Boston Celtics, Larry Bird famously commented that he "thought it was God disguised" as Michael Jordan. Some in the black community have referred to Jordan as the black Jesus. In the heyday of Jordan's unusual if not unprecedented global popularity, it was reported in the *Chicago Tribune* that Jews in Israel believed they were watching God on television when he played. A Parisian newspaper covering the Chicago Bulls' arrival in the French capital proclaimed, "It's God in person."[16] At one press conference for the 1992 Olympics, by then and forevermore associated with "Air Jordan" sneakers from Nike, Jordan seemed uncomfortable when asked if he was a god, with *Time* magazine reporting that "If Michael Jordan is God, then Phil Knight [president of Nike Inc.] put him in heaven." [17]

Chicago Bulls coach Phil Jackson reminisced about how the media director for the team joked about the intensity of fan adoration for Jordan by referring to "Jordan and his entourage as Jesus and the Apostles. 'Jesus goes to the bathroom,' [he] would announce in a mock broadcaster's baritone. 'Details at eleven.' " [18] But we all know Jordan is not God. He is not all-powerful and all-knowing; he did not create the heavens and the earth; he cannot raise the dead; he cannot walk on water. On the other hand, he has been known to fly through the air and defy the laws of gravity, rising above ordinary men and willing himself and his team to super-human, breathtaking heights.

Basketball, like baseball or football, is just a game. Like the others, it is organized play in carefully marked space using balls to score points, with time segmented according to a different logic than the twenty-four-hour day, and most importantly, rules that require opposing teams to conform to the exact same set of values—an ideal rarely fulfilled, so official arbitrators must stay in the action, on the field, with an eye on the ball. This game can also, like the others, bring religious language, behaviors, experiences, to the fore as well. It has its heroes and Hall of Fame; a myth of origins and All-Star game, an annual ritual that entails a much shorter duration of time than the seven games for the NBA championship but is as carnivalesque and religiously active as the Super Bowl; and its legendary teams and memorable moments that live on in the memory of fans and are repeated over and over on television sets with millions of viewers who relive them.

Michael Jordan is not just a basketball legend like Larry Bird or Wilt Chamberlain, nor only a sports icon associated with one franchise, like Red Auerbach and his cigar in Boston, or Kareem Abdul-Jabbar and his signature hook shot in Los Angeles. Voted the number one athlete of the twentieth century on ESPN's

Sportscentury, ahead of Babe Ruth, Muhammad Ali, and Jim Brown, Jordan has been referred to as the greatest athlete of all time, not just one century, by many commentators and fans. He is a superstar whose high-flying, tongue-wagging, gravity-defying body, at least for a decade or so, captured the public's attention and imagination, as well as the critical interest of scholars who claim Jordan has cultural as well as athletic significance in human history.

Books have been written on Jordan that place his body, whether soaring on a court or smiling into the camera, in color or in silhouette, at the nexus of momentous social and cultural change near the end of the century. Walter LaFeber's *Michael Jordan and the New Global Capitalism* is a work that examines the rise of multinational corporations, the spread of new global economies, the infiltration and dominance of new forms of media, and the impact of one man in all these trends; and David Halberstam's *Playing for Keeps: Michael Jordan and the World He Made*, a title intimating at divine creativity, is a remarkably careful study that both participates in and deconstructs the mythologization of Michael Jordan.[19] Pitchman and celebrity, family man and superman, Jordan's rise to cultural preeminence in the closing decades of the twentieth century was larger than life, greater than the sum of its economic, racial, or athletic parts.

Michael Eric Dyson, a well-known professor of humanities, cultural studies, and African American studies, wrote an incisive critical essay in 1993 called "Be Like Mike?: Michael Jordan and the Pedagogy of Desire." In this piece, Dyson explores the cultural meanings of Michael Jordan's fame, particularly his moral authority in the public arena as it relates to the culture of athletics, African American cultures, race and racial identities in American society, and late capitalism and globalization. But he also starts the piece on an unequivocally religious note that is left unexplored in his cultural analysis. After mentioning the "herculean cultural heroism" embodied by Jordan and comparable to Joe DiMaggio and Elvis Presley, Dyson writes, "There is even a religious element to the near worship of Jordan as a cultural icon of invincibility." [20] It is, in Dyson's words, this "cultural canonization" of Jordan that leads to his reflections on the multiple, often contradictory, symbolic, and material investments in Jordan's body from across the social body, emanating from the poorest urban areas to the wealthiest corporate suites on Madison Avenue.

What is religious about Mike? When does fan adoration transform into sacred devotion? Phil Jackson, a practitioner of Zen Buddhism and philosophically inclined head coach of numerous world championship teams, had this to say about Jordan's return from retirement and the pandemonium that transpired upon his presence back in training camp, in a chapter entitled "The Second Coming":

> What interested me was the religious overtone to the proceedings. Perhaps it was the fact that the nation had spent the last year caught up in the O.J. case, suffering the disillusionment of watching a one-time beloved sports great being tried for the murder of his ex-wife and her friend. Perhaps it was just a reflection of spiritual malaise in the culture and the deep yearning for a mythic hero who could set us free. Whatever the reason, during his hiatus from the team, Michael had somehow been transformed in the public mind from a great athlete to a sports deity. [21]

Jordan clearly aroused passions from white and black fans whose behavior could verge on, really cross over into, religious forms of devotion to his body and his image that resemble those found in churches and *masjids*, home shrines and synagogues. Here though, worship is enacted within a religious culture free from the authority of only one God and outside of institutional rules of ritual action, an appropriate state of being for people who believe they are in the presence of something extraordinary, breathtaking, and sacred.

A statue dedicated to the man called "The Spirit," weighing roughly two thousand pounds with the player in the distinctly familiar Nike airborne pose and an inscription that reads, "The best there ever was. The best there ever will be," is one site for evidence of popular worship. It has become a popular tourist attraction in Chicago where visitors from around the globe make time to stand in its shadow, take pictures, and occasionally engage in behavior more akin to pilgrimage rituals than meaningless tourist antics. A *New York Times Magazine* story in 1996 on the high-profile Bulls team that included Dennis Rodman and Scottie Pippin includes the following information about this peculiar statue carved from more than granite, weightier than just its mass for some pilgrims who have strangely meaningful exchanges with the sculpture of a man in perpetual flight: "The statue is wildly popular. People come to pitch pennies at its base, to make wishes, to kneel and pray." [22]

Other unusual acts capture the religious fervor that Jordan inspired in fans, who were compelled to give bodily, material expression to an interior, emotionally charged connection with the star. Jason Caffey, a Bulls rookie in 1996, gave one account in the same *New York Times Magazine* story of how fans resorted to behavior that in another time and place would be recognizably religious acts of devotion and veneration, kinds of actions and postures that can only be accurately described with a religious vocabulary. When practicing free throws in Los Angeles, where forms of celebrity worship generally run rampant, Jordan was interrupted by a fan who, Caffey claims, "dived at his feet and started kissing them. . . . The security had to come and pull him off of Michael's feet—he wouldn't let them go. I'd never seen anyone worshipped like that."

Later in the same article, one of the team assistants makes an odd, yet clearly fitting analogy to communicate the "synergy of hysteria" that could erupt when fans are in the physical presence of stars like Jordan, Pippen, and Rodman: "It's like pictures of the Kennedy funeral, the motorcade. . . . You see all these reactions from adults that you wouldn't normally see—people pointing, mouths open." [23] Although the three men had indescribable talent on the court and, for a short time, were treated as charismatic celebrities off the court by the media and fans, Michael Jordan will likely be the only one to live on in memory and continue to be an inspirational story—a story ripe for mythmaking that has already taken place in, for example, numerous children's books written about his life—for generations to come.

Jordan is not dead yet. One might think that with his career over, and his future devoted to the rather unglamorous life of running a basketball team, he would fade from the public eye until his death, when immortality would be realized and his iconic status confirmed. But that is clearly not the case. Jordan remains an irresistible figure in American and global cultures, one of the most renowned, recognizable faces in contemporary society whose body and voice continue to transport millions who consume, and are consumed by, his unique spirit. New ways to access the man and the myth include multiple DVD and video retrospectives and highlights of his life and career in basketball; additional commercially available merchandise, such as posters and jerseys, which keep Jordan's special body close to the fan's ordinary body; and books, authored or co-authored by Jordan himself, which are as value-laden as any sacred text, including his 1994 classic, *I Can't Accept Not Trying: Michael Jordan on the Pursuit of Excellence*.[24] Testimonials about the power of this book in readers' lives are posted on Amazon.com, including one that reads, "This is quite possibly the single most inspiring book by man, outside of the holy word of God"; another that asserts, "It tells goals you should have in your life"; and in still another emphasizing the value of this hero's words for youngsters who need moral direction, "Young people will be inspired by his words." [25]

The devotion to Michael Jordan is just another illustration of how sports can translate into sacred activities and religious attitudes. Throughout human history, predating even the rise of the so-called great religions of the Book, groups of people have ritually gathered together in contexts of intimate physical contact, or intense somatic exertions, for serious, often pleasurable, experiences between players but also, in little over a century, in that magical space between athletes and spectators in modern sports. Sports and the various kinds of organized games and contests that are as much about intellect as physicality are not always religious but can, in certain conditions, give life to sacred sentiments and transformative rituals. For reasons that cannot be fully explained but will always remain somewhat mysterious, Michael Jordan, like the Super Bowl or the Baseball Hall of Fame, enlivens religious sensibilities tied to play that find expression in culturally constitutive mythic narratives, regenerative rituals, and communal networks. God or no God, play can animate religious energies that bind communities of fans, athletes, and teams together around idols that are worshipped in ways that, for some, create shared experiences and memories as impressive and meaningful as any other sacred encounters in this life, but that for others conjure up biblical-based fears of the golden calf.

4

CELEBRITY

"You shall not make for yourself an idol, whether in the form of anything that is in heaven above, or that is on the earth beneath, or that is in the water under the earth. You shall not bow down to them or worship them." [1]

The second of the Ten Commandments seems rather unequivocal. The underlying message is straightforward for monotheists: do not worship other gods, or "bow down" to anything else in the cosmos. The Golden Calf incident from Exodus 32, in which Aaron and other ancient Israelites construct the dreaded idol at the foot of Mount Sinai, highlights the urgent need for this commandment and the easy slippage into a godless universe where the sacred knows no bounds. Moses was not pleased as he descended the mountain after forty days and nights transcribing God's commandments—you remember he smashed the original tablets of the sacred law upon seeing the robust religious practices of Hebrews in honor of the alluring, tangible, and familiar animal icon associated with the pagan culture surrounding the Jews. Although Moses and the law eventually triumph in reestablishing a monotheistic order, the victory is really only temporary. The rest of the stories in the Hebrew Bible and on into the New Testament, as well as the subsequent unfolding of history in the centuries following the appearance of these sacred myths up to the present, are replete with evidence of the utter failure of believers to keep the second, let alone the other nine, commandments.

Idol worship, on the other hand, is hard to shake. Sure, Moses destroyed the Golden Calf and, in his fury, forced his brothers and sisters who gave their bodies over to the false god to pollute their souls by making them drink the ashes of the ground-down idol. Yes, the myth also reports of God's righteous anger and religious violence in the slaughter of roughly three thousand revelers who are ultimately blotted from history. But despite this impressive cautionary tale, Jews, Christians, and others who value the Decalogue as the bedrock of moral behavior continue to bow down and serve graven images not crafted from gold but from larger-than-life stars worth their weight in gold and then some. Americans at the dawn of the twenty-first century are as easily led to venerate idols shaped by popular cultures as the Hebrews who were waiting for Moses to return from the mountain.

Celebrity icons arouse the religious passions of followers in modern society who find spiritual meaning, personal fulfillment, and awe-inspiring motivation in the presence of these idols. The early decades of the twentieth century witnessed the dawn of these new gods worshipped in celebrity culture, when fame and stardom in public and popular cultures could, in some instances, translate into religious categories with sacred implications in American lives. The sacred implications of worshipping at the altar of celebrity might include invigorating new forms of ritual commitment and devotional practice, or investing in mythologies that promise immortality and spiritual rather than material rewards, or even instigating a reformulation of personal moral values and ultimate concerns.

Celebrities in the twentieth century acquired sacred standing in American religious life as the mainline Protestant stranglehold on public culture began to loosen and technologically advanced forms of communication brought entertaining popular cultures into the private lives of listeners and viewers. Growing increasingly distant from the God above, these popular cultures of radio and television, film and music, sports and news, offer alternative divinities to Americans and inspire their own kind of devotional practices and religious investments. Leaving God behind did not simply mean that popular culture was now secular culture. Instead, celebrities were deified by fans and fanatics whose religious impulses and hungers remained active in a cultural field that could bring out the best, or the worst, in them. On some occasions, followers might venerate their idols in peaceful contemplation of the image in front of their eyes; on other occasions, however, followers fervently devoted to their idols can move in the opposite direction and be whipped into a frenzy of extraordinary—some might even say biblical—proportions.

The hysteria surrounding Rudolph Valentino's funeral is one of the earliest cases in which the religious power of entertaining celebrities transformed them into serious deities and will shed some light on the strange cultural brew mixing the sacred and profane. In 1926, Hollywood screen idol Rudolph Valentino unexpectedly died while in the hospital at the young age of thirty-one of complications arising from a perforated ulcer. When news of his death spread across the country, fans were stunned and saddened by the loss of this legend who came to life on the silver screen for millions around the world with absolutely nothing in common with him. The handsome and athletic Italian immigrant known as the "Latin Lover" for his smoldering cinematic presence is often identified as one of Hollywood's first screen legends, starring in such early film sensations as *The Four Horsemen of the Apocalypse* (1921), *The Sheik* (1921), *Blood and Sand* (1922), and *Son of a Sheik* (1926). At the time of his death, Valentino was one of the most popular and celebrated entertainment figures in the world.[2]

Millions of fans who adored the screen star desired full, unmediated access to his private life when the lights came on. Valentino's personal life contributed to a growing stargazing industry for fans and stimulated acts of worship from many of those fans that did not simply border on the religious, but literally crossed over into it. In addition to the films and tabloids, the public face—and physique—of Valentino consumed Americans who could not consume enough of him. He was one of the earliest entertainers to inspire both religious devotion among starstruck followers and profit-driven fervor to give those followers as many intimate details of his life as possible—the basic ingredients at work in the formation and maintenance of a dominant religious culture in modern American society: celebrity worship.

His image, his words, and his lifestyle transformed the everyday lives of legions of fans who dreamt of him at night, read about him in the day, wrote to him directly and to others about him, joined fan clubs, subscribed to fan magazines, and changed their own behaviors to follow his example and moral exhortations about how to lead a fulfilling life. In his case, Valentino instructed the masses about a fundamental feature of celebrity culture that ignited the spiritual zeal of many of his followers: obsession with exercise and disciplined care of the body, hypermasculine and militarized for men, youthful and highly erotic for women. Along with starring in films and leading an international, jet-setting life, Valentino promoted his own brand of exercise workouts in books and a newspaper serial, "Valentino's Beauty Secrets," which his fans ate up but also used as a measure, model, or ideal for their own lives.[3]

The events leading up to Valentino's death during his stay in the hospital were tumultuous for followers who had to rely on communication through selective, generally unreliable filters: the doctors and the media. The double operation for acute appendicitis and perforated gastric ulcers did not go well for Valentino, who avoided doctors most of his life and, like many in this era, had a deep suspicion of hospitals. While doctors kept the patient in the dark about the peritonitis that set in after the operation (a potentially deadly inflammation at the time), Valentino remained in good spirits and looked forward to getting out of the hospital. Yet, concerned fans were not so sanguine about the star's proximity to death: crowds held a vigil outside the hospital; many sent gifts and flowers; so many people called the hospital that two extra operators were hired; widespread preoccupation with his condition fueled the flames of sensationalism in the popular press seeking to capitalize on the public fixation, including the use of eerie, doctored photographs with the Latin Lover in a hospital bed and the premature headline in one rag announcing "Rudy Dead."[4]

But Rudy did die soon after the operation, traumatizing the nation and the world near the end of summer in 1926. The days following Valentino's death were marked by genuine feelings of profound loss and sadness for many Americans who shared little in common except their worship of the screen idol and their investments—financial, emotional, and spiritual—in his awesome image. But solemnity and decorum, cherished values in many religious traditions, did not prevail at Frank E. Campbell's famous New York City funeral home, which received and prepared the corpse. Instead, a crowd estimated at over fifty thousand people descended on the venerable funeral institution, desiring the kind of personal access they were used to in the darkness of the movie theater or the illumination of the news media. As newspaper reports, eyewitness accounts, and documentary film footage make perfectly clear, pandemonium erupted outside the doors of the funeral home, where the desperate, thronging crowds impulsively gathered to pay their respects and engage in last ritual acts of devotion to their dead idol.

The aftermath of Valentino's death is the stuff of legends, yet it is also a clear-cut, concrete historical marker of a new kind of sacred attachment, one based on fame and looks, personality and stardom as well as a new understanding of what counts as heroic deeds, moral leadership, or inner strength. While some can easily pronounce evaluative judgments about these shifts, making distinctions between signs of pathology and signs of authentic religious devotion, the behavior of fans at the death of this figure exposed their deep connection to him and the star's central role in the structures of meaning and feeling that make the most difference in their noncelebrity lives. Fans wanted to be near that body, to see it, touch it if possible, bring a souvenir from the room where it lay in state, before it disappeared, at such a young age, for good. With huge crowds in the tens of thousands in the streets surrounding the funeral home—including curiosity seekers as well as distressed fans, men and women, rich and poor, and police on horseback—and a downpour on the late summer day, rioting broke out before the doors opened, leading to injuries, broken windows, and an overturned car.[5]

After the crowd settled, many participants in this new religious culture of celebrity got the chance they hoped for, to see the star up close and personal. But in this sad case, a final close-up amounted to a final look at the fallen, embalmed star. By the end of the first day of public display, seventy-four people a minute passed the body so that by midnight, fifty thousand people had been through the doors of the funeral home; by the second day, twenty to thirty thousand got a glimpse of the mortal, though now sacred, remains.[6] Reports of frenzied fans, fainting individuals, sobbing mourners, and final gestures, such as touching the casket or kissing the various props surrounding the body, became national news and part of the lore associated with the funeral, which especially highlighted the actions of purportedly hysterical women. The degree and extent of this kind of unprecedented display of something more than mere affection for a familiar celebrity icon but clearly an utter stranger to the desperate, stunned followers can be seen either as a modern form of religious expression or, as is often the case when understanding new forms of religious life, as a delusional and irrational modern pathology.

In a short time, newspaper reports began questioning this seemingly strange behavior of the wild throngs descending on the funeral home, with commentaries frequently alluding to the uncivilized, godless, immoral attachments of these misguided fans. The deep concern that entertainment and Hollywood morality had replaced religion for the masses in the early decades of the twentieth century was reflected in the critical and highly elitist comments about the "gross irreverence" of the crowds who went to the body and particularly the actions of women who threw themselves at the altar of their beloved figure and were "prostrated before his tomb" at the funeral. Another bone of contention for the more sober, cultured social commentators was the shameful disregard for the passing of a significant public figure who was truly worthy of public displays of grief and commemoration: former Harvard University president Charles Eliot, who died the same weekend.[7]

But whether his body was embalmed and placed on display in a silver and bronze glass-covered casket in two funeral services, or whether his image was embellished and placed on the front page of popular magazines to give the appearance that the sensual star was now in the ethereal presence of angels, Valentino's spirit would not die with the man for thousands of seriously committed fans. The words of contemporary journalist Heywood Broun contrast dramatically with the righteous moralizing in the public press about pathological fanatics worshipping false gods: "It was not so much a motion picture actor who lay dead, as Pan or Apollo."[8]

In 1967, screenwriter and novelist Irving Shulman wrote a popular biography of Valentino that both captured and contributed to the enduring mythology around the by then long-dead star. The first chapters in Shulman's biography start with the star's death rather than his birth, perpetuating a strange but strangely familiar morbid attachment to the dead that is a common feature of many religious cultures, though in this case with all the fanfare and glitz of a Hollywood production. The author entitles the first section of his biography "Act One: United Artists Presents a Frank E. Campbell Production: The Great American Funeral," clearly tipping his hat to the public debate surrounding funerals instigated a few years earlier by Jessica Mitford's book *The American Way of Death* (1963). Shulman's narrative of these events is not only organized as a Hollywood screenplay, it reads like one too—dramatic, fast-paced, with heroes and villains, and a fabulous leading man. His account of riotous crowds in the streets near the funeral home emphasized bizarre group pathology rather than sincere personal devotion, even though Shulman does suggest there is a strange, irrational, unexplainable religious impulse at work in the dangerous swarm of bodies united in their passionate desire to see the dead star.[9]

This vision of fans going over the edge, of becoming fanatics driven by unacceptable religious sentiments that distort normal, rational perceptions of reality, is placed front and center in Shulman's book, which begins with an "Author's Note" to set the stage. Here Shulman observes that the impact of Valentino's short life on fans was a rather unique, though genuine, social phenomenon, a point driven home in 1950 when, according to the author, he visited a "little apartment-temple to the memory of Rudolph Valentino." He continues his description of this visit: "The temple was the private property of a lady not at ease in this world. The holy place, its artifacts, and the dithyrambic declamation of its curator, which alternated its verse praise of Valentino with a violent fishwife's denunciation of all the false high priestesses who dishonored the memory of the Great Lover with their fraudulent claims of election to his favor, so impressed me that I incorporated this visit and a description of the shrine in my novel, *The Square Trap* (1953)."[10] While some might question the veracity of this particular story, most of us know individuals who create temples and shrines to their celebrity idols, living and dead, as well as engage in a variety of ritual activities that invest these idols with sacrality often associated with saints, heroes, and other categories usually reserved for the special dead.

Are they crazy and in need of serious psychological intervention, abnormally fixated on and addicted to stars? Are they sadly lost, misguided, and susceptible to the temptations of false gods because their own lives are so empty and meaningless, without God but desperately seeking spiritual fulfillment in the lives and deaths of others they will never know but will remember for a lifetime? Or are they, perhaps, drawn to celebrities for other reasons, less absolute than each of these two positions separately but somewhere between them on a spectrum, where religious engagements and meaning-making exercises blur the boundaries between fantasy and stark reality, fanaticism and civil respectability, infatuation and mere entertainment?

The literature is decidedly mixed on these questions. Some look squarely at the numbers and are dumbfounded when they see Americans spending billions of their hard-earned and increasingly harder to save dollars to keep certain figures in the public eye and in their private worlds; others look probingly "inside the minds of stargazers," to borrow a subtitle from a recent book, to chart the borders between healthy encounters with stars and less rational attachments, if not pathological addictions, to celebrity;[11] and still others look disapprovingly at the attention given to a Brad Pitt, a Jennifer Lopez, or a Puff Daddy and lament the clear and unmistakable downward turn in cultural values, a decline signaling moral confusion, ethical relativism, and godless hedonism—idol worship in all its depraved glory. But one point shared by all commentators is that the fame surrounding celebrity is a pervasive and powerful force in modern society, magnetizing and tempting millions of people who make significant investments, not exclusively financial, in what is often seen as a historically unique, curious cultural phenomenon.

Celebrity culture, the cult of celebrity, celebrity worship— these and other phrases are regularly used to capture the elusive, irreducible power of celebrity in the present and recent past. From the early twentieth century, when celebrities primarily emanated from the Hollywood film industry, to the start of the twenty-first century, when celebrity status is available to anyone at a moment's notice, the public hunger for stardom marks a distinctive cultural trait that has evolved into a confounding, omnipresent source of capital, consumption, and community across the globe. It is also a source for sacred action and meaning to millions of Americans who are devoted to stars and who secretly yearn to be intimate with them, if not desire to actually become one of them, which in these days of *American Idol* fever is not so difficult to imagine.

In the most personal, inaccessibly private forms of devotion or in the most communal, spectacularly public displays of love and admiration, Americans look to the stars for guidance and inspiration, intimacy and ecstasy—powerful motives that bear on the sacred and can transform entertainment into revelation, escapism into liberation, and mortals into gods. Whether this power is tied to special charismatic qualities that mesmerize and attract others, or to compelling cosmic forces tied to fate and destiny, or to fundamental human desires for sex and companionship, one point is clear: it is a power that is not shared equally among all societal members, and those that do not have it will search for ways to get access to it.

The power of celebrities, on the other hand, may also have deeper roots in human history than the emerging popular and media cultures of the early twentieth century, roots extending to the earliest human communities and embedded in evolutionary traits geared toward basic survival needs. According to some evolutionary anthropologists and psychologists, imitating certain individuals who are the center of attention and endowed with prestige—acquired because of peculiar talents in hunting or sexual conquest, for example—had extraordinary value in the human struggle to adapt to changing environmental conditions. Humans are born to mimic others, they argue, especially prestigious individuals perceived to be the fittest and most successful by the group—individuals who stand out beyond the crowd and attract the deferential attention and admiration of others. One individual may be admired for specific traits or accomplishments, but the simple fact that others fix their attentions on the singled-out and admired individual only fuels the copying behavior of the rest of the group, who also want to be successful in the same ways and attain the same level of prestige. Additionally, and most relevant to the contemporary fixation on celebrity, in order to really know what behaviors to imitate, copiers want to be intimate with the model—to have a fairly comprehensive vision of the individual's private life.[12]

Whether or not components of contemporary celebrity worship can be scientifically grounded in evolutionary theory and psychological predispositions, a brief glance through human history offers up ample evidence of communities being riveted by certain figures who are subject to imitation and become objects of devotion. Greek heroes, Jewish prophets, Christian saints, military leaders, and other figures tied to specific cultural contexts rise above the crowd and, whatever the circumstances that propel them to this extraordinary position, enter a mythological terrain that inspires devotional practices, models cultural values, and frames the contours of what constitutes a truly meaningful life. Russell Crowe is certainly no Hercules, Charlton Heston is not quite Moses, Princess Diana is far removed from Saint Teresa of Avila, but these contemporary celebrities—whether living, aged and close to death, or long dead—share some things in common with their historical counterparts: they move people to action as well as contemplation, they bear on the emotional lives of large numbers of people, they embody power that far exceeds the material riches that can accompany fame, and their personal life stories become public morality tales instructing larger communities about right and wrong, success and failure, fulfillment and tragedy.

As historian Daniel Boorstin argued over forty years ago, however, modern celebrities are a different breed than heroes of yore, a distinction that he identifies in the cultural shift from a society with "ideals" to one consumed by "images." While true heroes from the past rose above the ordinary crowd through substantive individual accomplishments and achievements that embody the highest ideals of society, he contends, celebrities are media-created, ultimately empty vessels that provide only artificial, though captivating, images void of real purpose or value.[13]

Boorstin and other intellectuals understood this shift as being the result, in part, of the rise of popular cultures, new media technologies, and especially the stupendous growth of entertainment industries over the course of the early twentieth century. In this context, celebrities do more than simply capture the public's attention, whether for fifteen minutes or fifty years; celebrityhood has become a fact of life, embedded in everyday experiences from supermarket checkout lines to E! Entertainment, from water cooler discussions to incessant award shows. Could such a pervasive, profound, and personally compelling cultural phenomenon be without substance in people's lives? Perhaps it is too easy to follow Boorstin and uncritically assume that images of celebrities do not have ultimate, even religious, claims on us. Yet in the face of the overwhelming data—how people relate to celebrities, how they talk about them, how they dream about them, how they live with and for "intimate strangers," to quote the title of one book on celebrity culture[14]—it is equally possible that celebrities are not empty receptacles but fulfilling models who can give life purpose and embody a different set of strongly held, though less clearly articulated, ideals that many in society disagree with, if not find utterly disgraceful: the pursuit of physical beauty, the attainment of fame and wealth, and the desire to be loved by adoring fans.

Psychological profiles offer still another perspective on celebrity culture in contemporary society. A group of researchers recently developed a "Celebrity Worship Scale," a serious psychometric procedure to evaluate questionnaire responses and identify psychological attitudes toward celebrities, though the name of the scale retains its sacred and popular associations. Publishing their findings in a variety of scholarly journals in the last few years, including *Personality and Individual Differences*, *Journal of Psychology*, and the *Journal of Nervous and Mental Disease*, the authors have received widespread media attention as well, with popular communication outlets and news magazines enthralled by the possible academic legitimacy of "celebrity worship." Ironically, as the media began its feeding frenzy covering the social scientific findings, the "Celebrity Worship Scale" was morphed into a "Celebrity Worship Syndrome" by overzealous and sloppy journalists. Soon news reports were promulgating the mistaken notion that these researchers had established a new mental disorder when, in fact, they were only presenting evidence for a more complex understanding of personality traits associated with celebrity worship, which the authors contend covers roughly one-third of the population.[15]

The authors are quite concerned about this finding and argue in the book that while a spectrum of attitudes based on race, gender, class, age, and a variety of other factors exists toward celebrities, some forms of adoration can veer into neuroticism if not outright borderline pathology and psychosis. When one crosses the line from a healthy appreciation of entertainment to a pathological obsession with celebrities, the boundary is not only a psychological threshold, it is a religious one as well, hence the unproblematic designation of "worship" for these distinctive forms of behavior. Indeed, their studies suggest that celebrity worship is best understood as a peculiarly religious form of devotion, a kind of fanaticism most akin to religious fanaticism that can lead to extreme, unhealthy, if not delusional behavior. It is one thing to enjoy John Coltrane's music, they claim, but quite another to establish the Church of Saint John Coltrane.[16] By the end of their book-length study, the authors offer advice about "what can be done to reduce celebrity worship," and suggest that those who suffer from this form of idolization get a life, take up an active hobby, separate their welfare from that of a stranger, and realize celebrities are manufactured figures, not true heroes.[17]

Even *Psychology Today* ran a special article on the phenomenon and the increased popular and scholarly attention given to this inescapable, undeniable, irrepressible cultural force. "Seeing by Starlight: Celebrity Obsession" covered the innate, primordial drives associated with celebrities—such as to find romantic love, to admire certain members of society, to imitate those members and attain their status in the group, and even to gossip about others. But, the article notes, like spiritual guides in traditional religions, celebrities can also be inspiring to fans who realize they live in another world and who lack other sources of motivation to transcend current life circumstances and overcome life's obstacles. Summarizing the thoughts of James Houran, one of the authors of *Celebrity Worshippers*, the article also reinforces the notion that worshipping celebrities is somehow like religion, but not really religion—rather a secular version of more authentic religious devotional practices, a displacement of a deep human need onto stars rather than saints or more conventional and, it is suggested, deserving religious figures.[18] But who decides when a devotional displacement is secular or still sacred? What are the criteria in place to make these fine, though ultimate, distinctions between true religion and false, pathology and true faith?

In addition to social critics and social scientists, many on the religious and political right understand the power and popularity of celebrities in modern culture as a potentially delusional force wreaking psychological havoc, social chaos, and spiritual disease. From this perspective it is a seriously corrosive, corrupting cultural trend, reflecting the decline of true religious practice and the rise of false secularized religion. Celebrity worship is especially ripe for ridicule and satire from the right as well, though the terms of this kind of rhetoric belie a deep concern that this has, indeed, transmogrified into an appealing, and therefore highly competitive, religious culture based on the mistaken veneration of stars and stardom.

Eric Burns, host of *Fox News Watch*, recently wrote about this phenomenon on the FOXNews website. The article, "Celebrity Worship Turns Actors into Gods," hilariously trashes the popular acting cable show *Inside the Actors Studio*, hosted by James Lipton. Burns sees an assortment of familiar religious elements in this show, referring to it as "the official televised church service of the American secular faith," though to watch, for Burns, is "to long for the sound of chalk scratching a blackboard so that there may be some relief from the liturgy." Lipton's fawning and obsequiousness, his piety and adoration at the feet of Tom Hanks in this particular show, were too much for Burns and only confirmed the deadly serious observation in his piece: celebrity culture is built on perversely secular, not religiously ennobling values.[19]

Celebrity culture, the critics say, is a threat to social stability and moral order, part of a secular wasteland that draws on traditional religious forms and attitudes but misplaces genuine spiritual longing in inappropriate, imprudent ways. Today as in biblical times, it is feared that idol worship draws people away from God and away from true spiritual fulfillment, providing momentary animal gratifications but putting the soul, and society itself, in mortal peril. Yet celebrities continue to embody and impart sacred realities—not seemingly sacred, nor pseudo sacred, nor false sacred, but just plain sacred realities—that fuel instructive mythologies, generate ritual practices, inspire personal transformations, and establish meaningful and practical values for fans who identify with their heroes. Some may not like these heroes, our modern "cultural saints" in the apt phrase of religious historian M. Gail Hammer,[20] but like them or not, the power of fame and the spiritual dimensions of celebrity—a menace to some, salvation to others—constitute a distinctive religious culture with wide-ranging communities of participants. This religious culture merges entertainment and devotional rituals, commerce and sacred auras, in ways that transform public and popular figures as well as fans themselves.

The apotheosis of Oprah will serve as another illustration of this alternate form of sacred reality. Like many of her fans, Oprah Winfrey grew up in a household devoted to God, listening to and then learning to read from the Bible, and worshipping Christ in the church, first with her mother and grandmother in Kosciusko,

Mississippi, then with her father after she moved with him to Nashville, Tennessee. In the African American Progressive Baptist Church, her father served as a deacon and Oprah discovered the performer inside that loved to be in front of an audience.[21]

Her fan base, of course, reaches far beyond the African American Christian communities that figure so prominently in the telling and retelling of her life story, encompassing Jews as well as Hindus, Muslims, and Buddhists—New Agers and atheists too, no doubt. Indeed, the particularities of Oprah's individual life story are compellingly pertinent to millions of primarily but not exclusively female fans in America as well as the rest of the world. They hear repeatedly of her personal tragedies and triumphs, challenges and commitments on websites and in books, television specials, and magazines, in universal terms that many find deeply relevant to their own noncelebrity, ordinary lives—not quite hagiography in the traditional sense, but clearly sacred stories so familiar, so edifying, so archetypal for Americans of all stripes that they simultaneously personalize and canonize Oprah in the popular imagination.

From humble beginnings in rural Mississippi to media mogul with vast amounts of wealth and global power, Oprah has had an extraordinary life that is more than the sum of its parts to faithful fans. The struggles with poverty in her early years, abuse by relatives as a girl, diet and eating as an adult, and vicious critics for much of her career; her shape-shifting transformations in church as a young performer, in the media as an actor and talk-show host, in her physical appearance as a glamorous African American woman, in class standing from the lowest of the lows to billionaire status—all of the micro-details publicly consumed again and again do not add up to the banal "rags to riches" story so close to the hearts of Americans. Rather, in the context of racism and sexism, corporate greed and personal misfortunes, the familiar elements of Oprah's life and tremendous success as a celebrity with more to offer than entertainment to the masses is prime mythmaking material, uplifting and instructive, gripping and weighty, to those who listen.

Oprah is more than a source of religious mythology in celebrity culture, however. She is also at the center of a range of devotional practices that demonstrate the depth and breadth of her religious standing in this prominent culture of worship. Watching Oprah's talk show; reading her popular *O* magazine; buying the titles she includes in her book club; visiting her official website, oprah.com; journaling at her suggestion for greater self-awareness—these are only some of the ritual activities enacted in everyday life by millions of her followers. But how can watching, reading, buying, visiting, and journaling be religious ritual in this case when, in so many other circumstances, the same kinds of activity cannot be classified in a similar way? Are these deeply sacred bonds between an American idol and her starstruck fans, or consumer patterns manipulated by gross, profit-driven rationales to maximize earnings from this manufactured product?

Rituals are religious when they establish order for participants who return to them again and again; bind groups of disparate people into a unified community fixed on a common symbol or totem; empower individuals through expectations of personal transformation, transcendence, and fulfillment including but not limited to physical, embodied experiences; and teach followers about what is really real, especially meaningful, and genuinely insightful. In the religious culture of celebrity, public figures like Oprah inspire individuals to engage in ritual actions that meet these requirements because fans adore her as an intimate authority of sacred, spiritual matters and trust her guidance through the ordinary, everyday struggles in their efforts to achieve the same degree of transcendence and transformation idealized in the mythology surrounding her personal life story.

Oprah is not the pope, but as *Vanity Fair*, one of the primary sacred texts in celebrity religious culture, proclaimed in an article published over ten years ago, she may be a close second in terms of cultural authority in the personal lives of followers: "Oprah Winfrey arguably has more influence on the culture than any university president, politician, or religious leader, except perhaps the Pope."[22] As the recent book *The Gospel According to Oprah* argues quite convincingly, Oprah may indeed be considered the next Billy Graham, revivalist extraordinaire and twentieth-century national icon. Oprah is the nation's premier religious revivalist for the twenty-first century, though with more of a Christ-less message than evangelical Graham, and no less infused with moral teachings, spiritual promises, and healing wisdom for the national, and now certainly global, masses.[23] Her nonsectarian, Bible-influenced, spiritually based therapeutic power to transform individuals and society itself was fittingly on display during America's darkest hours after the 9/11 attacks. Oprah hosted the national memorial service after the tragedy, an intimate, familiar, trusted face who could lead Americans in the socially urgent rituals of death that did not exclude the expression of multiple religious traditions but, on the other hand, were sacred actions in their own right irrespective of the Christians, Jews, Buddhists, Muslims, and others who participated in the ceremonies.

Oprah is a rich celebrity, but that does not detract from her spiritual authority to help others live a more fulfilling, meaningful life, a point made starkly clear in her presence at the memorial service but also one that persists long after that moment. Indeed, her celebrity status and enormous wealth only reinforce her sacred standing in contemporary culture, and her trustworthy voice in intimate matters of love and romance, forgiveness and generosity, empathy and self-understanding, truth and transcendence makes people believe that following her lead can help them "live your best life," a familiar phrase to her fans but also one that sums up a fairly common goal in most religious traditions. Is she a celebrity savior offering salvation not just from the trivialities and boredom of everyday life, but from suffering, injustices, and even death itself? Is the secret of salvation to become rich like her and live in opulence? Oprah cannot make all of her fans rich—a truly base, secular desire in and of itself—but she does offer the promise to make their lives better, salvation of a different sort than found in Christian doctrine, and one that surely blurs the lines between sacred transformation and psychological therapy, spiritual healing, and healthy living.

For many Christians, the fear that Jesus Christ is not the only truly divine celebrity, the sole source for true sacrality for the modern world, is an ongoing challenge to contemporary theology which has found itself increasingly displaced by and ill-equipped to deal with an Oprah or a Valentino, let alone a Bruce, Marilyn, or Elvis. The confusion and fear over the commingling of sacred and secular, and the possibility that people have multiple religious identities and identifications, some of which do not require a monotheistic God, is expressed in public culture through diatribe and jeremiads, sermonizing and, in some cases, soul-searching reflection.

In the 2002 *Christianity Today* article "The Church of O," author LaTonya Taylor repeats the familiar elements of Oprah's religious life story, the notable influence of her vast media empire, and the well-known evolution of her spiritual teachings. It is this last strand in the Church of O that is the most vexing to Taylor and millions of Christians, to be sure. But rather than offer a harangue against celebrity worship like so many others, Taylor presents a more sympathetic view that clearly struggles with the implications of Oprah's popularity and rise to spiritual dominance, and underscores the fiercely competitive nature of this religious culture in the spiritual battle in the United States over what people should be finally seeking in this life: "The question for Christians is this: What can we do to help Oprah and her disciples find what they are ultimately seeking—the power, grace, and love that can only be found through a personal relationship with Jesus Christ?"[24] Oprah and her disciples may or may not be seeking this particular relationship, but they still struggle with ultimate relationships that matter most in contemporary society: between self and other, truth and deception, happiness and disappointment, idol and worshippers, product and consumers. What are the spiritual aspirations of Oprah and her disciple fans? Could it be that good Christians, Jews, Muslims, Wiccans, and a variety of others across the religious spectrum find either an enhancement to their own faiths or the discovery of an entirely new way of life in their personal relationship with Oprah, a relationship that may or may not include God in the spiritual equation? Oprah is not the only celebrity who forces society to reconsider the boundaries separating true and false religion and who also perfectly illustrates the powerfully religious reality of this culture. Public figures discussed in earlier chapters, such as Michael Jordan or Judy Garland, are also case studies in celebrity religious culture, each one human but superhuman in some way as well, mortals attracting devoted fan followers who transform personal life stories and individual accomplishments into instructive myths and cherished memories that have concrete, theoretical, practical, and spiritual effects in everyday life.

Besides Oprah, any number of celebrities can whip fans into a religious frenzy and demonstrate the sacred power of fame—Madonna and Brad Pitt, Johnny Depp and Anna Kournikova, all have legions of fan followers who find numerous ways to show their special commitments and spiritual allegiances. Whether fans build a shrine to Bob Dylan, as recently covered in an episode of National Public Radio's *All Things Considered*, or follow the humanitarian lead of Angelina Jolie, as reported in *Time* magazine's article "The Year of Charitainment," celebrities do something extraordinary to followers whose adoration is not simply analogous to religion, but is itself an example of religious activity.[25]

This is true for celebrities still living but even more apparent for the dead ones. James Dean and Jimi Hendrix, Marilyn Monroe and Frank Sinatra, Dale Earnhardt and Kurt Cobain, John Lennon and Princess Diana, Tupac Shakur and Elvis Presley—the list is not endless and certainly does not include every celebrity that ever lived, but it is rather limited to stars who shine even brighter in death, animating the imaginative and ritual worlds of fans in the most intensely personal, intimate ways as well as, in some cases, the most outwardly public, visible ways. The riots and mayhem surrounding Valentino's body were one expression of religious adoration for an icon; bidding outrageous sums of money for relics from a celebrity's life, like ruby slippers once worn by Judy Garland or kitchen materials that once belonged to Jackie O, is still another; ritually returning to the scene of James Dean's fiery and deadly crash and building a shrine on his death day also counts;[26] making a pilgrimage to the Dale Trail in Dale Earnhardt's hometown of Kannapolis, North Carolina, does too, a place where pilgrims can eat where the racing icon ate, visit the graveyard where his father is buried, and consume sanctified souvenirs all carrying the sacred, now brand name;[27] envisioning Tupac Shakur as a crucified Christ, as artist Tom Sanford has in his religious painting *The Entombment 2004*, does as well. Let's not even bring up Elvis, yet.

Celebrity religious culture does pose a real threat to traditional religions. The worship of these dead cultural icons as well as living successful stars from a range of cultural fields, such as sports or films, television or politics, is tempting to adherents of any number of religious traditions who find ways to participate in more than one religious culture at any time. Sometimes religious resources—myths, symbols, rituals, ethics, and so on—are found in the usual places, such as the Bible or Koran, the Book of Mormon or the teachings of Buddha. But at other times many Americans find religious resources—myths, symbols, rituals, ethics, and so on—in less conventional places.

The culture of celebrity is a form of idol worship, to be sure, but it is also a wellspring for religious living in contemporary society that is satisfying and meaningful to millions who are intimately familiar with the biblical story of the Golden Calf and experience no tensions or conflicts when they venerate a singer or movie star, a sports legend or a talk-show host. God is not crucial to this religious culture, scripture unnecessary for the sacred bonds between communities of fans and stars. The ease with which commerce and entertainment can intersect with devotion and reverence is a striking feature of celebrity culture, a spiritual-secular mixture that for many is as impossible to take seriously as the attempt to merge religion and science.

5

SCIENCE

Science is not a religion, but it can be religious.

In *The Sacred Depths of Nature*, the best-selling book first published in 1998, internationally renowned cell biologist Ursula Goodenough offers readers an unabashedly religious vision of the cosmos that does not depend on the existence of God. She calls her view "religious naturalism," a fundamentally human response to the primordial, awe-inspiring sacred myth at its core: the Epic of Evolution.[1] Goodenough is not hostile to God, or to any of the world's religions, but celebrates what she describes as a more spiritually effusive, more anthropologically relevant, sacred source of meaning and sentiment, ethics and orientation, fulfillment and wisdom. A scientific understanding of Nature, a word capitalized by the writer to emphasize its primacy in the religious landscape of human life, opens the door to spiritual wonder and reverential obligations rather than closing out the possibility that the cosmos is infused with sacred meanings.

In recent years, the public debates surrounding science and religion have erupted with a fury not seen for nearly a century. These debates often surface in the midst of gripping, controversial moral quandaries faced by communities struggling with the limits of scientific authority: the place of evolution in public education, human interventions at the beginning and end of life, the role of prayer in healing, and environmental crises in the face of diminishing nature. The pressing questions that bring science and religion together, or conversely, render them asunder, are in many ways similar to questions humans have faced for millennia: What is the relationship between humans and the surrounding natural environment? What is the nature and substance of the material universe, and how did it come into being? What is the nature and substance of the physical body, especially in light of birth and sexuality, pleasure and pain, illness and death? How does one account for change in physical bodies and the material universe, and the passage of time generally? What is the meaning of life in this world, and is there life in other worlds? The answers to these questions are as varied as cultures that have existed through time.

Despite the prevailing view in public media that science and religion are now and have always been at war, real world experiences suggest that they have much in common and intersect in myriad ways. Indeed, both seek to understand human life and the nature of the universe; both depend upon belief systems and ritual actions that impose order and ward off chaos; both are driven to better understand the truth about reality by combining theory with practice; and both are motivated by personal and social commitments that shape identities, bind communities, and lead to cultural revolutions.

They have more in common than people tend to recognize—so much in common in fact that the lines of demarcation begin to break down and the two separate domains can merge into one big mess. Some religions are not afraid of the authority of science, however limited it might be, including liberal Protestantism, the Catholic Church, and Tibetan Buddhism; on the other hand, and less familiar to most, science can be a sacred enterprise itself, sustaining religious cultures with critical knowledge about the world or, in some cases, generating new forms of religious life and ultimate commitments that arise from world-transforming scientific knowledge.

Science can become religious itself, a sacred portal leading to mysteries just as grand, to truth just as absolute, and to meaning just as ultimate as can be found in any of the world's religions. It is as authoritative as any one deity or pantheon of gods for scientists who live by its rules and rituals. To return to cell biologist Goodenough, these rules and rituals are invigorating, for they open up a cosmic vision of life and a universe filled with spiritual wisdom and sacred practical truths. For her the sacred truths of Nature are not found in any one text, but buried deep in the natural world around us, and within the evolving human species.

The scientifically discovered sacred truths in Nature can be a profound source for religious awakening and holy wisdom in the face of the usual array of ultimate questions answered by Christian teachings, Buddhist philosophies, Islamic verses, Jewish traditions, and other authoritative reserves in the world's religions. Death and the origins of life, reproduction and the mysteries of the universe, difference and the intricacies of consciousness—these are only a few of the fundamentally religious topics that are explained by Goodenough with a strange (at least at first glance) combination of scientific rigor and sacred devotion, both grounded firmly in a material world of protons, water, cells, enzymes, amoebae, as well as more complicated features like brains, Neanderthals, music, earth, and galaxies. But using science to uncover the particulars and processes of this material world does not lead Goodenough to a cold, mechanistic, reductionistic, nihilistic attitude toward life. Instead, she continues to see an enchanted, mysterious, spiritually invigorating universe that has meaning and purpose without God at the center of the Epic.

Perspectives on death and sex, two of the most basic yet vastly complicated biological facts of human life, often inevitably return to religious concerns expressed in myths that emphasize core values and meanings for communities of followers. Think of Eve and that apple, or the great bloody yet sensual epics contained in the Bhagavad Gita, or the royal then ascetic life and eventual enlightenment of the Buddha. Accounting for the existence of death and sex is a central preoccupation for most religious cultures, with some intimately linking the two corporeal though extracorporeal life experiences in myths of human origin. For Goodenough, the Epic of Evolution is itself a powerful, persuasive mythic story that can illuminate and give meaning to the human encounter with these two sometimes troubling, sometimes liberating realities, elemental to life regardless of your particular religious or scientific view, and indispensably linked together in the logic of the ultimate story of life.

Sex is, she writes, embedded in the course of evolution, necessary as an adaptive strategy in the survival and reproduction of eukaryotic organisms so long ago. For humans today, the often confounding, confusing intersections of emotions and sex, instincts and intentions, are not always easy to resolve but, according to Goodenough, they do set the stage for humans to experience love, a religious experience anchored in a sound biological understanding that does not require theology or the love of God. In the chapter entitled "Multicellularity and Death," she asks if an organism can be immortal and answers that yes, some organisms like a bacterium or an amoeba are immortal, though they are limited in complexity. But the more complex organisms in the evolutionary chain are built to die, a fate written into the life cycles in Nature and a persistent paradox for humans, who live only because we will die. Death literally gives us life in this scientific view; it produces consciousness and is a condition for the possibility and awareness of love and other kinds of religious experience and transcendent wisdom.[2]

Goodenough is quite at home in a godless universe where the great mysteries of sex, death, and the rest of life are not finally solved or clarified by science, but are confirmed and revitalized in ways that enhance religious sensibilities with practical, as much as theoretical, appeal to others enamored with the Epic—atheists, of course, but Christians, Hindus, and their fellow scientists who are intimate with the gods in sacred texts yet devoted to the wonders of Nature discovered through science, with many holding multiple, occasionally contradictory, oftentimes harmonized, views about the relationship between religion and science in their lives. Readers in America, as well as around the world, accept Goodenough's religious naturalism as a spiritually viable, valuable outlook that reconciles science and religion without compromising either, comfortably celebrating a sacred vision of Nature spied by both. Whether one publicly self identifies as a religious naturalist[3] or privately adheres to a worshipful appreciation of the natural world, evolution does not pose the slightest threat to robust, confident religious belief. The theory of evolution is an authoritative basis for security and order, values and liberation to inestimable numbers who follow the teachings of Charles Darwin. The Epic of Evolution, it should also be noted, can produce a spectrum of views from followers and disseminators of the myth. Like most sacred myths, it has generated interpreting communities that often do not agree and have a range of interests, from the more liberal, tolerant, ecumenical positions taken by religious naturalists like Goodenough, to the more conservative, narrow, closed-minded positions taken by evolution fundamentalists.

In the case of the latter, the fundamentals of evolution do not require an epic story to capture its power, but instead boil down to the incontrovertible doctrines of Darwinian theory such as natural selection, common descent, and the drive to survive. The orthodoxy here, as in most other fundamentalisms, is religious through and through, and even assumes more traditionally familiar forms of religious extremism in public debates about evolution, including strict adherence to the written text by believers, firm conviction that everything is at stake in this holy battle over ultimate truth, and easy slippage into demonizing the enemy. Biblical creationists who commonly charge that evolutionists are imposing their false religion—often identified as secular humanism or naturalism—onto others are imaginatively limited by the usual dichotomous thinking of monotheists, bound to simplistic notions of right and wrong, true and false. But, on the other hand, it is also clear that they are on to something. The public rhetoric in defense of evolu-

tion by many in the scientific community has an unmistakable religious flavor. Showing more than simply a family resemblance, the
public defense of evolution can often display the same kind of
rigidities, close-mindedness, and self-righteousness as the most ob-
noxious Christian fundamentalist.

Even the most orthodox of evolutionists manage to return to
the language of the sacred when describing their heavily contested
vision of the godless cosmos. In *Darwin's Dangerous Idea*, philosopher and champion of materialism Daniel Dennett explores how
the dangerous idea provided by Darwin, natural selection, could be
understood as a "universal acid [that] cuts to the heart of everything in sight." [4] He begins the book by questioning whether anything is sacred after Darwin, and ultimately argues with Sigmund
Freud, another dangerous thinker when it comes to religion, that
God, like Santa Claus, is a figment of the imagination, a fiction
from childhood that is a myth in the sense of being untrue, and
certainly something clearheaded, mature, rational adults do not
take literally. [5] But are meaning, purpose, the sacred also delusions
after Darwin, who introduced chance and adaptation, necessity
and mindlessness, into a larger cosmic frame of reference that has
challenged traditional religions to their core? No, claims Dennett;
the liberating rather than dangerous idea of the Tree of Life, referred to at one point as "the total fan-out of *offspring*," [6] unearthed
through Darwin's scientific studies, is the true, final source of eternal wisdom. "Is something sacred?" Dennett asks himself at the
end of the text. "Yes, say I with Nietzsche. I could not pray to it,
but I can stand in affirmation of its magnificence. The world is
sacred." [7]

The world is sacred, science can illuminate its sacrality, and
evolution is its sacral expression. Myths serve not in Dennett's
sense as a repository for lies and delusions, but instead as sacred
narratives all cultures must rely on to provide explanations for why
the cosmos is the way it is, how life came to be, and what, at bottom, are the driving forces in this world. Some myths are written

in sacred texts, others are oral and passed down from generation to generation. Others in more recent times are brought to life through film and new forms of visual media. Still others are products of history, pure inventions that erupt in a moment or emerge over *la longue durée*, germinating in cultural soil for decades only to take root and transform society.

The myth of evolution, this story about origins and orientations, destiny and detail is compelling to many, offensive to many, and utterly vital in the religious battles of the twenty-first century. Evolution is, for practicing scientists and nonscientists, a myth beyond myth, a meta-mythic story like no other that carries ultimate weight in solving the mysteries of life and death, a quest that is never purely secular, without religious sentiments and sensibilities, though commonly a quest carried on without God. For well-known biologist Edward O. Wilson, who does not believe in God, the scientific understanding of material reality and the scientific explanation of what is really real has more power, more substance, and more splendor than anything that can be found in the world's religions.[8]

Many other scientists recognize the necessary intersections between the two, including the great physicist Albert Einstein, who once said that "science without religion is lame, religion without science is blind."[9] Einstein had quite a bit to say about science and religion, sometimes referring to God, other times self-identifying as an agnostic, but often staking out a position expressing a non-monotheistic religious sensibility that, like Goodenough, denied the existence of a personal God but understood science as a means to encounter the sacred in nature. He wrote near the end of his life, "I am a deeply religious nonbeliever. . . . This is a somewhat new kind of religion."[10]

Einstein did not give up a religious view of the world for his science; science was a peculiarly powerful means to discover sacred wisdom and was intimately tied to his religious imagination and abiding moral and ethical commitment to human society. In this sense, he was very much an outcast, especially compared to others in the scientific community during the first half of the twentieth century, when sociologists tell us science fueled the engines of secularization in modern society. Unfortunately, Einstein would not live to see the public and popular transformation of science that took place in the second half of the century when godless spirituality merged with scientific endeavors and speculations, a spirituality not rooted in the monotheistic cultures of the West—how could it be?—but instead found in the great, mysterious teachings from the East.

At first glance, physics would not seem to be a likely source for religious innovation and inspiration. The highly esoteric worlds of quantum mechanics and chaos theory, big bangs and superconducting supercolliders, wave-particle dualities and uncertainty principles leave most people emotionally cold and intellectually perplexed. On the other hand, the revolutions in classical physics about bodies in motion, from Newton's consideration of a falling apple to Einstein's pursuit of a beam of light, have often drawn remarkable heat from many in the church for the cultural consequences of its truth-telling power: rational thought triumphing over blind faith; quantified experimentation trumping subjective spirituality; and, for critics of this mechanistic, deterministic, disenchanted explanation of the universe and its intricate workings, the authority of science displacing the authority of God. The cultural and political implications of modern physics have generally contributed to the public perception of irreconcilable conflict between religion and science in the modern era.

One of the early pioneers in quantum theory, Danish-born Niels Bohr, brought dramatically new perspectives to the elusive world of the atom. He introduced such ideas as complementarity, which paradoxically states that wave and particle are complementary and mutually exclusive ways of representing quantum objects, and the realization that experimental observations are always affected by the presence of the observer. When accepting his place in the prestigious Order of the Elephant, the highest order in the nation of Denmark, in 1947, Bohr decided to go with the Taoist symbol of yin and yang on his coat of arms and a Latin inscription that read "opposites complement each other." [11]

As classical physics gave ground to a radically different physics bound up with less tangible, more probabilistic, uncannily uncertain quantum theories in the middle and later decades of the twentieth century, the translations of these theories into appealing, popular terms increasingly and seamlessly blended scientific knowledge with religious wisdom and struck a chord in a wide range of communities after the 1960s. Pioneers in and translators of the mysterious, mind-boggling, even mind-bending science often found the right language to describe the complementarity principle and quarks, spacetime theory and nonlocality, and a host of other new concepts in the mysterious, mind-boggling, even mind-bending mystical and nontheistic traditions from the East, including Chinese Taoism, Zen Buddhism, and Advaita Hinduism.

Bohr and other groundbreaking scientists in the early years of quantum theory gravitated toward Eastern philosophies in their own personal lives or in the language they used when contemplating and translating the metaphysical implications of the new physics. These early years of the new quantum frontier, roughly the first half of the twentieth century, were also the last decades God would reign supreme in American public culture and the popular imagination as the primary reference for the sacred in religious cultures proliferating in the spiritually prosperous second half of the century. Godless spirituality grew by leaps and bounds in the consequential 1950s and 1960s, when people grew increasingly uninhibited about challenging authority and conventional forms of truth-telling, when growing numbers enthusiastically experimented in the public arena with alternative religious cultures transplanted from the East—the Beats and Buddhism, or the Beatles and Hinduism, to take two prominent examples, and as substantial increases in West, South, and East Asian populations around the country occurred after the 1965 Immigration Act.

These encounters and experiments were not limited to the visibility of new, unusual local practices in the neighborhood, or to the worlds of art and popular culture growing increasingly enamored with more global religious cultural models imported and adapted to American shores through music or literature. Science too became an arena where Eastern and Western trends and sensibilities creatively crisscrossed and interacted in inspired (though many would claim misguided) ways, leading to rather unique religious views of the world that the pubic eagerly bought in to and adopted as their own.

A pivotal moment in the fertile and profitable blending of Eastern spirituality and quantum physics came in the 1970s, when physicist Fritjof Capra had a few mystical experiences and then published his best-selling book *The Tao of Physics: An Exploration of the Parallels between Modern Physics and Eastern Mysticism*. The book, dedicated to the German physicist Werner Heisenberg, the Indian mystic Jiddu Krishnamurti, the anthropologist-cum-shaman Carlos Castaneda, and the musician John Coltrane, among many others, is a hodgepodge of basic physics, history of science, comparative religion, and philosophical speculation. The book ultimately argues that the rational insights from quantum theory affirm the intuitive wisdom of Eastern mysticism and vice versa.

The chapters lead the reader on a wondrous journey of discovery, bouncing back and forth between the two, but also thinking beyond a world of opposites and oppositions, identifying the unity of all things, discerning patterns of change in the universe, and imagining the dynamic relationship between emptiness and form.[12] In the epilogue, Capra writes that he hopes the reader will take away a central point from the book: "the principal theories and models of modern physics lead to a view of the world which is internally consistent and in perfect harmony with the views of

Eastern mysticism."[13] Capra and others like him, such as Gary Zukav, who wrote the best-selling book *The Dancing Wu Li Masters: An Overview of the New Physics* a few years later, have found avid, hungry disciples willing to consider a universe spiritually alive with compelling mysteries and revelations. Instead of the great myth from biology, the Epic of Evolution, quantum realities lead to the recognition of a sacred dance—a mystical, cosmic dance of energy and matter, subject and object, particle and field, time and timelessness.

Indeed, for Capra this cosmic dance finds one striking parallel with the dance of Shiva, the Hindu god whose rhythm is attuned to the never-ending cycles of death and rebirth, destruction and creation.[14] Similarly, internationally acclaimed theoretical physicist David Bohm probed the physical and philosophical implications of quantum theory and relativity, considerations that led him to Eastern gurus, including the spiritual master and popular philosopher after the 1960s, Krishnamurti, whom Bohm got to know very well as a collaborator and friend. In one interview, Bohm strives to describe the wave function, or the nebulous interactions of the electron and the multidimensional space surrounding it, before ultimately turning to the dance metaphor to capture the paradoxical essence of the quantum world:

> Electrons in a super-conducting state, for example, move in a regular, coordinated way so they don't scatter. In an ordinary state, they are like a disorganized crowd of people. Now if you compare this to the ballet, you could say that in the super-conducting state, the wave function is like the *score*—it's a kind of information—and the dance is the meaning of the score.[15]

What is cosmic about this "dance" for Bohm, other physicists, and the great mystics from the East? It is the unity in the cosmos, a grand but subtle interconnection that can be empirically demonstrated through either disciplined spiritual practice or rigorous mathematical computations.

The cultural reverberations of this mystical version of quantum theory in the American religious imagination have been profound. Like sacred texts in the monotheistic traditions, quantum theories have been the source of a great deal of conflict and contestation, with the result being an assortment of cultural products and movements. A variety of spiritual books with "quantum" in the title have appeared, such as the enormously successful publications by Deepak Chopra: *Quantum Healing: Exploring the Frontiers of Mind/Body Medicine* and *Ageless Body, Timeless Mind: The Quantum Alternative to Growing Old.* Additionally, the vast and complicated New Age and neo-pagan cultures look to quantum physics for scientific confirmation of the cosmic energy that unifies nature and the central role of consciousness in the construction of reality. The surprisingly popular independent film from 2004, *What the #$*! Do We Know!?*, which was rereleased in an expanded form in 2006 as *What the Bleep?!—Down the Rabbit Hole,* is another cultural phenomenon bringing quantum physics to spiritual light.

The film, understood as a lefty response to another religiously based blockbuster of the movie season that year, *Passion of the Christ,* is a heady brew of traditional storytelling, talking heads, and special effects. The story deals with a depressed and medicated photographer on the verge of a breakdown who ultimately arrives at a transformative spiritual awakening thanks to a healthy dose of quantum theory. The message promoted by the film, inspired by science but clearly framed as New Age revelation, is a simple one: we create our own reality—not with God from on high, but from below, so to speak, where personal consciousness influences quantum worlds of possibility from microcosm to macrocosm. The film declares near the very end: "If we can change, we can become the scientists of our life—which is the whole reason why we are here." Scientists, not priests or rabbis, gurus or monks, are the new authoritative figures in the religious cultures enamored with quantum mysticism, a sacred position anyone can attain, the film seems to suggest, given the proper understanding of the true, quantum-based nature of self and cosmos.

While quantum mysticism was already a popular, well-received imaginative prospect in a variety of New Age and non–New Age communities before the original release of *What the Bleep*, the film itself has become a national and even international cultural phenomenon in its own right. The website for the film, www.whatthe bleep.com, is a bustling, bountiful cyberspot for faithful or simply intrigued fans who want more than purely cinematic encounters with the quantum mystical truths offered by the filmmakers. The website has testimonials from viewers who rave about the spiritual awakening provided by the film; merchandise ranging from T-shirts to DVDs, jewelry to books, for material-minded spiritual seekers; and instructions on how to start "Bleep Study Groups" for those spiritually motivated, practically oriented people who want to meet other like-minded people.[16] Eventually, the film will likely fade from public consciousness, even with the current exuberance for proselytizing the film's version of quantum/spiritual truth. But for the moment, it is one very popular science-based sacred text inculcating Americans with a resoundingly religious message of hope and transformation, spiritual enlightenment and metaphysical edification.

While great religious mythology for many, *What the Bleep* is viewed as highly distorted science by a growing chorus of critics from the left and the right, atheists and theists alike, who see the makings of a dangerous, brainwashing cult behind the film. In one of many debunking pieces, Salon.com's John Gorenfeld reported on the growing skepticism surrounding the supposed experts interviewed on camera, including a physics professor from Columbia who renounced the filmmakers and publicly regretted his participation, a speaker whose identity as a former Catholic priest is not disclosed during the film, and one Judy Knight who plays a prominent role in explaining the connections between science and spirituality. She is identified only during the closing credits, along with the other talking heads, as a popular New Age figure who channels the spirit of Ramtha, an ancient mystical warrior, and serves as the leader of Ramtha's School of Enlightenment in Washington State. Gorenfeld outs the film's three directors as followers of Ramtha and confronts Meyer Gottlieb, president of Samuel Goldwyn Films, which owns the distribution company for the film, about the potential danger to the public good. Gottlieb responds candidly: "The question is, Is this movie promoting a cult? . . . The only thing we're interested in from a marketing perspective is creating a cult status for the film . . . cults, from my perspective, they deal with groups and leaders and that stuff. This movie is about individual thinking. Individual control over your future—and your own reality." [17] *What the Bleep* is a vehicle for the popular perpetuation of a religious culture that aspires to be legitimated on scientific terms, and one that inspires a vision of spiritual truth for the masses. Still, it has also been vehemently attacked as being pure fiction—science fiction—in other words, a genre of cultural production and activity that is yet another formidable wellspring for the curious blending of the scientific and religious imagination in the sacred landscapes of contemporary America.

Science fiction is a fixture in popular culture with deep roots in the Western imagination, including such nineteenth-century classics as Jules Verne's *Twenty Thousand Leagues Under the Sea*, Mark Twain's *A Connecticut Yankee in King Arthur's Court*, and H.G. Wells's *The Time Machine*. Science fiction came of age, so to speak, in the early and middle twentieth century through various short stories and novels, magazine publications, and films, but especially through critically acclaimed and popular works by such creators as Isaac Asimov, Frank Herbert, and Fritz Lang. As a genre of cultural expression, science fiction disrupts conventionally held boundaries separating science from fantasy, truth from fiction, past from future, humans from monsters, utopia from dystopia, and technology from morality. It also generally presents imaginative worlds void of God, even though many stories incorporate familiar, biblically centered religious themes tied to messiahs and saviors, apocalypse and salvation, and resurrection and immortality.

But in the fantastic, often futuristic context of science fiction, technology and scientific know-how are more important to mastering the universe than the presence of a Master of the Universe. These fictions are in part a product and an expression of unease and hope, distrust and faith, in a society growing increasingly dependent on the authority of science and decreasingly subservient to the claims of institutionalized religions. Some works of science fiction may be openly hostile to religion while others may be explicitly allegorical; some can transfix the imagination with action and drama; others may test the limits of boredom with obsession to detail. Regardless of the quality and content, stretching the boundaries of science along with creating far-fetched worlds of fiction can lead to engaged reflections on meaning and orientation in the cosmos, moral and ethical responsibilities in human communities, and the limitations and transcendence of the physical body.

Star Trek was a short-lived television series that lasted only three seasons, from 1966–1969.[18] Originally created by avowed secular humanist Gene Roddenberry—a celebrated icon and now, in death, a mythic persona in the *Star Trek* galaxies—the series has spawned numerous stories and characters. More than that, this television show enlivened a cultural industry that rapidly became a dynamic economic juggernaut and now spans the globe; shaped a familiar mythological touchstone that continues to stimulate the popular imagination; and developed a vision of reality that also has become a model for reality in the lives of millions of devoted fans who participate, body and sometimes soul, in the creation of new rituals and experiences. The original series itself; television spin-offs that included *Star Trek: The Animated Series, Star Trek: The Next Generation, Deep Space Nine,* and others; multiple films, fan magazines, conventions, books, novels, dictionaries, manuals, role-playing games, comics, computer games, and websites—the endless products and activities that satiate consumers hungry for *Star Trek*–related phenomena signal more than just entertaining social interactions or over-the-top fanatic behavior.

Like many other examples in the sci-fi genre, the power and persuasiveness of *Star Trek* in the lives of fans are intimately linked to the entertaining integration of scientific possibilities and advancements in technology with spiritual aspirations and inspirations in the search for meaning, purpose, identity, and order in contemporary society. It would be easy to disentangle religious themes and predicaments from the stories and characters found in the television shows and films. But even more intriguing are the various ways viewers entangle themselves in *Star Trek* realities that have nothing to do with scripts or special effects but everything to do with religious frames of reference and sacred content that offer fulfilling ritual activity, bonds of kinship, and means to personal regeneration. *Star Trek* conventions, to take but one example of fans blurring the lines between joyful entertainment and religious engagements, are unique gatherings where many followers seek and find meaningful, sometimes funny, but also frequently sad human experiences.

Numerous observers, commentators, and participants use religious language to describe the actions and meanings surrounding these conventions—for some it is tied to being with family, identifying with and experiencing an ideal form of community; for some it is immersion in an alternate reality—closer to utopia than the disordered, chaotic worlds left behind—that is full of possibility and promise; and for some it is on the order of pilgrimage, a journey outside of ordinary time and space, filled with lasting memories, joyful encounters, and embodied transformations. Attending these gatherings—which mix commerce and role-playing, philosophical reflection and stargazing—inspire legions of fans who realize that even though pilgrims must always, eventually, go back home, there are a variety of ways to keep the *Star Trek* universe enfolded into the elemental fabric of everyday life, including such routine matters as marriage or death.[19]

Conventions are only one means of routinizing sacred *Star Trek* investments. For dutiful followers of *Star Trek*, the ritual actions and mythic language employed after beloved cast members die off one by one are particularly poignant and unequivocally religious. When James Doohan, who played Scotty, died in 2005, the grief and sense of loss across the community was both palpable and immeasurable, leading to spontaneous and organized forms of mourning that moved the faithful to demonstrate the depth of their sorrow. A public memorial took place at Vandenberg Air Force Base before his ashes were to be shot out into space, the final frontier, on board a Falcon 1 rocket—the same destiny as Roddenberry's remains (though sadly Doohan's flight did not ultimately make it out to space). His wife, Wende, wrote a letter of invitation asking fans to attend the ceremony either in person at the base or virtually through the wonders of science on the web.

Testimonials from those touched by this actor, a celebrity but also an individual known for his personal connections to fans at conventions, were also going to be digitized and sent with Doohan's ashes as part of the shuttle payload, according to Wende. Close to ten thousand tributes have been posted at a website devoted to Doohan—whose role as chief engineering officer clearly inspired many to love science and see hope for the future—with words of love and gratitude, joy and appreciation for the special memories he provided to the countless fans.[20] *Star Trek*, like Doohan, is not bound by the material forces that give life in the world of entertainment—flesh and blood, sets and costumes, scripts and cameras—but instead, miraculously acquires a limitless afterlife unbound by the material world but supernaturally vital and vibrant in the lives of followers, who continue to find inspiration and hope, community and well-being in a religiously popular culture tied to a simple television show.

The wonders of an unbelievable future with science, as foretold in a series now over forty years old, continue to be a sacred source for religious belief and ritual action in America. The characters from the show have become icons in the cultural imagination—not static and one-dimensional roles masking the actors playing their parts, but multilayered, vivid, dynamic figures which transform actors into celebrities, and bring to life a whole universe of meanings and memories, morals and moods to viewers. Captain James T. Kirk—not just the name but also the image of William Shatner in his most famous role—conjures up a host of associations, including the spirit of adventure, the power and ethics of leadership, and the courage of convictions in the face of danger, that are embedded in a larger complex of culturally resonate, collectively vital webs of significance emanating from the memorable and hopeful journeys of the USS *Enterprise*.

Along with alluring celebrity actors who captivate fans, entertaining storylines with humanistic, inspirational messages of progress, and compelling worlds of action and meaning in distant galaxies but also accessible here and now, scientific know-how and technological innovations power these futuristic space journeys and transform them into sacred stories—myths, in other words. Faith in science takes many forms, from raving fundamentalists who look to science as the only source of absolute truth about life and the cosmos to committed consumers who find insight and knowledge about the true nature of human existence in science fiction. At the extremes and everywhere in between, science generates sacred investments and values with real cultural impact and social consequences. So in the case of *Star Trek*, for example, fans can have special attachments to a mythic television show and find religiously relevant lessons in their own worlds by caring about and identifying with these characters and their journeys.

6

MEDICINE

"Live long and prosper."

In a recent television commercial that premiered during the 2006 Super Bowl for the popular and profitable over-the-counter arthritis relief medicine Aleve, Leonard Nimoy is talking on the phone to his manager about pain. Nimoy played Dr. Spock on the original *Star Trek* series over forty years ago, and the role will always come to mind when we see an image of him. But he is alive and aging, a cultural touchstone in the lives of many—especially baby boomers who grew up with the young Spock from the series and know what it means to grow old in the early decades of the twenty-first century. In the commercial, Nimoy is backstage at a big *Star Trek* event, talking with his manager about his inability to move his fingers and make the signature Vulcan gesture, a salutation whose meaning is captured in the words above, "live long and prosper." His manager recommends that Nimoy take Aleve, and the actor immediately consents before walking into his dressing room and closing the door. After a fade to black, we see Nimoy walking out into a packed auditorium, full of Trekkies holding their breath in anticipation that the spirit of Spock, the fictional character, will make an appearance along with the nicely dressed (not in Starfleet uniform, but professorial slacks and a black turtleneck) aged actor. The iconic celebrity gets to the podium while the audience applauds; he lifts his right hand, which silences them; and though unable to perform the nimble finger move earlier, after a perfectly timed pause, he miraculously gives the Vulcan salute.

The crowd goes crazy while we hear the Star Trek theme and Nimoy's voice say, "That's good news. That's Aleve."

Like so much direct-to-consumer pharmaceutical marketing, this ad wants to spread the good news about modern medicines: they can cure bodily pains; stave off death, if only temporarily; bring happiness though with side effects; and generally allow consumers to prosper and find fulfillment—an optimistic gospel that many Americans buy into for spiritual rewards as much as somatic relief from pain. Medicine and medicinal cultures offer pathways to health, but health is much more than a physical condition.

The desire for good health in this life—a fleeting, ultimately unsustainable but intensely idealized state—has sacred significance for Americans regardless of institutional affiliations or religious identity, theological justifications or hedonistic pursuits. A body transformed—once afflicted by pain or distress or incapacity tied to genetic, mental, immunological, accidental, muscular, or any variety of sources, and then healed through swallowing a pill—is a body to celebrate. What constitutes "good health?" An athletic, chiseled, attractive body? An optimistic attitude and positive outlook? Harmonious relations with dead ancestors? The absence of disease? Balance with the surrounding ecosystem? The ability to reproduce? Just feeling better? Healing medicine provided by pharmaceutical companies or shamans, illegal drugs or experimental treatments, medical doctors or New Age healers, pharmacists or root specialists, addresses specific illnesses, but also seeks to keep the living alive, help them overcome the wear and tear of life, and ensure that individuals and communities live productively— perhaps a bit more complicated than "live long and prosper," but still touching on a fairly common religious sentiment associated with medicine across cultures.

The sacred pursuit of feeling better can depend, at least in part, on making sure you are taking the right meds. But good medicine, as we know all too well, can turn bad in a blink of an eye, when drug therapy becomes drug abuse. Rush Limbaugh can attest to that fact. His recent, heavily publicized bout with addiction to narcotic-based painkillers like OxyContin illustrates how easily a medication legitimately prescribed for the relief of pain can turn into an irrational obsession for something more than pain relief— even for one of the most moralistic, self-righteous champions of Christian values in American society. Limbaugh publicly acknowledged his addiction, as Patrick Kennedy did in spring 2006, when he admitted his abuse of the sleep medication Ambien after being arrested by the Washington, D.C., police.[1] Although in the glaring spotlight of public media, these two are far from alone, with estimates of Americans who abuse prescription drugs in the millions—exceeding even those Americans who are addicted to illegal drugs like cocaine or heroin, and an especially growing problem for young people who are experimenting with prescription painkillers like Vicodin to get high, using medicine to do something else than cure a symptom in the body.[2] Legal or illegal, the consumption of a wide range of drugs, organic or inorganic, with chemical agents that profoundly alter moods and change personalities, temporarily provide a balm for the pains and stresses of life, or dramatically induce ecstatic and euphoric experiences can be sacred activity. With this view the distinctions between good and bad medicine break down, the ideals of health begin to blur, and addiction looks more and more like religion.

Many people find that drug use and drug abuse provide corporeal experiences and mental states so powerful, so appealing, so gratifying, so healing that they are willing to lie, steal, deceive, and engage in all sorts of criminal activities to modify the body's chemistry and cross over from normal, ordinary consciousness into abnormal, extraordinary consciousness. From LSD to wine, marijuana to cocaine, peyote to prescriptions, drugs can be a means to encounter an expanding vision of reality beyond the material, offering medicinal access to a healthy dose of God the father or Jesus the son in the Peyote Church, to take the most blatant example, but also to sacred experiences of rejuvenation or restoration with no trace of God in any form at all.

America is a drug-obsessed society. The war on drugs, the billion dollar pharmaceutical industry, the pervasive illegal black market, the glorification of celebrities who overdose—these are only a few signs of our fixation on drugs and how truly integrated they are in everyday life. Coffee and alcohol, two staples of daily life for hundreds of millions of Americans, are acceptable, highly profitable substances that are so routine, so ubiquitous that many do not even recognize them as drugs which have pleasurable, and potentially harmful, effects on the body. Yet the heavily contested debate surrounding drugs, as a prominent feature of America's culture wars, as a volatile source of legal wrangling, as a potentially divisive presence in social relations, suggests there is more at stake than simply the state of health in the physical body and the body politic. Intoxication through drug use arouses and energizes the passions, subverts and confuses prevailing social values, and encourages and facilitates altered states of consciousness—sacred matters that can, under the right circumstances and in particular contexts, lead to prosperous religious experiences and participation in loose, diffuse forms of religious culture in any number of communal or private settings.[3]

The link between drug ingestion and religious cultures, medicinal therapies and sacred realities, is a common feature of social life in many cultures. Drugs of all kinds, initially drawn from the plant world in the form of mushrooms or tobacco, jimsonweed or soma, have been considered powerful and invaluable because they combine medicinal and spiritual goods; are embedded in meaningful, socially vital rituals and myths; and heal by way of cosmic revelation and personal as well as social regeneration. Sacred medicine is not only restricted to the pursuit of a healthy individual body but can have, in some cultural settings, powers not associated with modern medicines: divination and recovery of lost objects, enlightenment and transportation to the world of the dead, ecstasy and communication with the spirits and ancestors, transformation and social revitalization.

Take fly agaric mushrooms, for example. This powerful, psychoactive plant, scientifically known as *Amanita muscaria*, is distributed across a vast geographic expanse that includes Alaska, Canada, the northern United States, as well as northern Europe and Asia, and has played a critical role in the religious life of communities throughout this expanse for thousands of years. It is poisonous for humans, containing a variety of toxins including the alkaloid muscimole, which can produce symptoms such as dizziness and delirium, or hyperactivity and hallucinations, even euphoria and ecstasy, depending on the individual and the setting. The ultimate benefits this drug offers to consumers in Siberia or India, Alaska or the Netherlands, far outweigh the short-term dangerous side effects that accompany its ingestion: it can help diagnose illness, as well as cure ailments; it animates cultures of ecstasy as a sacrament that initiates altered states of consciousness and mystical flights out of this world; it also embodies the divine ("flesh of the gods" in a well-known phrase associated with the fungus), a botanical god in and of itself, allowing for invigorating, restorative experiences of communion. This hallucinogenic narcotic is religiously potent, a psychoactive sacrament providing healing and transformation on multiple levels of reality and meaning not limited to, but certainly encompassing, the physical body.[4]

Or smoke tobacco, a legal drug most of us are more familiar with and one which has a significant social and economic role in U.S. history. Today, a blight for America's health care system and a source of addiction for millions, tobacco and tobacco mixtures in the precolonial Native American past could provide sacred prosperity to individuals and communities who ritually integrated nicotine into their daily lives. For Cherokees in the southeast, the procurement and preparation of tobacco for smoking was a ritually precise, power-inducing process that transformed a mere plant into a supernaturally potent tool that could induce shamanistic visions, guide military planning in times of war, and serve as medicine to heal the sick and afflicted. The multiple uses of this drug make it difficult to assign its value to Cherokee society in singular terms, as only a medicine to cure, for example, or simply a sacrament to inspire.[5] *Nicotiana* in all its variations and regional distinctions served as a bridge between worlds, a sacred drug that bonded communities, expanded consciousness, compelled worship, and healed disease.[6]

Good medicine in one society is another society's scourge; what one society labels unhealthy addiction can be, in different cultural circumstances, a ritually religious way to provide community members with spiritual illuminations and mystical transportation. Yet one fact is clear: drugs have been used by humans throughout history for religious intoxication, leading some to argue that, like survival or sex, aggression or music, these experiences are also part and parcel of a primal, biological human drive.[7] Sacred, intoxicating, illuminating medicines are a proven, reliable channel to worlds of meaning and experience relevant to truths about the here and now, as well as truth beyond space and time. Regardless of the powerful, often harmful effects on the nervous system and neurological activity in the brain, consumption promises spiritual health and well-being that cut against the grain of twenty-first-century American standards of health often embodied and idealized in prescription drug advertisements—physically fit, firmly heterosexual, perpetually smiling faces, squarely at home in their body, their family, and the material world.

From its birth in 1776, the United States has always been a drug-devouring nation, with the help of indigenous Native knowledge and practice; or through cultural importation by immigrants from all over the world including East and Central Asia; or by way of slave routes from parts of Africa; or just as a result of European traditions brought from the Old World embracing alcohol, tobacco, and other well-known substances. By the first half of the twentieth century, however, Americans had become addicted to medications that included opiates in growing numbers and created black markets for drugs such as morphine and heroin after greater legal regulations criminalized certain forms of drug use.[8] Throughout the chaos and confusion surrounding drugs in American society, in spite of the contradictions and contestations in drug laws and medical classifications, Americans from all walks of life continue to find and consume illegal drugs that are perceived to be a dangerous threat to moral order, social responsibility, and cultural advancement. In modern America, drugs like marijuana or acid, mushrooms or morphine, can bring religious experiences to users that are not tied to formal institutions but arise from within another temple, not bound by biblical texts on the Divine, but emerge organically from altered states in the divine body.

One of the earliest and most important testimonials for drug use as a means to spiritual prosperity is from the famous American philosopher and psychologist William James. In his groundbreaking book from 1902, *The Varieties of Religious Experience*, James describes his experiments with nitrous oxide, an intoxicant that was generally used as an anesthetic for surgery, dentistry, or other potentially painful medical procedures. For James, however, nitrous oxide had other spiritually salutary effects beyond its analgesic properties—it also could induce a pronounced mystical experience that offered metaphysical truths to inhalers. James finds, as with most mystical experiences, that it is difficult to articulate the content of the spiritual insight though he comes closest by describing a particularly profound moment of ultimate, though transient, healing: "The keynote of it is invariably a reconciliation. It is as if the opposites of the world, whose contradictoriness and conflict make all our difficulties and troubles, were melted into unity"[9]—something close to the descriptions of raves in chapter 2 and very frequently echoed in other descriptions of mystical trips.

The religious possibilities associated with drug consumption and the cultural impact of using sacred medicine to facilitate spiritual awakening and rejuvenation really transformed the religious landscapes of the United States, of course, after the 1960s, when religious cultures flourished with psychedelics and pot, communal drug rituals and private inner journeys. In communities throughout America since the 1960s, drug use has often been connected with music and sex, aesthetics and alternative lifestyles, in ways that have enhanced the sacred dimensions of smoking dope or dropping acid, ritual activities that did not only alter consciousness and induce pleasures, but could revolutionize spiritual life itself.

The social dramas of the 1960s—race wars in the streets and military conflict in foreign jungles, political disintegration in the corridors of power and generational conflict between parents and children—eroded the social power of traditional sources of authority and institutions of control in public life, like government or the church. In these circumstances a narrow legalistic vision of mind-altering drugs did not hold sway for spiritually hungry Americans who were disenchanted with Western religions and external authorities. Instead, many were more intrigued by Eastern religious practices and the facilitation of inner and perspectival transformations, and they were eager to experiment with alternative spiritualities so appealingly displayed in the culture around them—in music, films, books, classrooms, and magazines.

No one captures the frenetic, confounding, multifaceted mix of desires and motivations, ideals and discontent intersecting with sacred medicine in the decades of the 1960s and 1970s better than Timothy Leary. Experimenting first with psychedelic mushrooms in 1960, Leary soon discovered the drug he would be associated with for the rest of his life, as well as beyond the grave: LSD. Albert Hofmann first produced the drug, lysergic acid diethylamide, in Switzerland in 1929, while searching for possible medications to use in obstetrics. Hofmann wrote about his own experiences with the drug but by and large LSD remained a pharmaceutical secret, seemingly destined for obscurity in the laboratory with no medical or social capital in the middle of the twentieth century.[10] Leary,

however, brought LSD to the bright light of day, first experimenting with it along with other hallucinogens at Harvard before being
dismissed there, and soon by initiating a cultural revolution with
the popular and remarkably persuasive gospel of turning on, tun-
ing in, and dropping out. LSD was for Leary and thousands of
other Americans sacred medicine that could unlock the mysteries
of the body, mind, and cosmos.

The spiritual wonder and vitality unleashed by dropping acid
was not exclusively an out-of-body, otherworldly experience. Indeed, Leary and other participants in this religious drug culture
understood the pleasures of sexuality, experimenting with myriad
positions and partners, as well as other hedonistic pursuits as an integral component in the encounter with God. Leary writes in an
early publication, *High Priest* (1968), "God and Sex are one" and
"You are God!"—blasphemous claims for most Jews, Christians,
and Muslims, though certainly a common refrain in this era of pop
psychology, commercialized Eastern spirituality, sexual revolutions, and impotent theology that cling to the word God for communicating godless religious truths.[11] The God within, this high
priest tells readers, is awakened with a peculiar sacrament, a psychedelic drug that taps into and chemically induces mystical experiences bringing immense pleasure and fulfillment, but also
wisdom and insight. From Haight-Ashbury in San Francisco to
communes in upstate New York, Americans discovered physical
pleasures and metaphysical truths by expanding their consciousness with sacred, medicinal drugs prescribed by cultural shamans
like Leary, who celebrated their religious implications and spiritual
potentialities.

Dropping acid in a sacred quest for expanding consciousness is one
thing, but prescription drugs are something else all together, far, far
removed from any type of religious pursuit. Right? Wrong. Today
biomedicine generally and pharmaceutical drugs in particular are
rooted in sacred myths and transformative rituals that shape how

Americans understand a common religious pursuit shared by
many of the world's religious traditions, Christian or Muslim, Jew
or Taoist: good health and long life. The ancient wisdom of an invented Vulcan culture, to return to Nimoy, even articulates the
sentiment, and Americans identify with it when they see Aleve
cure the aging pretend Vulcan from pain and distress and go
buy the product with a combination of faith and hope about its
powers.

Aleve is one among many medicinal products brought to the
public marketplace through direct-to-consumer advertising by
major pharmaceutical companies that spend billions of dollars sell-
ing their over-the-counter and prescription medications to a
drug-hungry, increasingly prescription-heavy America. Lunesta
and Paxil, Prilosec and Lipitor, Prozac and Viagra—these are a few
of the prescription drugs that work a special kind of magic on the
body, a scientifically grounded, potentially dangerous, highly expensive magic, for sure, but medicine that has an aura of the miraculous in public culture, as well as in individual lives.

The effectiveness of recent mass-market advertising by the
pharmaceutical industry pushing prescription drugs as the surest
way to treat disease relies as much on tapping into religious hopes
and aspirations as in couching the arguments in persuasive scientific language, a common mixture that often excludes the power
of a divine healer though retains something of the supernatural
in accounting for the tremendous—and for many, the awe-
inspiring—successes of modern medications. Modern medicines
like those provided by mega-pharmaceutical drug companies are
based on rigorous scientific research and experimentation, clinical
trials and quantitative analyses; they produce measurable biochem-
ical changes in the physical body, sometimes unpredictable and
clearly with potentially harmful if not deadly side effects, which
alter moods and behaviors as well as physiology in therapeutically
beneficial ways for many patients.

They may ultimately be worse for you than the ailment itself, as in the disastrous recent case of the pain medication Vioxx; or they may be created for questionable illnesses like the purported but not yet medically sanctioned psychiatric condition PMDD, a premenstrual dysphoric disorder that encompasses a range of symptoms experienced by young, menstruating women and legitimized by the Food and Drug Administration, which approved new forms of antidepressants like Prozac as acceptable medication.[12] Yet one common characteristic that prescription drugs today share with medicine in many human cultures is that the promise of cure is worth the risk, a notion often elaborated in strikingly religious practices and conceptions, rituals and myths, that underscores how true healing is more than just physical change and bears on nothing less than sacred visions of the good life, the pursuit of happiness, and the search for contentment.

Floating in the clouds or blissful under the covers, in love with an aging spouse and ready with a steady erection or gracefully performing tai chi in a beautiful green park—this is only a short list of memorable images from the often surreal, yet strangely effective commercials for these drugs.[13] The impact and significance of these ads can be measured in more than dollars and cents, though the fact that they cost billions and make billions is not unrelated to how they make religious sense.

The advertisements for Nexium, the "purple pill" put out by AstraZeneca, are an illustrative lesson in the creation and power of modern fetishism as much as they are a successful model of marketing a medication for gastroesophageal reflux disease, commonly associated with heartburn and acid reflux, an ailment plaguing millions of Americans. Part marketing magic, part religious commercialism, ads for prescription-only Nexium, a variation of the now over-the-counter Prilosec, answer some of life's most pressing questions about happiness, willpower, and the future. Rather than build a marketing campaign around substantive scientific details of the disease, rigorous dietary changes that might help with the problem, or painful accounts of people in distress—though all of

these are accessible at the heartburn-infocenter.com website—
AstraZeneca carved out a niche in the pharmaceutical landscape
by turning an ordinary pill into a colorful fetish object.
The purple pill is at the center of successful healing in these
ads. Indeed, the world is literally seen through a purple haze with
purple shades and purple hues and purple stripes and purple letters: the way to heal, and therefore find happiness, is via the purple
pill. The pill is framed in this media blitz as nothing less than a religious fetish containing special, life-altering, medicinal powers.

What is a fetish? Historically, the word has been used to distinguish true religion from false religion. In this case, the derogatory
word designated objects that aroused intense, irrational devotion,
and often fear and dread, in worshipers but that were ultimately
contrived, artificial, made-up, and unworthy of sacred investments.
In the less theological social scientific language of anthropologists
and psychologists, a fetish is a distinctive, inanimate artifact that has
special powers worthy of reverence and devotion. Whether in the
form of amulets or medicine bundles, carved stones or articles of
clothing, fetishes are objects of fixation and intense ritual activity,
sometimes quite erotic for people, other times a source of protection, and oftentimes employed for magical transformations, either
for good or ill.

The purple pill brings relief from and manages discomforts associated with heartburn and acid reflux, conditions that, according
to some ads, take the joy out of living, impede fulfilling relations
with loved ones, and interfere with prosperity in everyday lives.
Thanks to the scientifically proven, physiologically effective changes
in digestive processes and stomach acids initiated by popping the
pill, good health can be restored. In one ad, a woman suffering with
acid reflux tells the audience that she is a problem solver, while the
ad shows purple-infused images of her working around the house
and with her daughter fixing a broken bike. She could not solve
her acid reflux problem but, thanks to one purple pill a day, she feels
better and is healed, though we do not learn if she suffers from those

nasty side effects, like headaches or diarrhea, she warns the viewer about. All we know is that, by the end of the commercial—after we see a graphic of a damaged esophagus bathed in the color red and a healed one bathed in purple—she is smiling and seemingly rejuvenated in a well-running household and in a meaningful relationship with her daughter. The doctor writes the prescription, the woman is no longer a patient, and her life revolves around a fetish, a protective, health-inducing, liberating purple pill.

The fetishization of magic pills, operating by the placebo principle or not, transforms living conditions and instills hope that suffering can be replaced by joy, a life free of acid reflux in the case of the purple pill, or, to take another illuminating example, a life no longer plagued by erectile dysfunction, in the case of Viagra. The success of the fetish is based in part on faith, religious faith as well as scientific faith, in the power of modern wonder drugs to relieve and cure the body, but also to heal and restore the soul, or something else that cannot be measured by science but that is vital to life itself. At first glance, associating modern medical wonders with a discarded anthropological term tainted with colonial biases and ethnocentric disregard for nonindustrial cultures would seem confused if not downright ass-backward. But such a pairing makes a great deal of sense when the sacred is factored into the faith millions of Americans place in their doctors and the transformative power of authorized drugs. It brings to light the irrational superstitions undergirding modern rational drug consumption, now at record highs; throws into relief the passionate attachments to artificial products with extraordinary powers driving the logic of the health care marketplace, so out of control that health care systems are on the brink of collapse; and alludes to primitive mentalities ritually devoted to special *materia medica* prescribed by ritual specialists with the training and know-how to cure what ails us— doctors who have replaced priests and other religious leaders who struggle with the dominant moral issues of our day.

•　　•　　•

Most human cultures have designated healers who have the knowledge and skills to heal the physical, emotional, mental, and spiritual sufferings of those who are not well and save them from a life with stress, discomfort, and pain, and in many cases they save patients from death itself. The universal realities of sickness and disease, pain and illness, have to be addressed in all societies, but despite the universality of these conditions, societies have peculiar, distinctive classes of ritual specialists who are charged with this salvific task: shamans in states of ecstasy and medicine men with special knowledge of the plant world; conjurers who can contact the spirits and acupuncturists working with pins; voodoo priests possessed by gods and medical doctors in white coats who become gods, of a sort.

From the most ancient societies to those in the twenty-first century, healing is assumed to be a noble, humane, and oftentimes dangerous, activity. In many cultural contexts, it is also an inherently religious activity that bears on ultimate truths in the cosmos and consequential perspectives on bodies, spirits, and power. But in modern America, religion is assumed to be outside the purview of a good doctor, viewed as an irrelevant force in medical treatment that distracts from specialized knowledge and good clinical practice. The last century witnessed striking, dramatic revolutions in healing and medicine and the spread of one dominant system of healing with an undisputable source of authority: experimental science. From the early 1900s, with the rise of hospitals, professionalization of the medical field, and fantastic advancements in biomedical knowledge and technologies, to the late 1990s when health care systems teetered on the brink of collapse, medical costs soared to astronomical heights, and public awareness of alternative healing strategies openly challenged biomedical dominance, the cultural environment in which American doctors cared for the ill changed as never before.[14] But contrary to conventional wisdom about the twentieth century, these transformations did not simply

entail the triumph of science and the disappearance of religion
from the context of healing.

Instead, it seems clear that religious sensibilities and practices—
sacred engagements with healing and modern medicine that did
not begin and end with prayers for God's miraculous intervention or devotion to the cult of saints for protection while in the
hospital—were widespread in the biomedical world in the early
twentieth century. Another kind of religious cult flourished in
the early decades of the twentieth century: the cult of medical
doctors.[15]

The cult of doctors conveys both a popular religious phenomenon in the cultural imagination and a series of cultural practices authorizing religious webs of meaning and mystification to
make sense of ill health in the early decades of the twentieth century. In this cult, medically trained physicians were indoctrinated
with a narrowly defined set of universal principles by which to access ultimate truth, an education into unseen realities lying beneath the skin and sanctioned by the requisite socially powerful
sacred institutions that allowed the cult to flourish—in this case
medical schools and hospitals. On the one hand, the cult was an
exclusive group of primarily white men with very strict codes of
conduct, rules of initiation, and perceptions of self- and social
worth; on the other hand, changing social perceptions of doctors
and real-life experiences with them in technologically advanced,
physically intimate hospital settings contributed to the aura of
mystery and attraction, fear and sacrality, that has surrounded medical doctors—and especially surgeons—over the course of the
century and into the present.

Religious sensibilities played an integral role in the thoroughly
modern, scientifically grounded biomedical culture that emerged
and achieved social authority before the Second World War—an
authority embodied first and foremost by the medically trained
doctor and institutionalized in modern hospitals and medical

schools, both guided by the light of science. The cultural influence of religion in this medical culture goes far beyond the establishment of hospitals by religious institutions and the presence of religious figures in hospital corridors. A distinctive religious culture can be traced to numerous phenomena embodied by and radiating from the medical doctor, including the changing sacred spaces of healing, the growing faith patients have in science, the absorbing ritual dramas and indoctrinations of medical education, and the multiplying trajectories of devotion energizing the social relations between doctors and doctors, doctors and patients, and doctors and the larger public.

Throughout the twentieth century, the medical doctor was often portrayed in public culture as living in multiple worlds of reality and morality, embodying often conflicting but generally popular fears and desires about suffering and healing, health and death. Doctors are often heroic saviors, though they can be the most morally reprehensible villains; in some instances, they are the paragon of virtue and duty, in others, they are a more invidious presence; sometimes they are morally confused, just like the rest of us, other times, burning with absolute devotion to the welfare of fellow humans. It is difficult to think of another profession, often framed as a "vocation," outside of formal religious institutions that is so bogged down in the language of the sacred—the closest one that comes to mind, perhaps not so ironically considering they both require a peculiar kind of intimacy with the physical body, is the historically parallel role of funeral director.

Consider the following: on an early episode of E! Entertainment's *Dr. 90210*, an intimate look at the world of cosmetic surgeons practicing in Beverly Hills, California, the focal point of the show, Dr. Rey, made a striking comment: plastic surgery was a religion, and he had the power to transform his patients' lives. One grateful patient of pioneering brain surgeon Harvey Cushing wrote after a successful surgery in the early twentieth century, "I can never begin to tell you just what you have meant to me and

what a debt of gratitude I owe you for saving my life by your op-
erative skill and for encouraging and helping me through the years
since then. You have been a blessing to the world." [16] In *The Scalpel
and the Silver Bear*, Lori Alvord's 1999 memoir of her journey to
become the first woman Navajo surgeon, from reservation life to
dean of Dartmouth Medical School, the author writes powerfully
of the "awe and reverence" she feels when looking into the body
of a patient and how, from the patient's perspective, "surgery . . .
was magical and . . . made us [surgeons] the modern-day equiva-
lent of shamans." [17]

The extraordinary lives of doctors have been a fixture of public consciousness for most of the twentieth century: from the life
of extraordinary doctors like the publicly venerated doctor-
celebrity Harvey Cushing in the 1920s through 1940s to television
fixations on the lives of medical doctors as evident in such recent
shows as *ER* or *Scrubs* or *House*; from the familiar iconography of
harmless, and often humorous, physicians with children in Norman Rockwell's paintings to the disturbing imagery in David Cronenberg's film about twin gynecologists, *Dead Ringers* (1988); from
the intense and commanding figure in Thomas Eakins's iconic
painting *The Gross Clinic* (1875) to the fresh and impressionable
Young Doctor Kildare (1938), the first of a series of popular films.
The public fascination with these lives, coupled with the peculiarly fraught personal interactions with private doctors increasingly successful at diagnosing disease and sickness, endowed the
medical profession with a special magic when the stakes are highest in someone's life or when a person is dealing with health or
possible death, prosperity or decline.

By the closing decades of the twentieth century, however, the
cultural traction of the cult changed and in many ways dissipated,
thanks to the rise of pharmaceuticals and direct-to-consumer advertising, where this chapter began, as well as the corporatization
of health care and diversification of students graduating from medical school. Indeed, the cult of doctors diminished in religious

power as these new trends led to a greater, more widespread diffusion of religious sensibilities in the larger arena of health and healing, transforming medicine in twenty-first-century America but in many ways resembling the exceedingly diverse, highly contentious state of medicine and medical practice in America before the Civil War. Perhaps most significant to this process of sacred diffusion beyond the socially authoritative realm of medical doctors has been the growing popularity and legitimacy of alternative healing practices less beholden to the powers of biomedically trained male gods in white coats and more besotted with spiritual influences that only occasionally emanate from any gods, let alone one God.

Alternative medicines have a faithful following of millions of Americans who willingly turn away from medical men and women in the pocket of pharmaceutical giants deeply invested in cure by prescription. The desperate search for health and well-being leads Americans away from traditional modern institutions for healing, like the hospital or the clinic, to private homes and strip malls, massage parlors and sweat lodges where medical authority and therapeutic interventions are more openly, explicitly tied to religious sentiments and sacred engagements. On the other hand, it is true that in the last decade or so, mainstream medicine has also been willing to incorporate some alternative medical perspectives into biomedical settings and research agendas, including the National Institutes of Health's increasing financial support for complementary and alternative medicines. Compared to the monolithic and hegemonic status of biomedicine in the first half of the century, contemporary American society displays a unique, but not unprecedented, medical pluralism that often combines spiritual with physical healing.[18]

Whether the medical options are coming from other parts of the world, like China, India, Mexico, or Jamaica, or arising by way of indigenous cultural streams, like Native American practices, homegrown metaphysical movements, or New Age cultures that combine one, two, or several of these sources, Americans today are willing to embrace or at least try so-called alternative approaches to healing.[19] These approaches transform afflictions and illness through changing lifestyles rather than ingesting a pill, or by attending to the spirit as much as altering body chemistry. Sometimes these alternative medical strategies invest all of their faith in the healing power of God, as in the case of Christian Science, but many make a faith investment in therapies that do not require belief in a personal God at all, as in the case of transcendental meditation. The vast, public presence of alternative healing systems in twenty-first-century America contributes to the growth and development of religious cultures that offer sacred medicine to folks increasingly disenfranchised from and disenchanted with biomedical orthodoxy, which can be ineffective, make things worse, and even more disappointing, avoid completely the nonmaterial dimensions of feeling ill.

The body is only one piece of a medical puzzle for alternative healers, who provide a larger cosmic frame of reference in which to put pieces together to form a picture of health. Microcosm blurs with macrocosm, matter with energy, and individual self with spiritual realities. Who needs a scalpel or a pill when your aura is diseased or energy blockage brings back pain or the God within remains undiscovered? Instead, to take one example, crystals can be used for medicinal purposes, a healing therapy that purifies the body as well as revitalizes the higher self. Advocates look at crystals as conductors of spiritual energy and power that bring balance and harmony to more than just the physical expression of reality, but other expressions less susceptible to physical measurement as well, including the etheric and the astral.

Like other alternative medical technicians, crystal healers may or may not invoke God or Jesus, a higher self or a great soul, in their highly ritualized and profitable healing sessions, workshops, or books. But they do offer mystery and enchantment, as well as bright-eyed metaphysical speculation, to the curious and convinced who are searching for the right remedy to heal their pain and discomfort.[20] While too New Age–y for some, use of crystals is but one of myriad alternative healing approaches present in the medical landscapes of modern America and popular enough to draw people into religious cultures with meaningful myths and transformative rituals, whether they are also Jewish or Hindu, Buddhist or Christian, atheist or agnostic.

What matters most is that sacred knowledge existing beyond the realm of medical science is available and relevant in diagnosis and treatment, not an esoteric, abstract knowledge but one that can have practical, concrete effects that bring spiritual transformations as well as physical succor in this life. The Bible is irrelevant when the sacred is not limited to the word in a text or to a God on high but is an immanent, dynamic feature of life in this world that can be manipulated with the right techniques and knowledge, either by oneself or with the expertise of trained specialists, to convert sickness to health and suffering to peace.

7

VIOLENCE

"War! What is it good for?"

Absolutely nothing, according to the still-popular anti–Vietnam War song "War," originally performed by Edwin Starr in 1968. But war has played a vital role in human history, shaping the destinies of individuals, families, societies, and empires, and violence remains an ever-present reality embedded in the fabric of daily living. America is one of the most violent nations in the world, a country gripped by fears of violence from others, propped up globally by threats of violent force, and fascinated by graphic depictions of violent acts. Its history and present is rife with the attendant bloodshed and murder, hatred, and oppression that accompany violence. America also displays a remarkable obsession with representations of violence, from early Puritan sermons to contemporary interactive computer games. Even though many glorious counterexamples of compassion and peace from the nation's history can be listed, this penchant for violence in times of peace but especially in wartime pays many social dividends that are essential to American life—economic for sure, political of course, and religious as well, though perhaps in some unexpected ways.

The intimate, troubling connections between religion and violence have preoccupied historians, filmmakers, theologians, poets, anthropologists, novelists, and others since long before 9/11, a day now seared into consciousness and forever marked on the terrestrial and imaginative landscapes. But we would be overlooking so much of human history if this is only understood as an exceptional case of religious extremism, an act of terrorism fueled by delusional fanaticism or monotheism gone all wrong. Violence has long been a potent source for sacred activities, identities, and transformations in religious traditions like Judaism and Buddhism, Hinduism and Christianity—all of their sacred histories and myths provide evidence that religion and violence go hand in hand at times. Anyone familiar with the general contours of human history must acknowledge this fact as well, for the past is undeniably delineated by endless religious persecutions, hatreds, and wars that brutally kill young and old, innocent and guilty. Even if violence, a clear evolutionary trait found primarily in males whose DNA drives them to be naturally aggressive, is hardwired biologically as some suggest, it does not rule out the possibility of sacred experiences, though it might overrule the belief in a benevolent, loving God.[1]

So if violence is indeed an inescapable reality in social life, war can be good for a great many things in human cultures. Can the violence of modern war be sacred? Is it ever anything but religious when the lives of so many are at stake? Every time America goes to war, theological questions arise about whether or not the current engagement counts as a holy war, leading in many, though not all, cases to public debates and institutional disagreements over God's role in all the cruelty and carnage. This discussion, however, is missing the larger point: all wars are holy with or without God, inherently religious because the violence of war places everything that matters into bold relief—values and territory tied to group identity, of course, but also more immediate life or death concerns for the individual soldier, like maintaining the integrity of the physical body for as long as possible or risking life and limb to save a wounded comrade. Even when God is not invoked to justify violence—a rarity in Western history considering the biblical rationales for God to take sides in times of war—deadly battles between groups arouse religious sympathies and sensibilities that are as deeply embedded in personal transformative experiences as they are widely dispersed across a community that is held together by shared loss and common cause.

The experiences of soldiers in the midst of battle are often indescribable. From the most ancient societies to the present new world order, warfare has given warriors a glimpse of something the uninitiated will never know, a separation that cannot be bridged by language or representation or empathy. Some experiences in war defy easily accessible translation, yet transfix both the soldiers who have them and the noncombatants who want to hear about them over and over and over again—think of the poetry and novels, plays and films, paintings and music inspired by and devoted to life in war.

Many accounts from American soldiers, like those of warriors in other armies throughout history, claim that the ugliness and savagery wrought by the violence of war can at the same time provide something sublime and revelatory, a mystical vision piercing the real physical surroundings and sensations and illuminating something quite beyond this world. Proximity to death and corpses figure into the sacred equation, as does the suspension of conventional social norms while in the military and especially in combat zones. The heightened awareness of one's own body and the bodies of others, comrade or rival, along with the simultaneous responses of fascination and revulsion, awe and dread, in the face of violent spectacles and horrific bloodshed, establish extraordinary conditions as well for individual soldiers so far away from ordinary peacetime routines and relations. Communal bonds forged in battle and the shared memories of the living of soldiers lost in the fight also bring to life religious sentiments and sensibilities on the fields of battle, making sacred experiences possible and often transforming scarred earth into hallowed ground.

Mixed together in the realities of battle, the combination of potential religious factors associated with warfare can bring soldiers to weighty spiritual revelations and strangely liberating mystical encounters, often transporting the warrior beyond good or evil and into an unforgettable realm at once ecstatic and aesthetic, arousing exceptional feelings of love and remarkable perceptions of beauty alongside abject disgust or repulsion. From the jungles of Vietnam to the beaches of Normandy, the fields of Antietam to the deserts of the Middle East, the streets of Paris to the wastelands of Hiroshima and Nagasaki, American soldiers have often struggled with appropriate language to describe and capture the strange allure, mysterious profundity, and compelling exhilaration that can arise during battle.

Marine William Broyles Jr., for example, fought in Vietnam and wrote in his essay "Why Men Love War": "Part of the love of war stems from its being an experience of great intensity; its lure is the fundamental human passion to witness, to see things, what the Bible calls the lust of the eye and the Marines in Vietnam called eye fucking. War stops time, intensifies experience to the point of a terrible ecstasy. . . . War *is* beautiful. There is something about a firefight at night, something about the mechanical elegance of an M-60 machine gun. They are everything they should be, perfect examples of their form."[2] Or take the words of J. Glenn Gray, reflecting on the forceful appeal of violent spectacles during his service in World War II: "It is the fascination that manifestations of power and magnitude hold for the human spirit. Some scenes of battle, much like storms over the ocean or sunsets on the desert or the night sky seen through a telescope, are able to overawe the single individual and hold him in a spell. He is lost in their majesty. . . . An awareness of power that far surpasses his limited imagination transports him into a state of mind unknown in his everyday experiences."[3] In these and other war testimonials, told in works of literature or news reports from the front, through the lens of a camera or the stanza of a poem, violence in the heat of battle is an awful, extraordinary power, a force to be reckoned with so far from normal that it can, in a flash or after long, sober reflection, open up new levels of perception and meaning about reality that were inaccessible before the violence.

Violence in war is sacred, but also from very early on the tools of destruction have been objects of veneration containing special powers that awe and inspire the men who hold them or see them in action. The handgun is sacrosanct in American life, as American as baseball and apple pie, and cherished in ways that arouse heated religious passions. The atomic bomb too is shrouded in religious imagery and understandings, with many from the very beginnings of the Manhattan Project appreciating but not always agreeing on and having quite the right words to express the religious implications of this world-altering weapon of mass destruction.

Thomas Farrell, brigadier general in the U.S. Army, observed the first atom bomb test in Alamogordo, New Mexico, in July 1945. In his report he came close to but stopped short of attributing what he witnessed to the Almighty: "It was the beauty great poets dream about but describe most poorly and inadequately. . . . Thirty seconds after the explosion came, first the air blast pressing hard against people and things, to be followed almost immediately by the strong, sustained awesome roar which warned of doomsday and made us feel that we puny things were blasphemous to dare tamper with the forces heretofore reserved to The Almighty."[4] The religious implications of the awe-inspiring sight, not part of God's natural creation, as well as the indescribable power of the bomb itself were open to wide-ranging theological and nontheological religious interpretations.

The old adage "There are no atheists in foxholes" is on to something, not about how mortal fear drives unbelievers to God, but about how warfare is intrinsically sacred. First and foremost is the sacrificial principle at the heart of any war: the idea that an individual soldier's violent death has special power for the larger group and is indeed noble but holy as well, a form of martyrdom in modern times not necessarily for the glory of God but generally for the glorious nation. More than just an idea, this principle is put into practice in every American war when presidents and other leaders establish the spiritual truth that young men and women who give their lives fighting to preserve the nation's ideals, such as freedom and democracy, do not die in vain. Instead, in the famous words of the sixteenth president, Abraham Lincoln, delivered while standing among fallen Union soldiers at Gettysburg, they have the power to consecrate—to make sacred—the physical landscape and also the military resolve to continue fighting and dying for the ultimate cause, national continuity and progress. While God is often invoked in this sacred equation, the religious consequences of sacrifice in war are not always theological elevations of the soul but can often be quite primitive urges, when the spilling of real blood becomes a primal resource for establishing social order and political authority through rituals and myths that give meaning, ultimate meaning, to violence.[5]

War is a sacrificial ritual that simultaneously promises social chaos and human destruction as well as moral inculcation and miraculous transcendence, a ritual act that transforms individual death into a source of cultural regeneration, cruel acts of violence into noble acts of virtue, and gratuitous killing into a vehicle for social revitalization. But the religious potentialities of warfare are not limited to the sacrifices of men and women who are willing to exchange their individual lives for the good of the country and for the promotion of national values.

Violence in war establishes sacred bonds between the living and the dead that are foundational to national life and public memory, for sure, but it also creates a special kind of sacred community for soldiers within the military itself, one built on the close, intimate reality of death, the complex relations and rituals among soldiers and officers, and a peculiar form of love that undergirds the phrase "brothers in arms." These intimate connections between soldiers in peacetime but especially during combat, perhaps experienced erotically, perhaps only in terms of kinship, perhaps with the Divine in mind, bear familial fruit—in other words, new families are born from war that are as equally sacred as the bonds that tie biological families together.

Finally, sacrificial violence produces glorified, revered heroes, cultural icons who are a special breed of warrior, intimately tied to the birth and protection of the body politic. War heroes like George Washington or Stonewall Jackson are figures to emulate if not worship, warriors whose courage and character, deeds and daring, inspire the armed forces to face the threat of violence that is always present in our world. Throughout United States history, warriors who prove their mettle in battle with heroic acts, who are transformed by their encounter with violence in war either by surviving or by dying, are sacred exemplars that have brought into national focus ultimate questions the nation might not otherwise ask itself, such as how to distinguish good from evil, right from wrong, valor from cowardice.[6] Perhaps no other cultural hero is as bound up in sacred violence in the American imagination as the soldier, except for possibly the other great icon saturated in violent bloodshed and death, the cowboy.

John Wayne, a "reel" cowboy, was never a real one. Though now long dead, he still personifies the cowboy spirit like no one before or since. Wayne starred in some of the most well-known westerns from the late 1950s up through the end of the 1960s. His celebrity star power as a particular and peculiarly American cowboy had achieved such mythic proportions in popular culture during this time that soldiers in Vietnam and elsewhere had the Duke in mind on patrols, in firefights, and in camp. Many extolled the frontier virtues and courage of his cinematic characters, who bring justice through violence on-screen, though others ridiculed the conservative, militaristic values Wayne the actor stood for in real life.[7] Regardless of the particular political meanings associated with Wayne and his cowboy image, the westerns that he starred in, like *The Searchers, True Grit, How the West Was Won,* or *Hondo,* recapitulated a dearly held, though often contested, sacred American value long associated with but not limited to the cowboy: violence outside of warfare can be righteous too, whether conquering the frontier, exacting vengeance against others, or protecting innocent victims.

Imaginary cowboys like those portrayed by Wayne project the sacred, heroic value of regenerative violence, not purely through an entertaining and long-adored storyline made formulaic in westerns but as a religiously vital myth central to American identities that reinforces certain values and rationalizations surrounding the use of violence. Cowboy stories do not ignore history but reframe the historically real savagery enacted to conquer and control the territorial western frontier over the course of the nineteenth and early twentieth centuries.[8] The deceptions at work in the cowboy myth imaginatively transform acts of violence into noble and morally uplifting responses to the basic facts of life in a hostile world—injustice and suffering, heartache and misfortune— understood in clear terms separating right from wrong though not necessarily lawful and unlawful. But myths are not simply about deceptions, or truth for that matter; Hollywood cowboys from *The Virginian* to *Brokeback Mountain* are of abiding interest to Americans who flock to theaters and DVDs to see men act out against the very moral strictures that are perceived to be necessary for the social cohesion, prosperous communities, and commercial expansion they are fighting and killing for.

The western is as old as the film industry itself, born with the release of the first narrative-driven film, *The Great Train Robbery*, in 1903. Cinematic cowboy heroes evolved over the twentieth century, however, ranging in type from glorified frontiersmen from times past, like Davy Crockett, to the aggrieved outlaw seeking righteous revenge, like Ringo Kid in the classic *Stagecoach* (1939), to the lone gunfighter eradicating evil from good society, like the memorable *Shane* (1953), all the way to the more politically cor-

rect, Indian-loving westerns, like *Dances with Wolves* (1991). Yet
what remains stable in the midst of all these variations is that in
many westerns violence can have extraordinary, transformative
power, not solely through force of will and skill by the cowboy
hero, but also through brutal acts of bloodshed and killing that
make things right again in the world or at least in the imagined
world of frontier America.

In many western films, strong men with loaded guns restore
order to the disordered, dangerous boundaries separating civilization from wilderness, humans from animals, God from godlessness,
allowing civilization to follow on the heels of slaughter or at least
murder in these "reel" versions of American history and national
destiny. Hollywood cowboys, like their literary and folkloric pro-
genitors tied to such famous cultural icons as John Filson's *Adventures of Col. Daniel Boon* in the late eighteenth century or James
Fenimore Cooper's durable *Leatherstocking Tales* soon after in the
early decades of the nineteenth, do not live squarely in one
world—the civilized or the wild—but somewhere in between,
where men often strive to be faithful to the Lord but also live by a
more primal, though equally sacred, code of honor that is nothing
without righteous violence.

Violence drives the narrative of these films and structures the
experience of time, invigorating actions and motivations that captivate an audience from the opening credits to the closing frame.
But true myths live on long past the end of their telling, and some
western films retain their vigor in culture when audiences leave
the theater or turn off the television, when the values embodied by
the cowboy heroes teach behaviors that viewers bring to their
daily lives and shape perceptions about not only the American
past, but its present and future as well. The moral universes inhab-
ited by imagined cowboys invest violence with sacred powers of
redemption or damnation, restoration or desolation, and illumine
circumstances in which violence ultimately becomes the only re-

course, when negotiations fail or calls for peace fall on deaf ears, or even when God must be taken out of the picture to ensure proper justice in a dangerous world.

The best and most enduring religious cowboy myths are not limited to celluloid frames but shift to a much larger cultural frame of meaning, either as stories with characters who become personal heroes to individual viewers, as storylines that get repeated again and again in various popular cultural settings and teach the same messages, or as storied tales that have multiple layers of possible meaning and yield no consensus over their true and clearly enduring significance to society. But violence—the anticipation of violence, the thrill of it, and the consequences of it in the films—is a critical ingredient in its success as a movie genre. Another reason for its success is the presence of one of the most beloved items in the United States, a material object that defines the very existence of the cowboy and soldiers for that matter: the gun.

In American culture, the gun is a sacred object. It is a distinctive source of cherished cultural activities, from hunting to collecting, as well as consecrated social values, like protecting the family and preserving individual freedoms. But perhaps more than anything else, a gun is a source of power—ultimate power, considering it can end life with minimal effort—that many Americans will never surrender under any circumstance. Guns are ubiquitous across the American cultural landscape—a crucial element in historical memory, across myriad forms of popular entertainment from Hollywood films to rap music, and throughout political and civic discussions about crime and crime prevention. But they are also embedded in the physical landscape, safely and not too safely stored in homes and businesses in every corner of the nation.

The sacred aura permeating gun culture is spiritually infused by a peculiarly American religious text: the United States Constitution. For gun lovers, the Second Amendment to the Constitution is especially sacrosanct and the ultimate authority on gun ownership: "A well-regulated militia being necessary to the security of a free state, the right of the people to keep and bear arms shall not be infringed." These words, so highly divisive in current policy and legal debates surrounding gun control and individual rights, undergird the emergence of gun culture in America and mythically frame the deeply religious attachments and justifications of gun owners.

Guns are sacred because they are intimately linked with the redemptive power to confront fundamental dangers that are perceived to be constantly present in American life, like individual crimes that may require self-defense or government tyranny that may require revolutionary actions from armed citizens. For participants in this cult, violence is an inevitable fact of life one must always be prepared to counter with violence. With this primal vision of human nature and the concomitant moral understanding of the role of government and the rights of individuals, a gun is not simply a tool for protection and survival but a cosmic means of purification in the never-ending battle against the forces of evil lurking throughout good society. The potential for righteous violence contained in the plastic and steel, ammo and casings offers sacred security as a bulwark with these social dangers ever-present, even when folks who own guns also use them for the sheer pleasure of visiting the local firing range or tracking and killing wild, defenseless animals.

Perhaps no other American institution embodies and articulates these sacred principles about gun ownership and the sacrality of the Second Amendment better and more powerfully than the revered and feared National Rifle Association, or NRA. This organization is the center of a religious culture built on a right to violence, a characterization that one of its lobbyists conveyed by stating, "You would get a far better understanding [of the NRA] if you approached us as if you were approaching one of the great religions of the world."[9] Indeed, the gun in this culture is a totem that ritually and mythically unites living Americans with dead

Founding Fathers, past generations with future generations, and individual families with a national family, with all mystically linked together around the godless, sacred Second Amendment in the Constitution.[10] The persistent fear that this amendment is under siege and must be defended motivates and animates the social energies—tied to more secular activities like lobbying and fundraising, but also mixed up with literally worshipping the gun—that drive the NRA and ensure its continued existence.

No doubt many NRA members are God-fearing Christians and even Jews, or at least in the case of celebrity and former NRA president Charlton Heston, a Christian who played the role of a Jew in the film *The Ten Commandments*. While God may or may not be invoked by NRA members and leaders, the religious messages about freedom and patriotism are easily established without recourse to elaborated and detailed theological rhetoric; like any good religious commitment, truth is self-evident, for all to see. Aging rock star and avid hunter Ted Nugent, for example, made the point in an opinion piece published in the *Waco Tribune Herald*, proclaiming that the self-evident truth at the foundation of the NRA family is that "self-defense is an imperative and a responsibility for good, thoughtful people everywhere. America's founders, having fled the horrors of tyrants' enslavement, wrote down a list of these conscientious, overtly obvious, self-evident truths for a new nation."[11]

Or listen to the words of former NRA president Wayne LaPierre, who asserted that after many setbacks in the 1970s and 1980s, the members of the NRA can be proud of all the accomplishments and victories the organization has seen recently in restoring the threatened integrity of the Second Amendment, including ensuring that John Kerry is not president and that Hillary Clinton will never be president. He sermonizes, "Because you restored the Second Amendment, this freedom can be passed on to your children, and to their children and to their children's children. The most precious of birthrights can be conferred upon every infant whose first breath is drawn beneath our American skies."[12] The most precious of birthrights in this mythology is not the right to religious freedom or equality under the law, or even to shelter and clothing, but instead to own and shoot guns.

It is not too much of a stretch to move from this type of religious mythology surrounding guns among NRA members to the real-world extremism of militia movements who amass large numbers of weapons in states throughout the nation. On the other hand, and in a radically different direction, reverence for the gun can also be found in gangsta rap culture where street violence and weaponry are mythologized as basic dimensions of everyday life, with guns as a potent symbol of sacred meaning and action as well as a concrete instrument containing real-world powers and therefore of practical as much as spiritual value.

Of course critics of militias, gangsta rap, and the NRA would strongly object to this kind of religious interpretation of gun culture in each, stating that these are in fact examples of worshipping false gods or illustrations of misguided values in a secular, relativistic society. Yet the tenacious commitment to gun power within each of these very different communities, along with the larger American context in which violence historically has been revered and spiritually generative, makes such evaluations and judgments quite suspect: what is seen as gratuitous violence from one point of view can, from another vantage point, be a wellspring of spiritually gratifying ritual action.

Violence is a potent instigator for religious reflection on ultimate questions about morality and death, social order and supernatural power. Aztec culture ritualized mass human sacrifices; ancient Greece mythologized heroic warfare; Jews philosophize about their suffering at the hands of others; Hindus visualize the destructive forces in the cosmos through the iconography of the ferocious and terrible Hindu goddess Kali. Today, Americans have video games to anchor their primordial religious urges to see destruction and be aggressive, as well as instigate public reflection on the sacred meaning of violence in our lives. Not all video games are religious or played religiously, but their stupendous growth in popular culture and near universal presence in everyday life—raking in more billions than Hollywood films in recent years—can potentially take them far beyond purely secular entertainment that helps to pass the time. Not all video games are rooted in violence, though most of them and clearly the majority of the bestsellers allow players to carry out graphically stimulating, aesthetically captivating, surprisingly fulfilling acts of horror and terror against virtual others, human and nonhuman. Are these just harmless fantasy games with no bearing on the really real? Surely games like *Doom* or *Star Wars Battlefield* or *Evil Dead* have nothing to tell us about the state of religious life in the nation today, right?

Video games do, in fact, reveal quite a bit about the spiritual state of America. Video violence is made sacred and worshipped by large numbers of primarily young and old males who lose track of the lines between fantasy and reality but who redraw the boundaries between the two in a religious miasma of pleasure and desire, morality and chaos, transformation and continuity. One indication of just how spiritually powerful violent video games have become in contemporary society is the high-spirited vitriol they inspire from many who condemn the lessons being taught in these alternate, virtual worlds; they do not merely entertain—they are also dangerously fertile spiritual ground where the eternal souls of players can be lost or found.

In these games violence rules the universe in never-ending battles between good and evil. It does not matter what virtual environment the player enters—Middle Earth or a World War II unit in Normandy, deep in outer space fighting alien monsters or the gang-infested streets of Los Angeles. What matters is that killing can take place regardless of where it all begins or where it all ends—violence is both the means and the end point in these games, and when a player masters one, he can move on to another

just as long as more killing challenges are guaranteed. The thrill of
the kills and the variety of weapons available for virtual violent
engagements are meaningful not just for individual players but,
collectively, for larger communities beyond cyberspace, literally
bound together by shared enthusiasm for *Splinter Cell* and *Halo*,
Ghost Recon and *Strike Force*.

The dead do not always stay dead, the living often get away
with murder, unknown and unseen forces are at work, power is
fluid but must be mastered to triumph over others—the religious
logic operating in many of these violent games is equal to any cultural product that engages the imagination with fantastic stories
like being transported to heaven or hearing a burning bush speak
or seeing a Jedi master use the power of the Force. The ethical
quandaries found within these games, where players are often first-
person shooters, are glaring and blatant religious dimensions that
reflect shifting collective values about play and imagination, responsibility and desire. In *Grand Theft Auto*, for example, players
can participate in a carjacking, kill the innocent driver, then hire a
prostitute and have sex with her in the backseat; or, in the western-
flavored game *Gun*, which boasts on the box that the only thing a
player can trust is his gun, the gunslinger-actor can use a range of
weapons, including shotguns, rifles, dynamite, and even, if you are
of the mind, a scalping knife to claim a special souvenir of your kill.
Are these just violent fantasies catering to adolescent male suppressed urges to indiscriminately screw and kill the rest of the
world? Or do such scenarios vicariously give players a taste of what
not to do and therefore reinforce moral lessons about loving your
neighbor or helping others in need?

Whether one believes that engaging in this kind of virtual activity encourages real-life aggressive behavior toward others or
oneself or allows individuals to play at being destructive in ways
that reinforce improper distinctions between right and wrong, an
ethic is at work every time players wrap their hands around a joystick or other controller to wreak havoc in other worlds. Some

play for the sheer visceral pleasures that can make them lose track of time, placing such ultimate value on the enjoyment of violence in the timelessness of virtual reality that real-life, time-bound relationships and responsibilities become secondary. Some play for more technical reasons, planning to master the skills necessary to triumph in conflict-ridden, mortally dangerous environments that turn space inside out for players who seamlessly coexist in their multiple realities. The moral drama unfolding within and around violent video games is not fixed or uniformly experienced for all American gamers, but now, more than Hollywood films or traditional bedtime stories, quite possibly more than the church and the school system, these games are teaching lessons about the hardcore reality of violence in their worlds.

It is exactly in these kinds of spiritually charged environments, virtually real and seriously fantasy, where the absence of God to make sense of violence and differentiate righteous from unrighteous acts is a religious matter of supreme importance—an importance to consumers, but also to evangelicals who have crossed oceans and now will enter other virtual worlds to bring the message of the Gospel, even if they have to use an M-16 or laser-blaster to do it. Many in these and other religiously conservative communities are rightly concerned about the alternative spiritual and sacred commitments that pervade the gaming world, where violence draws normal, seemingly innocent people into perilous virtual territory with temptations of hedonistic gratification in mass killing, graphic stimulation when carrying out heinous acts, and debased satisfaction from wallowing in scenes of gross destruction. Judgmental, yes, but these religious critics are also onto something very real and socially meaningful: video games operate with a different set of principles about how and where to derive pleasure, questions bearing on sacred decisions about authority over the body that the church and other institutions do not want to give up; they also lead individuals to invest in them in ways that create bonds of attachment so strong, so ritually empowering, that the game is no longer

just a game but constitutive of social identities and intricately entangled in consciousness and everyday life.

With the rapid growth of massively multiplayer online role-
playing games like the *World of Warcraft*, which allow large numbers
of players to interact together in virtual otherworlds by assuming
often fantastic alternate identities as shamans or undead warriors,
evangelicals are heartily biting the bullet and entering these dangerous, tempting environs as players to win over virtual and, they
must assume, real souls to Christ. Even some entrepreneurs and in-
vestors within the Christian community have decided to create
their own versions of these appealing, profitable violent games that
absolutely ensure God's presence in what has been traditionally
godless yet abundantly religious virtual worlds. *Left Behind: Eternal
Forces*, for example, is based on the best-selling series of books that
tell of impending Armageddon and the destinies of the damned
and the saved as foretold in the book of Revelation.[13] In the video
game—really only one of many now catering to a distinctly Christian market—the deadly environment is New York City, with
Tribulation Forces, the good guys left behind after the Rapture,
fighting the bad guys, the Antichrist's Global Community Peace-
keepers, with armies and arsenal fit for a king, or at least a small
nation.

As A. Larry Ross, the president of a Christian-based public relations firm involved with Mel Gibson's film *The Passion of the
Christ* and the three *Left Behind* films puts it, parents can be assured
some forms of violence in video games have social value: "In addition to the youth audience—that's the primary target—there are
parents who are concerned about what their children are exposed
to and are encouraged by products that are biblically based. . . . I
would assume, if there is violence, it is the cosmic struggle of good
versus evil, not gratuitous violence."[14] Christianity never looked so
good to the younger generations, whose virtual escape from the
real world via flesh-eating demons or grenade-launching tanks can
have real-world spiritual consequences. Video games allow them

to be warriors, warriors for Christ in cosmic battles with righteous violence as the ultimate solution to the virtual confrontation with evil mayhem. The problem, of course, is where the lines are drawn between "righteous" violence that saves and "gratuitous" violence that damns. In either case, violent video games can be a sacred source of imaginative play and moral formation for many young warriors today, orienting them to a long and deep tradition in national culture.

American history is a tale of death and destruction from the get-go, a warrior's story unfolding in the New World that establishes violence as a fundamental ingredient of social progress and as fundamentally religious in its social consequences. Video games, popular films, iconic heroes, gun worship, and the long, long history of warfare in the United States all speak to this elementary form of religious life. The present post–9/11 terror wars are no exception, and once again Americans are reminded in political terms how the lifeblood of the nation, its spiritual vigor and moral convictions that move the social body onward in time, is nourished by broken bones and bodies of soldiers who die violently in bloody combat or preparation for battle. In the midst of war or during times of peace, sadly, violence is in the blood circulating throughout the body politic, as a recurring historical condition and as a distinguishing cultural feature of the popular imagination. It can give birth to sacred rituals, sacred spaces, sacred myths, sacred attachments that shape religious life for Americans and bind them to the military or a gang, to a gun or even a joystick.

8

SEXUALITY

"Oh god, Oh God, OH GOD!"

A common refrain in many porno clips, this verbal expression of otherworldly ecstasy and deep personal fulfillment is not a literal cry for God in the act of sex, though many familiar with the erotic portions of the Hebrew Bible, especially the Song of Songs, know that the Divine is not necessarily out of mind when it comes to sexual pleasures. But pornography is surely not about God, nor does it have any possible religious significance that might signal the presence of the sacred in the lustful, lascivious, labor-intensive physical exertions and excitements associated with this enormously popular form of cultural activity.

Like death, which will be discussed in the next chapter, sexuality is a biological fact of life—an inescapable reality of the world we live in, a force at work in every nook and cranny of society and culture, found in the home, office, mall, classroom, hospital; imaged on television, computer, theater, and mental screens; aroused at sporting events, clubs, parties, funerals, and weddings. It is no wonder sex, along with death and health, is of the utmost importance in the world's religious traditions, most of which seek to regulate and monitor the body generally but most especially the terms on and by which sexual desires can be fulfilled or transgressed. Is adultery prohibited? Can a man have multiple wives? Do different positions bear spiritual fruits? What is the meaning of orgasm? Religious traditions thrive on intimacy with and access to the body, its experience of suffering, sorrow, and sickness, as well as rapture, delight, and bliss. Sexuality's obvious and overwhelming role as a primary, primal factor in evolution and communication throughout the animal kingdom makes it even more confounding to humans who are animals but not only animals, a species that makes much more of sexual relations than a biological imperative to secure a fertilized egg.

Pleasurable intimacies with the sexual body, like healing intimacies with the suffering body or mortal intimacies with the dead body, are charged with real-world powers that shape the contours of the sacred in cosmic space and time. The boundaries between self and other, inside and outside, animal and human, ordinary consciousness and ecstatic states, dissolve or at least blur during sex, producing extraordinary experiences that are physically tied to tactile intimacies, changes in respiratory rate and blood flow, and chemical and electrical processes in the brain. Indeed, there is a burgeoning science of the orgasm, with physiological evidence suggesting that the orgasm itself is a richly complex neurological phenomenon with brain stimulation in some regions and complete neural shutdown in others—brain activity just as mysterious and revealing as other measurable, mystical, and altered states of consciousness induced in more conventional religious practices, like meditation, prayer, or the ingestion of sacred medicine.[1] The powers of sex, its potentially empowering pleasures and mindblowing transportations, however, are entangled in phenomena that cannot be reduced to bodily processes or easily measured with brain-imaging technologies.

How these powers are defined and understood varies across and within cultures, but they are never simply neutral and always bear on the sacred. The intricacies of sexuality in human cultures—its political, economic, mythic, moral, ritual, emotional dimensions—belie any easy generalizations. Ascetics who practice celibacy in Buddhism, Christianity, Hinduism, and other religious cultures see the sexual body as a distraction, or obstacle, in the pursuit of spiritual fulfillment and empowerment. In the biblical story of David and Bathsheba, the adulterous sexual union between the two initiates a chain of bloody, violent acts and violations, including rapes, murder, and even civil war in ancient Israel; but the sexual union between the two also brings life to another son, Solomon, who becomes a great king and propels sacred history forward under the powerful hand of God. Practitioners of some forms of yoga engage in sexual exercises that not only arouse vital life energies, but also lead the way to profound spiritual enlightenment and liberation from the self. The examples of sexual diversity are endless across the world's religions.

Millions and millions of American men and women, including churchgoers, temple members, and those with no formal religious affiliations at all, love to watch pornography. A dizzying, incalculable number of Americans—professional but increasingly "amateurs"—perform in and provide a spectrum of shamelessly hedonistic activities that are viewed alone or with other consumers transfixed by visual images of often outrageous, often intimate, sexual escapades of one, two, three, or many more actors. Pornography and pornographic-related activities generate billions and billions of dollars from Americans who will not admit the degree of their investments, while many publicly advocate for strong legislative action to protect society from itself, believing that nothing good can come from heart-pounding, sweat-inducing, erotically charged sexual activity available to all with a click of a button.

There is evidence, however, that suggests Americans have their fill of pornography to fulfill religious payoffs. Sex acts that include but go far, far beyond the conventional heterosexual missionary position can not only be outrageously pleasurable, they can also be spiritually liberating and a sacred experience as powerful, transformative, and meaningful as any to be found in the church or temple. The sexual ecstasies for those performing as well as those watching porn open the body to sensations and transportations that transcend everyday physical experiences and routines, a form of tran-

scendence for some that can only be captured through religious
language and ritual. Many, of course, strongly reject this connection and take up the crusade against pornography as an antireli-
gion scourge that destroys marriages, families, and reputations, as
well as a social force that encourages violence, immorality, and de-
bauchery. For the more conservative segments of society, religion
only enters the action when people walk away from the degrada-
tions and depravities of pornographic pictures and, in the more familiar story, find Christ, moving out of the carnal, hedonistic filth
and into a new, pure, and elevated spiritual home.

Deep Throat is one of the most revolutionary porn films of all
time and, having grossed over $600 million, one of the most prof-
itable films of any kind. It is also a popular cultural touchstone in
the culture wars that provides a deeply moral, cautionary tale
about pornography as a gateway to hell and damnation. The
cheaply made porn flick about a woman with a clitoris in her
throat made its stars, Linda Lovelace and Harry Reems, instant
celebrities in 1972 and catapulted fellatio into the public eye as
never before. After some time in the celebrity limelight, as well as
some time in the bedroom with other celebrities at the time—like,
in the case of Lovelace, Sammy Davis Jr.—both stars moved away
from the world of porn with all of its dangers and entrapments and
found spiritual relief through Christianity.

For Lovelace, who for a time became an antiporn crusader
and also wrote a controversial tell-all about her experiences in the
film, Ordeal, it was only after a shameful life of licentiousness and
abuse that true religion could enter her life.[2] Lovelace learned over
time that the harsh, physically demanding life in adult films had
nothing at all to do with spirituality and the sacred, but finding
Christ saved her soul in the end when she turned against porn, at
least for a time. She lived out her remaining years unable to find
steady work and facing seriously declining health before her untimely death at the age of fifty-three in a car accident in 2002.[3]
Reems's life too is the stuff myths are made of, especially a partic-

ularly familiar version of mythmaking not about the size of his
penis but the capacity of his soul. After bursting onto the public
scene in *Deep Throat*, Reems went from the Playboy mansion and
high living with the celebrities of the day to living in a dumpster
and serious alcoholism before the Jewish-born cult figure became
a born-again Christian. And compared to the sad, regrettable ending for Lovelace, Reems comes out smelling like roses as a dedicated family man and successful owner of his own real estate
business, Reems Real Estate.[4]

Surely the horror stories surrounding this film offered Americans a palatable moral lesson that could serve as the last religious
word on uninhibited sex: the spiritual desolation associated with
pornography can be overcome by individuals who find true religion and are then forgiven for their scurrilous, evil impulses,
which found enjoyment in fellatio, cunnilingus, anal sex, orgies, or
masturbation—an especially blasphemous activity, for that matter.
Yet as popular as this form of moralizing has been with regard to
pornography in American life, it simply fails to put even the slightest dent in the behemoth, multibillion-dollar industry, which
caters to an ever expanding range of tastes and proclivities, desires
and enthusiasms.

Professionals and blue-collar workers, educated and unedu-
cated, patriots and criminals, married couples and singles, upstand-
ing citizens and administrators—up to 40 percent of Christian
clergy and 18 percent of born-again Christians, according to recent surveys, visit sexually graphic pornographic websites.[5] And
this is nothing new. Long, long before videos and smut magazines,
websites and DVDs, Americans hungered for sexually explicit
themes and experimented with the erotic imagination. The antebellum North, for example, saw the rise of highly profitable forms
of sensational and subversive literature—filled with graphic, explicitly sexual, often violent scenes in pamphlets, the penny press,
and best-selling books of the time—which were avidly consumed
and read, then as now, in secret.[6]

So what accounts for the popularity of pornography in American culture? Is it simply a matter of amoral, lustful, decadent appetites run amok in an otherwise virtuous society? An example of how base, prurient attractions overwhelm, if only temporarily, the puritanical, typically American need to control and regulate physical bodies, and especially the boundaries of reproduction? Or might pornographic sex offer Americans personal pleasures that in some circumstances arouse sacred experiences and moral lessons bearing on a search for fulfillment and transcendence not offered or allowed in the presence of God? In America today, porn has become mainstream, no longer limited to guys in trench coats at local movie theaters or magazines hidden from spouses or parents in closets and under beds, with content much more varied than the stereotypes of being just for male pleasure and phallic dominance, saturated with violence and perversion—though there is, no doubt, still a lot of that as well.

Some Americans are religious about their pornography consumption and proclivities, but how they are religious about it cannot simply be explained through biblical verses or church teachings. Sexuality in pornography has religious ramifications in the spiritual and moral lives of men and women who do not always find God or Christ or Bathsheba in their encounters with this explicit material. Some find sacred meanings in the strange pathways to spiritual liberation and mystical encounters emanating from the orgasmic ecstasies of wild, unbridled, often unromantic sex between consenting adults or as a result of solitary sex. Annie Sprinkle is a public advocate of pornography, a sex-positive, self-proclaimed sex therapist who has been at various stages of her career a prostitute, porn star, and performance artist. Born Ellen Steinberg in 1954, Sprinkle is a sex icon not only for her work in popular porn films, including *Deep Inside Annie Sprinkle*, but also for the way she embraces sexuality as a form of spirituality and sacred healing, perhaps most glaringly and graphically expressed in her infamous performance art routine, "The Legend of the Ancient Sacred Prostitute."

In this performance piece, with the stage set as an altar with candles, dried cow dung, and numerous dildos, among other props, Sprinkle first informs the audience about ancient sacred prostitutes who lived before the rise of monotheism in cultures from Mesopotamia and Greece and who could initiate forms of ecstasy that induced visions, produced miracles, and connected humans to the gods. She then engages in a rather elaborate masturbatory ritual—what she terms a sex magic masturbation ritual—that taps into those long-repressed energies and powers for purposes of healing and transformation until the final climax, an orgasm in which, in her own words, she "is not in Kansas anymore. . . . It's a very real, intense, wild ride, a close encounter of the fourth kind."[7] This link between spirituality and sex in a rather pornographic frame is not limited to her activities during her performance— Sprinkle now offers sacred sex workshops including one called "Fun with Ecstasy Breathing and Energy Orgasms" for women who are eighteen or older and want to learn these sexual technologies for reasons that are explicitly religious as well as sexual: spiritual growth and self-realization, personal transformation and emotional healing, cosmic unity and world peace.[8]

Sprinkle is someone who seamlessly brings pornography and spirituality together in more positive, less condemnatory ways. But many other folks soften the impact of porn in everyday life and, indeed, glorify it as a potentially lucrative and ultimately morally uplifting path away from home. *How to Make Love Like a Porn Star: A Cautionary Tale*, written by the porn "sex goddess" herself, Jenna Jameson, made it to the *New York Times* bestseller list in 2004. An honest look at the business that made her a millionaire, Jameson provides readers with the ups and downs of the pornography industry but also, by the end of her story, renders a cautionary tale out of her sordid yet salutary past, with twenty-first-century

pornified family values that do not run away from sex but head-
long into it.⁹

From the other side of the porn divide between actors and
viewers is the story of consumer Richard Easton in a recent defense of viewing sexually explicit materials on Beliefnet. Easton, a
pseudonym, we learn at the end of the piece, for a writer living
somewhere on the East Coast, informs readers that coming clean
about his secret habits to his wife, though not to the public, saved
their marriage and gave them a much healthier outlook.¹⁰ Porn
values are not from these perspectives limited to vice and sinfulness
but can provide a morally viable, religiously reasonable way to live
life that can, in fact, save you, while letting you enjoy sex and sexual fantasies in a manner seemingly impossible for adherents of the
monotheistic traditions. In the land of religious freedom and diversity, non-monotheistic religious traditions and cultures, sacred
perspectives on sex abound and do not necessarily interface with
the theological ruminations of Augustine or the fire and brim-
stone evangelism of Billy Graham.

Most Americans are familiar with a prevailing monotheistic take
on sex—associated with sin, temptation, and paradise lost. For
Christians, the savior was born from a virgin, abstained from sex,
and had followers convinced that the body was corrupt if not
downright demonic, leading to a volatile ambivalence about but a
constant fixation on sexuality. Monogamous sex in a marriage for
the purposes of reproduction, ideally with the man on top of the
woman, makes sense and is given a sacred stamp of approval.
Celibacy and the glorification of sexless bodies spiritually more intimate with God, Jesus, and the Holy Spirit than fellow humans
are also authorized in many Christian communities, though these
spiritual intimacies can erupt into full-blown mystical ecstasies
often described in quite sexualized terms and images. Any other
kinds of sexual relations or imagery are taboo, signs of moral transgressions of the worst order, and vigorously, yet also obsessively,

scrutinized in the effort to promote proper Christianized versions of family values that are not defiled by the pursuit of carnal, sacredless pleasures.

Indeed, American history is plagued by sexual obsessions of Christians gravely concerned about sexual order, as though the proper functioning of society, if not the cosmos, depended on making sure sex was limited to husbands and wives having babies, assuming people were going to have any intercourse at all. It is also, of course, peppered with contradictions and hypocrisies when it comes to sex, an activity which opens the chasm between ideal moral virtues and real human appetites in social relations between Christians and others. When Catholic missionaries encountered Pueblo Indians in southwestern North America beginning in the sixteenth century, for example, they were particularly offended by a radically different view of sexuality, one that knew no God but was integrally tied to the surrounding natural world they lived in and bound to cosmic conceptions of fertility and renewal.

This was also a matriarchal culture, with women and women's sexuality especially powerful in the daily lives of the community not just for reproduction, but for economic reasons associated with agriculture, spiritual relations concerned with maintaining social harmony, and regenerative rituals based on mythic female creator figures. If this was not enough to challenge the limits of the missionary position and imagination, the many other honored mythic spirits who were bisexual, literally both male and female, such as the Hopi Kawasaitaka Katsina, and the orgiastic festivals ritually performed at certain times of the year, only fueled the fires of the missionary spirit and convinced them of the desperate need for spiritual redemption through sexual purification.[11]

Throughout the colonial period and into the nineteenth century during westward expansion, Catholics and Protestants were troubled by the sexual practices of indigenous cultures. Many were no doubt tempted by these practices as well, with some likely joining in the alternative enjoyments offered by these cultures, others violently raping Indians for the personal pleasures and assertions of power provided by sexual control over the subjugated women before heading back to church and God on Sunday. Regardless of what was taught about sexuality in local churches or the Christian home, sexual relations between conquered and conqueror, subjugated and subjugator, operated according to a very different set of rules than those governing civilized monogamous heterosexuality but no less engorged with ethical demands and ultimate values.

The historical record of plantation owners in the South (most claiming to be Bible-based, God-fearing, Jesus-loving Christians), speaks of similar desires to have forbidden sex with young and old female and, no doubt, male slaves who had radically different cultural perspectives on sexuality—perspectives that were shattered but not forgotten in the slaveholding South.[12] In this "peculiar institution," any form of sexual intimacy between blacks and whites, even the tender, long-lasting attachments of slave owners like one of the nation's revered Founding Fathers, Thomas Jefferson, was soiled by hypocrisy and injustice. These secret intimate relations, with good and bad Christians taking sexual liberties with enslaved Africans, had sacred ramifications for the whites, who were confused about their own sexuality let alone clueless about the blacks among them. But they also made an impact on the slaves whose families were torn asunder, cultural traditions decimated, and spiritual lives beaten down—all central aspects of life in African cultures that integrated sexuality in ways that posed a mortal threat to their owners, yet also aroused them to act on impulses that were embedded in violent and fearful responses to these alternative views on sexuality and religious life.

The recurring battles and conflicts over the terms of sexuality have been a well-worn pattern in American religious history, with pagan Indians, polygamous Mormons, perverse Jews, predatory Catholics, and an assortment of other villains and sexual deviants, at one time or another representing a serious threat to American society and especially vulnerable women and children. Even with the herculean efforts in America to keep sex in line with an ideal moral order and under the control of institutional authorities, the seductive powers of sexuality have been too strong and deep-rooted to be managed according to monotheistic standards. Instead, the potentially sacred expressions of sexuality find cultural authority in a diverse range of voices and texts, with communities of people engaging in intimate relations and erotic practices outside America's purported sexual ideals tied to heterosexuality, monogamy, and reproduction. Historically through time but also across the social map today, from the homogeneities in the Bible Belt to the radical pluralism of cosmopolitan centers like New York or Los Angeles or Atlanta, sex is celebrated in ways many would find offensive to God.

But for participants in sex acts that are more sacrament than sacrilege, penetrating the spiritual depths of a godless universe can be meaningful and fulfilling, with moral purpose and cosmic insights more profound than any to be experienced by reading the Hebrew Bible or New Testament. Sexuality unhinged and detached from the Lord is just as sacred, just as transformative, just as redemptive to many as the romantic love experienced by a husband and wife successfully conceiving a new life under the watchful eyes of God.

Sexual diversity in many forms is now accepted or at least tolerated in American society. Many Americans who are white or black, Christian or Jew, Muslim or Native American, fundamentalist or atheist, and on across racial, ethnic, and religious communities can grant social legitimacy to women giving blow jobs and couples wife-swapping, group sex and one-on-one action, yet there remain fundamental transgressions that will not be tolerated. Men engaged in anal sex or women penetrating each other with dildos or their own tongues can become a cause for outrage and moral panic. While the sexual revolution no doubt led to greater sexual permissiveness in American cultures, the sacred line separating heterosexuality from homosexuality still holds—even if Ellen

DeGeneres scripted a lesbian kiss for a temporarily adoring television audience.

For those opposed to gay and lesbian sexual freedoms and rights, sex between members of the same sex can never be anything other than perverted and godless sex, a cultural perspective rooted in the Bible and the language of sin. The other source for cultural authority on sexual matters in the twentieth century, science, no longer condemns homosexuality and gay and lesbian lifestyles as necessarily pathological. It is clear that the current firestorm over same-sex marriage, though rhetorically tied to preserving a conservative concoction of ideal family values, is primarily about obsessive fears with deep, deep roots in Western Christian history about men pleasing men and women pleasing women. The confusing history of the word sodomy and its varied application by the church in the sexual behaviors and desires of the flock highlights the persistent difficulties posed by these sexual preferences, or "orientations" as we like to say today, within Christian communities let alone outside of them.[13]

Sex between men and sex between women can be about more than physical pleasures, erotic transgressions, or sensual explosiveness; much to the chagrin of conservative moralists devoted to the only sacred value in sex, reproduction, it is often described in deeply religious terms and explicitly spiritual language. Compared to the situation before the Stonewall riots, when the pleasures and desires of gay and lesbian sex rarely made their way into public culture, these communities now have a voice on the social stage and a presence in most media, including journals, videos, books, television, and websites, which allows them to offer alternative visions of homosexuality than those coming from the state house and the pew. This alternative vision, however, is far from uniform, providing a range of perspectives within a complicated, heterogeneous community, where many self-identify as Christians or Jews or Muslims and see their sexual preferences and experiences as unproblematic to their religious commitments and incorporating rather than excluding God.

But many also speak of divine sex that does not lead to the Divine One in heaven; instead, it leads to cruising the bathhouses in the Castro district of San Francisco or experimenting with leather while role-playing with a lover or having a night of romantic passion as an integral dimension of monogamous life with a lifelong partner. All of these real-world experiences can arouse and inspire a spiritual dimension to sex that lives beyond but does not deny the physical body. While this sentiment about sexuality is promoted by gays and lesbians within the many monotheistic traditions, many others do not need the comforting presence of God to understand the extraordinary experiences that can emerge when members of the same sex make love, or inflict pain for that matter, down below.

Guy Baldwin is a writer and expert on gay male leather culture and sadomasochistic rituals who speaks of S/M as a form of "holy fire" and characterizes it as a spiritual experience. In one interview, Baldwin emphasizes a mystical element at the core of what for him, and a good many others who concur with the assessment, is a sacred act infused with sexual eroticism. "When I am with a partner with whom I can achieve a nearly perfect synchronous dance, my 'self' becomes stripped of all of its external trappings. . . . What I am left with is an ecstatic contact with Self." [14] The specifics of his religious experience vary, depending, he says, on whether he is on top and in control, in which case Baldwin keeps his wits about him and does not lose consciousness. But make no mistake, the entire ritual does have an otherworldly, spiritually liberating quality whether Baldwin loses control of sensory processing or not: "the ecstatic, transformational event can occur for me on either end of the top-bottom, master-slave, sadist-masochist dynamic." [15] Pain and leather, power and submission, can all play a part in the sacred dance of S/M ritual, but connections between spiritual elevation and sexual intimacy can occur in less extreme, more mundane bedroom settings of same-sex couples as well.

Many Americans see any alternative form of sexuality as hedonistic and devoid of spirit, displaying only base carnality and salacious immorality. Yet a persistent refrain from within homosexual communities is that, *au contraire*, this alternative path often brings them right smack into a sacred, uncharted realm. Robert H. Hopcke, a psychologist and Jungian scholar, is convinced that sexuality and spirituality can overlap seamlessly in the lives of gay men and understands both in terms of universal archetypes deeply embedded in consciousness and through his own personal experiences as a gay man: "In my adolescence and early adulthood there was absolutely no question to me that eroticism was a divine gift. The most important relationship I had in high school was with the Italian-American captain of the soccer team. . . . My relationship with him was clearly erotic and yet sacred at the same time. . . . Gay sexuality, gay eroticism, is as transformative as any transformative sacred event." [16] The spiritual life of gays and lesbians celebrates and embraces eroticism and sexual play, intimate romantic passions and outrageous rituals, as a means to transform consciousness and transcend physical experiences. In other words, sexuality can be a viable pathway to sacred experiences and meanings, liberating the self from the material and social prisons that inhibit true spiritual awakening but also reinvigorate social ties that bind individuals and communities together in a discriminatory political context.

The sacred values associated with sexuality, however, are not simply celebratory. Without question, the impact of AIDS on the gay community has been devastating and dramatic, with momentous consequences for the spiritual lives of community members who have struggled with HIV-related illnesses. And in the early years of the disease, soon after the pivotal death of Hollywood icon Rock Hudson in the early 1980s, many straight Americans were quick to attack alternative, nonreproductive sexual practices within gay communities in biblical terms.

•   •   •

Nonreproductive sex may or may not be sacred in the eyes of God, but in the hands of the goddess, sexuality is transformed into a ritually cosmic event brimming, if not overflowing, with sacred powers that heal and reveal, enlighten and inspire, those who follow Her prescriptions and techniques. Sex and spirituality come together in other thriving cultural settings along with gay and lesbian cultures in contemporary America. In neo-pagan and New Age communities many individuals look to goddesses and witches rather than God the Father to unlock the mysteries of the universe and discover sacred powers, particularly as these relate to the human body. Neo-paganism is a scholarly designation covering a wide array of activities and beliefs, though generally identifying a movement that seeks to revitalize ancient, pre-Christian religious cultures that venerated nature and bring them into the modern world, usually borrowing concepts and rituals from Celtic Druids, the Greeks, Romans, and Egyptians, as well as an assortment of imagined sacred worlds tied to Native American and Tibetan cultures. New Age does not do justice to the diversity of views and opinions it brings under one label, but many who participate and invest in this movement seek individual, social, and cosmic healing transformations. Like the neo-pagans, New Agers draw from a wealth of traditions and cultures, including Native Americans, occult and metaphysical movements, and Asian religions, matching practices with needs in the quest for inner wisdom, spiritual growth, and sacred power.[17]

Both neo-paganism and New Age celebrate nature and interact with numerous spiritual beings, live happily with spiritual eclecticism and often rigorous practices routinely incorporated into everyday life, and tend to reverse prevailing gender imbalances by creatively overturning biblical-based patriarchy and tapping into distinctly feminine sources of power and authority. They both also understand sexuality in sacred terms, providing yet another alternative set of practices and attitudes that can not only spice up someone's sex life for nonreproductive reasons, but also unleash the spiritual potentialities of physical intimacy. For neo-pagans, the seminal 1979 book, *The Spiral Dance: A Rebirth of the Ancient Religion of the Great Goddess* by Starhawk, is one key authority on these ultimate matters. It contends, among other things, that sex can be seen as "numinous and sacred," with lovemaking between a husband and a wife only one variation of the spiritual and magical set of relations between individuals.[18] Multiple partners in neo-pagan festivals, what one adherent calls "A Bouquet of Flowers," is another sexual variation with spiritual potential tied to natural cycles and psychic rhythms opening up participants to sacred experiences taking place within the material world of bodies and nature, but transporting souls far, far beyond them.[19]

New Agers will often turn East, rather than return to nature, to pursue the frontiers of sex and spirituality. Many advocate experimenting with tantric practices, which provide disciplined sexual procedures often made accessible with pictures and easy-to-follow steps that can produce ecstasies of a sacred order, though often defined in terms of kundalini energy rather than the work of a Holy Spirit. Even the paragon of New Age wisdom, Deepak Chopra, has deemed sex spiritually valuable. He writes in a short blog, "Sex and Spirituality," how "sexual desire is sacred and chaste. . . . During sexual union, there is union between flesh and spirit. . . . Sexual intimacy is the road to the taste or experience of true freedom. . . . When we have restored the sexual experience to the realm of the sacred, our world will be chaste and divine, holy and healed."[20] No leather or orgies, secret rituals or dildos, and no God, at least not the monotheistic one found in the Hebrew Bible, New Testament, or Koran. Instead, coming from an increasingly mainstream New Age sensibility, Chopra offers a view of sexuality and spirituality that is rather palatable for a sex-hungry, but theologically confounded, American public.

• • •

Oprah too approves of sex and spirituality. At least she brought it to the glaring public light of day in an interview with Gina Ogden, a marriage and sex therapist who has been conducting extensive research on women's sexuality. The interview took place on the show, "Wives Who Don't Want Sex," and focused primarily on Ogden's 1999 book *Women Who Love Sex: An Inquiry into the Expanding Spirit of Women's Erotic Experience*. Oprah.com provides the bullet points of her arguments, including what she sees as the overmedicalization of sex through prescription drugs like Viagra and her reminders that sex is about much more than physical contact alone.

But at its core, the message is clear and simple: sex and spirituality go hand in hand, leading to both a satisfying sex life and fulfilling spiritual encounters with the soul.[21] From the fringes of society during the sexual and drug revolutions of the 1960s to the newfangled rituals emerging in gay and lesbian cultures from the late 1970s, from the birth of popular pornography in easily available magazines and videos in the mid-1970s to the no longer so mysterious witches' covens and esoteric New Age practices of the 1980s and 1990s, the spiritual dimensions of sexuality have become more and more visible and mainstream. With or without God, sacred sex has passed a threshold in religious cultures across the land, with the work of Ogden and the approving nods of Oprah only the tip of the iceberg.

The current infatuation with sexual practices from Asia, initially limited to furtive glances or close, private readings of the *Kama Sutra* (an ancient Indian text popularly understood as a sex manual but culturally steeped in spiritual traditions), is one indication of the widespread desire to inspire sexual activities for religious but not reproductive fulfillment. Cultural translators of Eastern practices, most commonly centered on tantric yoga, cater to an increasingly uninhibited consumer base that flocks to workshops, purchases DVDs, visits websites, and buys lots and lots of

books. Margot Anand, a disciple of the well-known Indian guru
of sex and spirituality, Bhagwan Rajneesh, has written two popular books on the topic, *The Art of Sexual Ecstasy* and *The Art of
Sexual Magic*, both instructing readers about how to breathe, reduce inhibitions, build trust and communication, and discover the
spiritual potential of consciousness-expanding good sex with a
partner.

Just what kinds of people read these books and attend her
workshops? In one interview from the late 1990s, Anand gave an
example of a female client she was helping in her yearlong training
session. This client had a great deal of material wealth and corporate power as the head of a large business, but she remained unful-
filled and without truly meaningful power. Anand's specialized
training was the trick and helped her turn a spiritual corner. "She
said that the ability to clear her yoni (as we call the female sexual
organ) of tensions through the practices that we do . . . opened
her up to an incredible understanding. . . . When she cleared herself and was able to access much deeper levels of orgasm and, in the
process, was able to guide her partner and tell him how to give her
what she needed sexually, she suddenly found that now she was to-
tally empowered." By attaining those deeper orgasmic levels, this
client could do more at the office professionally as well as tap into
sacred energies with unimagined powers for individual, professional, social, and cosmic transformation.[22]

The spiritual possibilities imminent in intercourse and fore-
play, in sexual situations and erotic interactions, and in good, old-
fashioned romantic lovemaking between a man and a woman have
been fondly celebrated in American popular culture in recent
times, whether through consumption of esoteric spiritual practices, discussion of the subject on talk shows or in books, or seduc-
tion of the opposite sex in Top 40 music in ways that blend
sensuality with sacred longing. When Marvin Gaye soulfully sings,
"Get up, get up, get up, get up, let's make love tonight," in the 1982
smash hit "Sexual Healing," the combination of his vocal perfor-

mance with the music, his emotional tonalities and the musical rhythms, strikes a chord in many listeners, today as well as twenty years ago, that is as spiritually charged as it is erotic. Indeed the sexual healing which Gaye yearns for when he declares, "I can't wait for you to operate," is sacred medicine that heals the body but also fulfills the spirit. A haunting voice from the past, a ghost still alive in the public imagination, Gaye continues to remind an American audience about sexuality unhindered by traditional religious preoccupations with fertility and propagation or increasingly psychological language about syndromes and addiction.

Even the enormously popular, now iconic book from 1972, just revised and reissued in 2003, *The Joy of Sex*, brings sexual pleasure into otherworldly realms where God is not necessarily a player in the erotic imagination—though some have written similar books helping Christians and Jews enjoy sexual pleasure with positions and postures that are more God-friendly. While the original book, written by Alex Comfort and containing memorable graphic illustrations, was rather technical and procedural in tone and style, an especially surprising heading in the table of contents brings the world of the beyond to mind. Here, alongside topics ranging from "rear entry," "foursomes and moresomes," "bondage," and "earlobes," to name only a small portion of the sexual cornucopia, is an entry entitled "little death." [23]

In this entry, Comfort alludes to a phrase well-known in French literature, *la petite mort*, which attempts to capture the experience of orgasm in words that are not entirely metaphoric. A little death, as opposed to the big Death, is not real death, the cessation of life, but a momentary break from normal time and space in the heights of ecstasy. Indeed, Comfort cautions the reader that the phrase was associated with fainting, not just entering an altered state of consciousness, but losing it completely, when the orgasm erupts. This kind of passion is overwhelming, and when people begin to lose their sense of self in the act, when the body is literally brought to its limits, when the passage is made into what can only be described as another order of existence, death just may be an apt reference point.

This intrusion of death talk into a manual on sex might strike many readers as odd and strangely out of place. Orgasms are not usually deadly when you get right down to it, and their indescribable pleasures keep people in this life, not catapulted across the threshold never to return. But sex and death may have more in common than it appears at first glance. Both bring humans into close proximity to the sacred because the integrity of the body is at stake, and the experiences with each bring individuals beyond their physical and imaginative limits. The interconnections between death and sex, in fact, are not so uncommon in many societies, where the corpse is symbolically tied to regeneration and fertility, and funerals can easily fall back on rituals either implicitly or explicitly sexual in nature.

9

DEATH

A Ghost Is Born

The rock band Wilco used this line from the song "Theologians" as the title of their 2004 release. With its chorus, "Theologians, they don't know nothing, about my soul," the song evocatively suggests that the study of God really offers no clue about the spiritual life, nor reveals anything about the end of life. The leader of Wilco, Jeff Tweedy, sings about the gulf between specialists who may illuminate some elements of faith, but who are also far, far away from the truth about death: "Where I am going you cannot come, no one is ever going to take my life from me, I lay it down, a ghost is born, a ghost is born . . . I am a cherry ghost." In a simple, straightforward way, Tweedy richly combines images of fertility and birth with notions of death and spiritual resurrection. His lyrics point to fundamental issues surrounding the human experience with death—the afterlife and souls, of course—but he also challenges those who claim to be experts about life's most impenetrable mystery.

From the earliest archaeological evidence of ritual funerary activity in the Paleolithic era to the current scientific experimentations with cryogenics, or freezing the dead, human cultures have invested a great deal of their spiritual and material energies in penetrating and mastering this mystery, with or without experts to guide them. Something that remains constant across time and space and in the midst of all the incredible diversity of human responses to death is that it is sacred and requires religious modes of acting and thinking to ensure psychological well-being, social continuity, and cultural vitality. What is sacred about death—mummification or cremation, interaction with spirits or acts of memorialization—varies depending on the social milieu, imaginative frames of reference, and ritual strategies survivors must work with to do right by the dead and heal their own emotional and psychological wounds and disruptions when faced with the loss of life. Without question, what is sacred about death in one social setting may be an outrage in another, which is why in times of war the profanation of the dead can be such a horrible symbolic and material offense. But in times of war or peace, death remains sacred across religious cultures, including those with one God, those with many gods, or those with no gods at all.

Monotheistic cultures familiar to most Americans place God squarely in the center of this sacred event: the God of Abraham, Isaac, and Jacob; the Holy Father; Allah; the ultimate power, who brings forth life and defines the terms of death, is the bottom line. Throughout American history, God, biblical texts, and theological authorities have provided many in grief with the necessary solace and meaning to carry on and not cave in to the desperation, hopelessness, or unimaginable sadness brought to life by death. Yet the monotheistic vision today and for much of American history does not exhaust the spectrum of religious cultural resources available for artists like Jeff Tweedy and many other Americans who may or may not identify themselves as Christians, Jews, Muslims, atheists, or agnostics. What is beyond this life and what survives the death of the body can be understood without theologians, and for many, without the Lord above. Endless examples from popular culture frame death and the presence of the recently dead—cherry ghosts, to use Tweedy's wonderful phrase—in a distinctly a-theological way.

Ghosts are born and inhabit worlds of public culture and private memory, a familiar ethereal mode for imagining how the dead live and still matter even though a once living, embodied identity transitions to a decomposing corpse. The moral lessons of death, stories about the dead, tributes in their honor, the emotional education when grappling with their loss—all of these crucial social and psychological matters take shape and acquire relevance in and through fields of popular culture and mass entertainment. Music, film, television, cyberspace, and literature all serve as primary teachers helping us orient to and focus on what really counts when it comes to death, loss, grief, and healing. What really counts?

One of the elementary lessons from American literature about death is that the boundaries between the living and the dead are permeable, interactions and intimacies with the dead made possible through words and plot devices and imaginative settings that not only draw readers in but also ring true with their own fantasies and dreams, real-life experiences, and expectations. From Washington Irving's "The Legend of Sleepy Hollow" (1820) to Louise Erdrich's *Tracks* (1988), from Louisa May Alcott's "A Whisper in the Dark" (1863) to John Cheever's "Oh Father, Father Why Have You Come Back?" (1956), from Edith Wharton's "The Eyes" (1910) to William Kennedy's *Ironweed* (1983), from Nathaniel Hawthorne's *House of the Seven Gables* (1851) to Toni Morrison's *Beloved* (1987), the dead are present to haunt, reassure, frighten, disturb, and inspire the living. Ghosts are now and have always been a staple of the literary landscape, an entertaining presence not inconsequential to the most serious religious questions about morality and transformation, justice and transcendence, and of course life after death.

Alice Sebold's best-selling, highly acclaimed 2002 book *The Lovely Bones* is one fairly recent example. In this story a fourteen-year-old girl ghost describes her horrible rape and murder by a neighbor and its consequential aftermath among the living. Susie Salmon, the young narrator of the novel, is not an ethereal presence on earth but is instead located in a godless heaven suited just to her peculiar circumstances. Readers learn early on that, according to Susie, the dead live on in heavens of their own making, based primarily on their own visions and hopes shaped while they are alive. Susie's heaven is created from the life of a young teenage girl, eternally existing on the grounds of a school, though not quite mirroring the reality below: "There were no teachers in the school. We never had to go inside except for art class for me. . . . Our textbooks were *Seventeen* and *Glamour* and *Vogue*."[1] Here, in this afterlife, Susie will never grow into a woman but will forever remain imprisoned in early adolescence.

Sebold draws from spiritualism, a rich, and pervasive, religious movement in American cultural history that does not require a biblical God to confront the reality of death and imagine possible relations between the living and the dead. The book represents the line between the two as blurred and porous, rather than segregated and distinct, with descriptions of generally comforting spirit possessions, communications, and visitations that bring the dead within reach of the living. No institutional authorities here to mediate connections between spirits and the living, no saints who hear the prayers of the living to assist the dead, no educated theologians and mystical leaders with direct access to the other world, just a young ghost girl whose eternal identity is primarily defined by a domestic portrait of grief, heartbreak, and ultimate reconciliation with the facts of life. In this religious novel, which resonated with a nation obsessed with child abductions and murders, death is never the end but truly a new beginning and the birth of new, potentially healing relationships across the great divide.

Like American literature, Hollywood films offer an assortment of stories that bring the dead to life in the form of ghosts or phantasms, spirits or zombies. The dead are present almost from the cinematic get-go in early films transfixed by mummies and vampires, and have had starring roles in such films as *Topper* (1937), *Heaven Can Wait* (1943 and 1978), *The Ghost and Mrs. Muir* (1947), *The Innocents* (1961), *All of Me* (1984), *Beetlejuice* (1988), *Ghost* (1990), *Truly Madly Deeply* (1991), *Heart and Souls* (1993), and just recently,

Ghost Town (2008), to name only a few. One of the major block-buster films depicting the integrated worlds of the dead and the living was M. Night Shyamalan's 1999 work, *The Sixth Sense*. The memorable tagline in the publicity for the film, "I see dead peo-ple," summarizes the essential predicament for the protagonist in this story, Cole, yet another youngster with preternatural abilities and cosmic insights about the nature of death, and life.

The story follows Cole's relationship with child psychologist Malcolm Crowe, who a few months before their meeting was at-tacked and shot by a former patient whom he could not cure and who had similar difficulties as Cole. After the attack, the ex-patient kills himself. Months later, though Malcolm is seemingly recov-ered from his injuries, his personal and psychological life are now in pieces. The young boy, Cole, comes to Malcolm for help with his dilemma, the "sixth sense" in the movie title: he can see dead people who do not know they are dead and, besides being teased at school and worrying his single mother, is haunted by unsettled, malevolent spirits. Malcolm seeks to help him and comes to un-derstand that his own fate is somehow mysteriously tied up with the boy.

The surprise ending that gave this movie such a buzz in popu-lar culture and kept viewers returning to watch it again is Mal-colm's realization that he, in fact, is dead, a ghost who until that point could not face the truth of his condition. In addition to the expertly crafted, evocatively moody and, at times, downright scary elements of the film, *The Sixth Sense* provided viewers with a story Americans have told themselves over and over again throughout the nation's history: the dead are not just dead and gone but can re-turn as frightening ghosts to haunt the world of the living or sometimes as less malevolent ghosts to heal the living's wounds and provide them with wisdom and insight about the way the world really is. In this film, like many of those listed above, God is not a factor in the sacred details of death and the afterlife. Literature and folklore, children's stories and poetry, music and film—all forms of cultural expression that capture the fancy, entertain, and educate Americans often return to the religiously captivating notions of a life beyond this life, ethereal spirits mingling with corporeal bodies, ghosts who stay close to the living instead of returning home to God.

Along with the birth of ghosts in the American imagination, community members face another sacred labor when facing loss, a universal chore in all cultures that initiates religious actions and ignites the fires of the religious imagination: disposal of the corpse. In the history of the United States, cultural responses to the dead have exhibited a range of religious characteristics, including traditional rituals tied to the church and synagogue, and more innovative practices untethered from any institutional authority. From the colonial era to the present, religious preoccupations with death and keeping the dead in place have also made an indelible mark on material cultures in cemeteries, sites of worship, war memorials, public shrines, and other sacred spaces.[2]

The strong ties between religious cultures and death in America, both yesterday and today, should not be surprising; like societies around the globe and throughout time, American society has long been concerned with the delicate task of managing relations between the living and the dead, and drawing social sustenance from the extinction of life. But in a pluralistic society like the United States, it is difficult to argue for a singular American "way" of death, as Jessica Mitford tried to do in her popular 1963 book, *The American Way of Death*, published only a few months before the assassination of JFK.[3] Rather, from the earliest years of national life to the present, the dead have always acted as a sacred resource for communities establishing or reaffirming their identity and social solidarity, sometimes with the hope of maintaining the status quo, other times searching for ways to turn the world upside down.

America is often described as a Christian nation or, to stay away from too narrowly identifying with one tradition, as a nation of faithful monotheists with one of the highest percentages of people in developed countries who believe in God. Most Americans who are adherents of monotheistic traditions will turn to God or Jesus or Muhammad in their encounter with death and how they imagine the plight of the dead. Yet the popularity and potency of American religious cultures that do not rely on God or any textual revelations found in the Hebrew Bible, New Testament, or Koran speak to pervasive and wide-ranging, viable and appealing, godless, sacred possibilities available to communities across the social landscape. These religious cultures make sense of death and locate the dead in worlds where God is absent, or not necessary, for the living to find the strength and tools to carry on in this life with reassurances that moral order can overcome chaos, personal integrity remains in place instead of disintegration, and social relations do not succumb to ultimate corruption—negative possibilities so powerfully represented by the decomposing material corpse but symbolically redeemed, of course, by the powers of culture and social effervescence.

African slaves in antebellum southern states, middle-class spiritualists in the second half of the nineteenth century, theosophists in urban areas at the turn of the twentieth century, first-generation Buddhists from Southeast Asia in the wake of the 1965 Immigration Act, late twentieth-century New Agers with crystals and medicine wheels—these are only a few examples of cultures that draw on religious principles and spiritual practices to transcend biological death and imagine the transition out of this life without turning to a personal God. But many other less distinguishable, more diffuse forms of cultural activity can also wring religious transformation from human finitude, converting death into vital, dynamic spiritual life and commitment for Americans who may publicly identify as secular atheists, reform Jews, Southern Baptists, Roman Catholics, Methodists, or Buddhist meditators, or who claim no institutional affiliation at all. Godless sacred feelings and investments are aroused in Americans who are not only spiritual but also voracious material consumers stimulated by films dealing with the topic of death, sports figures who pass on and are remembered as heroes, literature of all kinds built around dead bodies, and musical idols who die young and other revered dead entertainers—special engagements with popular culture that do not show up on surveys or personal interviews but are signally responsible for inspiring sacred rituals and notions with immeasurable value in the inevitable encounter with the corpse.

Historically, funeral homes have played an especially important role in shaping the sacred contours of death in American life, from their earliest appearances in private houses and on busy streets during the second half of the nineteenth century to the current multinational presence of the death industry around the globe.[4] The undertakers who became funeral directors during this evolution and now serve as ritual specialists in the business of *ars moriendi*, or the arts of death, have carved an indispensable and relatively unchallenged niche in American life. Sometimes embarrassed and disgraced, often ridiculed and reviled, morticians, as they used to be called, have been greatly appreciated by Americans for the vital cultural work they do: putting the dead in their place. In some cultures, ritual death specialists are revered and esteemed; in many others, they are outcasts and polluted. In American culture, funerals generate a vast economic network of merchandise and services, therapies and investments, with the funeral director at the center of it all, directing the body's exit from living sight. Some hate him, but many are materially as well as spiritually satisfied in his care. Clearly if any so-called secular social institution brings church and God to the mind, it is the funeral industry.

But God does not always define the boundaries between secular and sacred, nor exhaust the peculiarities of the holy in the face of the profane when the body makes its exit from living communities. Undoubtedly, most funeral directors will state that they believe in God and have an institutional affiliation with a religious organization or two. Surely a majority of Americans will feel the presence of a personal God during this difficult, inevitable separation from the physical body, a rending so fraught with ambiguity and weight that the one in charge is less important than the One in charge. Yet the details of the transaction to remove the body, the implements used to prepare it for disposal, and the ritual actions enforced or invented to ensure its transition are sacred on all counts, religious work in any cultural setting, monotheistic or pagan, ancient or modern. Yes, the cost of caskets makes your skin crawl; true, the cosmetic touches boggle the mind; certainly the merchandise and services available to customers are staggering; but the material investments do not exclude spiritual rewards, and the economic logic makes sense for religious reasons.

The venerable funeral home, a staple of the social landscape for now over a century, is a social institution that was born from the death and carnage of the Civil War and the strong, primarily Northern desire to hire someone to bring the dead home. It came of age with simultaneous support in public culture through the years, where famous dead like Lincoln, Valentino, and Elvis were prepared by funeral directors and displayed before a transfixed nation, and in private lives, where undertakers proved themselves worthy to families who returned again and again. And the funeral home has reached maturity with the globalization of death, where local independent and small business mentalities are in tension with multinational forces based on economies of scale, stockholder confidence, and the outsourcing of jobs to more cost-efficient parts of the world, and the clientele are increasingly pluralistic in terms of their country of origin and stated religious proclivities. Perhaps even more significant to the institution's religious plasticity and transformative potentialities is the peculiar, quite confusing mixture of sentiments and rational thought, functions, and identifications that are contained within the space—and are in many ways constitutive of the sacred within the space—of the funeral home itself.

By the early years of the twentieth century, undertakers rapidly turned their own homes into a location that combined domestic space with commercial enterprise, turning away from other possible practices like making house calls and keeping the dead in their own homes, or transporting the dead to an office or place of business outside the home, where most American men worked. Instead, the American funeral director placed the dead in a suitable home away from home, made a living with the dead out of his own house, sought to help the living feel at home with death, and ensured the business remained a family affair. Rites of passage generally take place in only a few social locations, familiar structures where, generally speaking, everything is at stake in the care of the body: home, church, hospital. The lifeless body often made its way through all of them in the twentieth century, fittingly finding its way back home, not necessarily a specific home, but a home where emotions are high, values reassessed, and rituals can work magic.

Dramatic changes have occurred within the industry from the closing decades of the twentieth century, including growing numbers of funeral directors who do not bring their work home but leave it behind at a separate establishment; a diversifying population of individuals who are not born into this line of business but instead choose to enter it without family connections; and an ever-expanding range of ritual requests from customers with radically different hopes and expectations, desires and tastes, at the time of death. Now more than ever, a cultural shift in the mortuary landscape is highlighting how the sacred persists with or without God in the mix, and how the sacred work of ushering the body out of sight from the living takes place whether the body is burned to ash and deposited in artificial corral reefs; or quickly disposed unceremoniously before the memorial service commemorating the passing of a family member or close friend; or placed in the ground and celebrated with an extravagant display of wealth or by purchasing funerary mementos and merchandise. The Lord was a likely presence in funeral homes before the 1970s, but by the end of the century He was not automatically assumed to be on the premises, playing a role in the drama of death either implicitly or explicitly. Even without His named involvement in the proceedings, funeral homes continue to arouse and tame sacred powers and impulses initiated by the brute remainder at death.

Some dead do not stay dead, in spite of the ritual work of the funeral directors, the sincerest wishes of friends and family members, and the consoling words of theologians and other religious leaders. Some dead take on a life of their own, present in material as well as spiritual form, culturally resurrected and religiously viable to thousands of Americans who interact with them in ritually specific ways that open up the world of the sacred but do not necessarily close the door on God. Saints in the Catholic Church are a sacred class of holy figures, in another world but distinctly active here in this world across a vast, complicated, culturally varied field of regional practices, community ideals, and influential iconography brought to the New World from the Old. The war dead from any nation are also clearly a distinctive class apart, representative of the citizenry but extraordinary in making the ultimate sacrifice perhaps for God but always for country, and therefore worthy of collective mourning and memorialization rituals that are geared toward social unity and solidarity but often fall into easy political grandstanding and exploitative partisanship. Ancestors are another category of the sacred dead, worshipped by family members, not only through long-standing traditions—for example, customs imported from Asian countries that draw on Buddhist attitudes or Confucian practices, or African customs and philosophies forcibly suppressed though not extinguished in the fertile religious soil of the New World and now as American as apple pie—but also through a more indigenous, Americanized, bourgeois valorization of the domestic family unit and its value to memory, identity, security, and ultimate meanings.

Along with Christian saints, sacrificed soldiers, and departed ancestors, dead celebrities can acquire sacred standing; attain the

status of religious icons; overcome death itself to instigate initially
odd, but upon reflection very familiar cultural activities that build
communities, declare affinities, model values, and demand investments. In popular culture the chosen few are easily identified with
Christian images and rituals, but in no way can they be exclusively
defined in relation to God and church. The names Tupac Shakur
and Elvis Presley would rarely be said in the same sentence, let
alone held up for comparison of their musical contributions while
alive, but in death the two share many things, and their life stories
and physical traces, mythic mysteries and material products, bond
them not quite as brothers but more like spiritual kin. Not simply
ghosts, Tupac and Elvis are more like gods for the large and culturally powerful communities energized by collective effervescences
of a peculiar sort, living a spiritual life as sacred as the gods of distant times and places, some that faded long ago and others still
arousing the faithful to this very day. How do you measure the sacred in the afterlife of Elvis? Where is the religious data from the
postmortem presence of Tupac?

In 2006, ten years after his death, a waxen, though remarkably
lifelike sculpture with the name "2Pac Eternal" was unveiled at
the world famous Madame Tussauds in Las Vegas, the city where
the gangsta, with "thug life" tattooed on his living body, met his
untimely end in a hail of bullets. The fate of his real body, in
contrast, less tangible than the wax body, has taken on an aura of
mystery and reverence while concretely grounding rituals and
material investments informed by its brief time in physical form.
Mortally wounded in an attack that injured the driver of the car,
Death Row Records founder and convicted felon Suge Knight,
Tupac remained on life support machines for several days before
dying an all-too-common death for young black men in America.

The fate of his body after death, however, was far from common for anyone white or black, Christian or Muslim. His body
was cremated and his ashes very deliberately placed in the sacred
spaces of Tupac's life, some scattered in his mother's garden, for ex-

ample, some in the Pacific Ocean off the West Coast, a critical geographic distinction in the rivalry with East Coast rappers, and
some smoked in a blunt by his band, the Outlawz (per Tupac's own
explicit instructions to them in the event of his death and found in
the lyrics in "Black Jesus" as a last wish).[5] Some have even been
preserved and recently dispersed by his mother, Afeni, on the
grounds of the Tupac Amaru Shakur Foundation Memorial Park
in Stone Mountain, Georgia, and in a special, ten-year anniversary
ceremony in his ancestral home, Soweto, South Africa. The symbolic weight of these remains, and the ritual import for others in
their dispersal, were evident from the moment the young, promising star passed on.

Tupac's brutal slaying may have been foreshadowed in his own
music and predicted based on his own experiences leading up to
the murder, but no one could have imagined the extraordinary religious power Tupac would exert on the living from beyond the
grave. These powers cannot be only measured in dollars and cents
but have to include other spiritual variables which surface in cultural expressions and are tied to personal and social transformations, or deeply moving and meaningful this-worldly somatic
experiences by an adoring public that assume otherworldly significance, or relevant moral and ethical precepts fans draw from his
music and words, anchored in reflections and actions building
moral communities.

As is often the case with hallowed religious figures who die
young, many refuse to believe that the individual is dead. The truth
is much less complicated and prosaic in some quarters—it is all a
hoax or a strategic economic scheme or the ultimate slap in the
face of racist white American society or just a playful joke, as de-
picted in a 2006 broadcast of one of Dave Chappelle's "Lost
Episodes" on Comedy Central. A far greater number of followers,
however, see in his death certain spiritual truths that speak directly
to the heart and head of people alive now, ten years on, and are relevant to moral, philosophical, ethical, even theological sensibilities

pervasive today. These truths are not merely tied to the trove of
music and writings he left behind, nor to the invaluable merchandise more than worth its weight in gold to consumers, nor to the
special memories conjured up by his visage or tattoos.

Indeed, Tupac's theological portrait was not fully appreciated
while alive, but in death—for many theologians, philosophers, and
cultural critics—the gangsta has a bit of the Old Testament
prophet in him, and his angry rap lyrics carry a theodicy about
God in the face of suffering, pain, and death.[6] In life, Tupac on the
radio, the television, the movie screen, and across the media was
magnetic for so many, but also repulsive to others. His words and
his body aroused fear and confusion in the early 1990s, as well as
awe and allegiance in black and white communities throughout
America. God is not absent in this life story: his mother, Afeni, was
a young, single militant Black Panther who gave up the revolution
to support her son and now embraces God as the driving force in
her life and in his cultural legacy; his knowledge about religion,
learned from the streets in various communities and the books he
read that ranged from Nietzsche to the *Tibetan Book of the Dead*,
Zen and the Art of Motorcycle Maintenance to Thomas à Kempis's *Imitation of Christ*, as well as key texts from black literature and culture, including Richard Wright, Maya Angelou, and W.E.B.
Dubois;[7] his lyrics, prose, and poems, which sometimes only allude to, other times cry out to, the Lord above. Even his body
serves as a theological tableau, with tattoos that include a cross and
"Exodus 1831," the familiar biblical myth and the year of Nat
Turner's slave revolt.

But the meanings of God are not always so clear in the complex, contradictory life and body of Tupac, who also had a tattoo
that read "Fuck the World," and especially in songs like "Only
God Can Judge Me" or even better, "Black Jesus," with a starkly
divergent image of the son of God than what is served up in most
white and black Christian churches then or now: "Searchin' for
Black Jesus. . . . Somebody that understand our pain / You know

maybe not too perfect, you know / Somebody that hurt like we hurt / Somebody that smoke like we smoke / Drink like we drink / That understand where we coming from / That's who we pray to / We need help y'all." Tupac was quite well-read and informed by religious interests that included but did not end with the God found in the Bible. His growing knowledge about his African heritage as well as more diffuse, less theologically focused expressions of religious life that applied to street life and gang banging, moral systems unfamiliar to most Americans though renounced by many, paints a complex picture that is not easy to categorize as monotheistic or nihilistic. Tupac led a thug's life that at times corresponded to his gangsta image but also acted in inspiring ways that demonstrated profound love and concern: he sang about bitches and hoes as well as Jesus and Judgment. The God identified in his life does not seem fixed nor entirely stable, a point of certainty or source for ultimate meaning—qualities which more often come from the street and a code not found in any sacred text.

The spirit of Tupac is alive and thriving, a cornerstone of industries and inspirations for fans throughout the land and around the globe. Looking back on his tragically short life and bringing lessons from that life into the present and future, fans heartily consume postmortem merchandise ranging from clothes to coffee mugs, DVDs to mouse pads, and of course the best-selling musical releases, transforming Tupac into one of the top grossing dead celebrities in entertainment and far, far outselling anything he produced while alive. All of these commercial items are available in the mall at Tupac's official website, 2PacLegacy.com, just one of numerous sites devoted to more than the memory of the young man's short life, each one dedicated to communicating and capitalizing on the "spirit," "legacy," "truth," and other religious markers reminding fans that Tupac transcends time and space, like other prophets or shamans, gods or visionaries.

The website thuglifearmy.com, "Sparking minds of youth around the world," is a website fixated on Tupac. Images of Tupac dominate the screen, both close-ups of his visage and longer shots of him shirtless, and fans can hear music, see additional images, watch videos, and read up on extraordinary facets of Tupac's life and death, all neatly listed on the screen under the heading "2Pac's Life": "Is Tupac Alive," "Tupac Tattoos," "Tupac Poetry," "Tupac's Wild Side," "Tupac Tributes," "Takedown of Tupac," "Tupac Autopsy," and "Tupac's Reading Library." What makes this and other fan sites so critical to the formation of religious cultures centered on Tupac is the expression of a set of values either implicitly or explicitly tied to the flesh and blood person turned larger-than-life spirit.

At thuglifearmy.com a veritable moral system for respectable living is provided to visitors, inspired and written down by Tupac originally as an effort to bring peace to the deadly rivalry between the Los Angeles gangs the Bloods and the Crips. Leaders from both sides signed on at a peace picnic in California in 1992, but now and always it will offer "do's and don'ts for being a righteous thud and banger" to a more general and much larger following brought together virtually and in reality after his death. Similar in some respects to the Ten Commandments for Jews and Christians, the Four Noble Truths for Buddhists, or other more recognizable religious laws in any number of religious traditions, the code of Thug Life is a rule book for living with practical import and guidelines on the streets as well as ethical urgency and guidance for the spirit. Like other guiding principles in religious cultures, this code reminds participants that they are mortal ("All new Jacks to the game must know. . . . He's going to die"); identifies clear-cut offenses to the spirit of the community ("Snitches is outta here"); encourages a vital and intensified us/them mentality ("Know your target, who's the real enemy"); proffers appropriate relations with others ("Respect our sisters. Respect our brothers"); and offers sage advice in matters of life and danger ("Protect yourself at all times").[8]

The World Wide Web is only one strand in the webs of mean-

ing associated with the Tupac phenomenon. Across other media
and works of art, a figment of private and public imaginations,
Tupac lives a peculiar kind of spiritual life that has the power to attract many and still repel some. Often associated with Christ in
image and in word, Tupac is present as no mere mortal but as a singular figure who can, like the Christ figure, arouse faithful communities who interpret his life and messages in more ways than
one and imagine a life beyond the grave. Tupac with a halo and
angel's wings in one painting; a thoughtful theological reflection in
the journal *Black Renaissance* entitled, "Time on the Cross," by
womanist theologian Jacquie Jones;[9] traffic in chat rooms compar-
ing 2Pac to JC—the allusions to martyrdom and sacrifice for the
disenfranchised and to a suffering body and redemption, naturally
draw from the Christian well of mythical sources and ritual frames
that predominate in U.S. society. But Tupac's death has a surplus of
meanings, taking interpreters far outside the reach of Logos and
engaged fans out of sight from a not quite omniscient God.

The recent outpouring of newspaper coverage and social commentaries celebrating the ten-year anniversary of Tupac's death attests to both his staying power in public culture and private lives,
but also the religious meanings that persist, if not expand, with
each year. Tupac is offered to the public as a visionary, revered by
fans, the source of a dynamic mythology, a controversial rapper
who has achieved iconic status, a heroic, one-of-a-kind individual,
who inspires faith, a following, communities that return to him
again and again.[10] His death also continues to evoke mysteries that
blur the lines between the living and the dead. Alive or a ghost?
Fully materialized or spiritually present? Many still speculate that
Tupac is somehow not really dead but still living, a heated bone of
contention provoking theories about conspiracies and hidden secret clues in his music, as well as counter statements that urge fans
to leave the dead in peace and remember the spirit.

Thuglifearmy.com includes the following quote from Snoop
Dog on these lingering theories: "People need to let him rest in

peace, let that rumor rest in peace. Because . . . the public don't
want to accept it, so they gonna keep that myth or that philosophy
going on as long as they can because his music lives on and he's a
legend, you know what I'm sayin'. When you make legendary
music, people don't want to believe you're gone. Like Elvis, they
keep saying Elvis ain't dead you know what I'm sayin', but it's just
all about the individual himself, he was a legend and everybody
don't wanna let it go." [11] Indeed, Snoop and others are correct that
the best comparable phenomenon, seemingly secular but abun-
dant with religious meanings in fact, is Elvis. In death, Tupac may
be something of a prince to many followers, but there is still only
one King ruling in the world of dead celebrities.

Elvis lives. Elvis is everywhere. Elvis is a phenomenon unsur-
passed by Tupac or Marilyn Monroe or Princess Diana or Kurt
Cobain or Jimi Hendrix or any other figure in human history, save
one or two. A cultural force that bears economic but also spiritual
fruit, Elvis saves and satisfies, entertains and enlightens the masses
with more than charisma or savvy marketing. The cult of Elvis
knows no bounds, has no hard and fast boundaries that distinguish
it as only an industry or entertainment; it is worthy of church but
cannot be institutionalized. From Graceland to cyberspace, the
ghost of Elvis haunts and transforms the lives of millions of Americans who have developed a sacred, meaningful bond between
themselves and the King. The annual pilgrimage to Memphis on
August 9, Elvis's death date, the conventions celebrating his music
and life, and the holy relics so highly valued by fans give expression
to the religious devotions so powerful in the lives of communities
in the southern, northern, western, and eastern United States, as
well as far, far beyond national borders.

The material and the ethereal mingle in the sacred wake of
Elvis in death. Religious traces in cultural products and practices
span the globe and energize meaningful relations between a long-
dead entertainer and communities enlivened by his ghostly image
and familiar spirit. The Elvis born poor in Tupelo, Mississippi, in

1935 and who died rich in Graceland in 1977 fades from view
with each passing year and as generations come and go. But that
Elvis, the physical man with the guitar and lips, hip-shakes and
sideburns, the one embalmed and displayed before crowds of people congregating around the corpse, is only half the man now, less
and less significant compared to the spiritual body that, unlike
other cherry ghosts that rivet the public's imagination after death,
cloaks his presence as a cultural saint, or perhaps even better in this
case, a popular god.

What more is there to say about Elvis? Books, films, websites,
documentaries, photographs, insignias, stamps, music, museums,
shrines, and articles say it all: Elvis is a cultural institution, making
money for the Elvis corporation for sure, but also a pervasive point
of reference in the onslaught of information in everyday life, icon-
ically familiar with multiple, wide-ranging meanings and emotional resonances that are still magnetic and energizing to many
consumers.[12] His religious status is also obvious and openly discussed across cultures in testimonials and analyses that require the
language of the sacred, routinely ritualized in myriad public and
private activities that confer the sacred on its object of devotion,
and imaginatively endowed with mythical qualities that bring the
sacred to mind when contemplating his visage or hearing him
sing.[13] The God above may or may not be a part of the religious
equation; a personal God beyond Elvis, transcendent but imminent and present for many Jews, Christians, and Muslims, does not
always put the sacred in its place here in this world nor determine
the afterlife of celebrated figures who capture and hold the public's
eye. In the case of Elvis, the sacred does not remain tied to the
Bible or Koran nor have anything to do with the sayings of Buddha or the Rig Veda, but is instead generated and regenerated by
less disciplined cultural forces and deep-seated human desires at
play in his curious, ghostly presence today.

Elvis and Tupac, funeral homes and ghosts, cherry or otherwise, provide religious data of a peculiar, though by now quite fa-

miliar sort: God does not constitute nor exhaust the sacred when it comes to American responses to death and expressions of community and commitment in the face of mortality and loss. Religious life is animated by music and entertainment, the powers of the corpse, the reaffirmation of values in ritual and myths, and other kinds of activities and beliefs transforming the finite into the infinite, the biological into the cosmic, matter into spirit. Death is one marker among many outlined in this book where godless religious cultures flourish and decline, take hold as full-fledged social movements or impact individuals one at a time.

The sacred without God has a great deal of potential in America, where cultures are not bound to one source of authority, restricted by institutional logic and order, or inhibited by a single moral frame of reference. The true story of the sacred in America is one that breaks from the familiar overriding monotheistic plot and instead admits that one religious story cannot be told. The truth is the sacred assumes multiple forms, is grounded in vastly different categories and diverse value systems, and overflows institutional boundaries and margins on a page. In America, proclaiming one true religion can be used to judge the spectrum of religious expressions is a fiction, a dream that once may have been effectively asserted but now is impossible to maintain. This state of religious affairs may provoke some people to ask, "Is nothing sacred?" even though the answer is abundantly clear.

NOTES

Introduction

1. This discussion and indeed the entire book are shaped and informed by Emile Durkheim, *The Elementary Forms of Religious Life* (New York: The Free Press, 1995; originally published in French in 1912).

1. Film

1. A fascinating story found at various online sites dedicated to the history of film; outlined, for example, at http://www.pbs.org/wgbh/ amex/eastman/timeline/index_2.html and http://www.pbs.org/ wgbh/amex/eastman/timeline/index_3.html (viewed June 30, 2005), both from PBS *History of Photography* website; and also at http://www.adherents.com/people/pg/Hannibal_Goodwin.html. See also Barbara Moran, "The Preacher Who Beat Eastman Kodak," *Invention and Technology Magazine* 17, no. 2 (Fall 2001), available at Americanheritage.com, http://www.americanheritage.com/articles/ magazine/it/2001/2/2001_2_44.shtml (viewed July 2, 2005). On Goodwin's motivation, see Rev. W.H. Jackson, "An Indictment: The Moving Picture, a Clergyman's Child, Has Been Neglected by the Church," in Terry Lindvall, *The Silents of God: Selected Issues and Documents in Silent American Film and Religion, 1908–1925* (Lanham, MD: Scarecrow Press, 2001 [1918]), 189.
2. A number of books give useful overviews of this period, including Randall Balmer, *Religion in Twentieth Century America* (New York: Oxford University Press, 2001); Mark Hulsether, *Religion, Culture, and Politics in the Twentieth-Century United States* (New York: Columbia University Press, 2007); Charles Lippy, *Pluralism Comes of Age: American Religious Culture in the Twentieth Century* (New York: M.E. Sharpe, 2000).
3. Lindvall, *The Silents of God*, xiii.
4. John Margolies and Emily Gwathmey, *Ticket to Paradise: American Movie Theaters and How We Had Fun* (Boston: Little, Brown, 1991), 54–55.

5. Ben Hall, *The Best Remaining Seats: The Story of the Golden Age of the Movie Palace* (New York: Da Capo Press, 1988), 8.

6. Ibid.

7. Margolies and Gwathmey, *Ticket to Paradise*, 25, 107, and 44, respectively.

8. M. Darrol Bryant, "Cinema, Religion, and Popular Culture," in *Religion in Film*, ed. John R. May and Michael Bird (Knoxville: University of Tennessee Press, 1982), 101.

9. See for example Lary May, *Screening out the Past: The Birth of Mass Culture and the Motion Picture Industry* (New York: Oxford University Press, 1980).

10. Many scholarly studies chart the connections between religion and film, including John C. Lyden, *Film as Religion: Myths, Morals, and Rituals* (New York: NYU Press, 2003); Margaret R. Miles, *Seeing and Believing: Religion and Values in the Movies* (Boston: Beacon, 1996); and S. Brent Plate, *Representing Religion in World Cinema: Filmmaking, Mythmaking, Culture Making* (New York: Palgrave Macmillan, 2003).

11. Steven Watts, *The Magic Kingdom: Walt Disney and the American Way of Life* (Boston: Houghton Mifflin, 1997); and the more recent Neal Gabler, *Walt Disney: The Triumph of the American Imagination* (New York: Vintage, 2007).

12. Much of this discussion is from my article "The Disney Way of Death," *Journal of the American Academy of Religion* 68, no. 1 (2000): 27–46.

13. L. Frank Baum, *The Wonderful World of Oz: The Wizard of Oz, The Emerald City of Oz, Glinda of Oz* (New York: Penguin Classics, 1998; originally published in 1900).

14. In addition to Christian attacks on the populist politics of Baum or the sinful celebration of witches, flying monkeys, and other signs of paganism in the film, numerous books have been published offering the public the deeper meanings of the movie, including Lawrence R. Spencer, *The Oz Factors: The Wizard of Oz as an Analogy to the Mysteries of Life* (Lawrence R. Spencer Publisher, 1999), or Joey Green, *The Zen of Oz: Ten Spiritual Lessons from Over the Rainbow* (New York: Renaissance Books, 1998), or Darren Main, *Spiritual Journeys along the Yellow Brick Road* (Morayshire, Scotland: Findhorn Press, 2000).

15. Quotes taken from the website for the Internet Movie Database:

http://www.imdb.com/title/tt0032138/usercomments?start=0 (viewed June 22, 2005).

16. See Oprah's website for the story: http://www.oprah.com/slide show/oprahshow/oprahshow1_ss_20080123/15 (viewed September 1, 2008).

17. See Ruby Slipper Fan Club website: http://users.deltacomm.com/ rainbowz/rubyslipperfanclub/introduction.html (viewed June 27, 2005).

18. Salman Rushdie, *The Wizard of Oz* (London: BFI, 1992), 18.

19. Ibid., 12.

20. Ibid., 23.

21. See, for example, Andrew Gordon, *"Star Wars:* A Myth for Our Time,"* in *Screening the Sacred: Religion, Myth, and Ideology in Popular American Film,* ed. Joel W. Martin and Conrad E. Ostwalt Jr. (Boulder, CO: Westview, 1995), 73–82.

22. See Will Brooker, *Using the Force: Creativity, Community and Star Wars Fans* (New York: Continuum, 2002), for one exploration of the cultural productivity of the film.

23. Bill Slavicsek, Andy Collins, and J.D. Wiker, *Revised Core Rulebook (Star Wars Roleplaying Game)* (Renton, WA: Wizards of the Coast, 2002).

24. See Star Wars Chicks website: http://www.starwarschicks.com/sith chicks/ (viewed June 28, 2005).

2. Music

1. Lyle V. Harris, "Raves: At Unconventional Parties, Devotees Express Themselves Through a Rousing Mix of Dance, Technology and Spirituality," *Atlanta Journal Constitution,* March 24, 2000, C1 and C4.

2. Walter Freeman, "A Neurological Role of Music in Social Bonding," in *The Origins of Music,* ed. Nils L. Wallin, Bjorn Merker, and Steven Brown (Cambridge, MA: MIT Press, 2000), 420.

3. Anthony Storr, *Music and the Mind* (London: HarperCollins, 1992), 17.

4. See Freeman, "A Neurological Role of Music," 420, as well as the more recent work by Daniel J. Levitin, *The World in Six Songs: How the Musical Brain Created Human Nature* (New York: Dutton, 2008).

5. David P. McAllester, "Music," in *Native American Religions: North*

America, ed. Lawrence E. Sullivan (New York: Macmillan, 1987), 187. Also see David W. Stowe, *How Sweet the Sound: Music in the Spiritual Lives of Americans* (Cambridge, MA: Harvard University Press, 2004), 3; and Stephen A. Marini, *Sacred Song in America: Religion, Music, and Public Culture* (Springfield, IL: University of Illinois Press, 2003).

6. Stowe, *How Sweet the Sound*, 21 and 4–5.

7. Christopher John Farley, "Rave New World," *Time*, June 5, 2000, http://www.time.com/time/magazine/article/0,9171,997084,00.html.

8. Harris, "Raves," C1.

9. Scott R. Hutson, "The Rave: Spiritual Healing in Modern Western Subcultures," *Anthropological Quarterly*, 73, no. 1 (January 2000): 35–49.

10. Letter to the editor, *USA Today*, November 19, 2002, 20a.

11. Hutson, "The Rave," 42.

12. Proclaimed loudly on the back cover of Jimi Fritz, *Rave Culture: An Insider's Overview and a Primer for the Global Rave Phenomenon* (Canada: Small Fry Press, 1999).

13. Jon Michael Spencer, "Introduction," *Blues and Evil* (Knoxville, TN: University of Tennessee Press, 1993).

14. James Cone, "The Blues: A Secular Spiritual," in *Write Me a Few of Your Lines: A Blues Reader*, ed. Steven C. Tracy (Amherst, MA: University of Massachusetts Press, 1999), 231.

15. Ibid., 241.

16. Teresa L. Reed, *The Holy Profane: Religion in Black Popular Music* (Lexington, KY: University Press of Kentucky, 1993).

17. Lawrence W. Levine, *The Unpredictable Past: Explorations in American Cultural History* (New York: Oxford University Press, 1993), 117.

18. Yvonne P. Chireau, *Black Magic: Religion and the African American Conjuring Tradition* (Berkeley, CA: University of California Press, 2003), 145.

19. Natalie Hopkinson, "Rap Gets Religion, But Is It Gospel?" *Washington Post*, September 24, 2004, C1.

20. "Lil Jon Is the King of Crunk," Associated Press, November 16, 2004, http://www.msnbc.msn.com/id/6505027/ (viewed July 19, 2005).

21. Greil Marcus still has one of the most compelling cultural studies of

the Elvis phenomenon, and rock in general, in *Mystery Train: Images of America in Rock 'n' Roll Music*, rev. ed. (New York: Dutton, 1982), 141–210.

22. Greil Marcus, *Dead Elvis: A Chronicle of a Cultural Obsession* (Cambridge, MA: Harvard University Press, 1991), 154.

23. Michael Ventura, *Shadow Dancing in the USA* (New York: Tarcher, 1985), 156. Also see references in Marcus, *Dead Elvis*; and Gilbert B. Rodman, *Elvis after Elvis: The Posthumous Career of a Living Legend* (New York: Routledge, 1996).

24. Robin Sylvan, *Traces of the Spirit: The Religious Dimension of Popular Music* (New York: New York University Press, 2002), 94–102; also, for broader cultural analyses of the band, see Robert G. Weiner, ed., *Perspectives on the Grateful Dead: Critical Writings* (Westport, CT: Greenwood, 1999).

25. Grateful Dead page at the Rock and Roll Hall of Fame website: http://www.rockhall.com/hof/inductee.asp?id=113 (viewed July 22, 2005).

3. Sports

1. Johan Huizinga, *Homo Ludens: A Study of the Play Element in Culture* (Boston: Beacon, 1955), 28.

2. Ibid., 1, 8.

3. George Orwell, "The Sporting Spirit," available online from "The Complete Works of George Orwell," http://www.georgeorwell.org/The_Sporting_Spirit/0.html (viewed September 9, 2008).

4. Ibid.

5. Michael Novak, *The Joy of Sports: End Zones, Bases, Baskets, Balls, and the Conservation of the American Spirit* (New York: Basic, 1976), 19.

6. Michael Mandelbaum, *The Meaning of Sports: Why Americans Watch Baseball, Football, and Basketball and What They See When They Do* (New York: Public Affairs, 2004).

7. Ibid., 4.

8. Dan Holmes, "Hall of Fame Debuts *Sacred Ground* Exhibit, Celebrating Ballparks and the Fan Experience," Baseball Hall of Fame website: http://web.baseballhalloffame.org/news/article.jsp?ymd=

20070307&content_id=3780&vkey=hof_news (viewed August 8, 2005).

9. Buzz Gray, "New Look Puts Shine on Shrine," *Times Union* (Albany, NY), Saturday, July 30, 2005, C1.

10. Audio of the ceremony is available at the Baseball Hall of Fame website: http://www.baseballhalloffame.org/history/index.htm (viewed August 8, 2005).

11. Steve Hummer, "Halls Aim to Be National Destinations," *Atlanta Journal Constitution*, July 9, 2005, D1.

12. See, for example, Allen Guttmann, "Eros and Sport," in *Essays on Sport History and Sport Mythology*, ed. Donald G. Kyle and Gary Stark (College Station, TX: Texas A&M University Press, 1990).

13. Clifford Geertz, "Deep Play: Notes on the Balinese Cockfight," in *The Interpretation of Cultures: Selected Essays* (New York: Basic, 1973), 448.

14. Erik Brady, "Continuity of Sports Helped Heal the Times," *USA Today*, September 9, 2002. Found at website: http://www.usatoday.com/sports/sept11/2002-09-10-ccover_x.htm (viewed August 19, 2005).

15. Jack Santino, *All Around the Year: Holidays and Celebrations in American Life* (Urbana, IL: University of Illinois Press, 1994), 55.

16. All noted in Edward G. Armstrong, "Michael Jordan and His Uniform Number," in *Michael Jordan, Inc.: Corporate Sport, Media Culture, and Late Modern America*, ed. David L. Andrews (Albany, NY: State University of New York Press, 2001), 17.

17. "Time 25," *Time*, June 17, 1996, 79.

18. Phil Jackson and Hugh Delehanty, *Sacred Hoops: Spiritual Lessons of a Hardwood Warrior* (New York: Hyperion, 1995), 17.

19. Walter LaFeber, *Michael Jordan and the New Global Capitalism* (New York: W.W. Norton, 1999); David Halberstam, *Playing for Keeps: Michael Jordan and the World He Made* (New York: Random House, 1999).

20. Michael Eric Dyson, "Be Like Mike?: Michael Jordan and the Pedagogy of Desire," in *Michael Jordan, Inc.*, 259.

21. Jackson and Delehanty, *Sacred Hoops*, 16–17.

22. Jeff Coplon, "Legends. Champions?" *New York Times Magazine*, April 21, 1996, 8.

23. Ibid., 7.

24. Michael Jordan and Mark Vancil, *I Can't Accept Not Trying: Michael Jordan on the Pursuit of Excellence* (San Francisco: Harper, 1994).

25. Sample customer reviews at Amazon.com: http://www.amazon.com/gp/product/customer-reviews/0062511904/ref=cm_cr_dp_2_1/103-9829198-8563060?%5Fencoding=UTF8&customer-reviews.sort%5Fby=-SubmissionDate&n=283155 (viewed August 31, 2005).

4. Celebrity

1. *The New Oxford Annotated Bible*, ed. Bruce M. Metzger and Ronald E. Murphy (New York: Oxford University Press, 1991), 95.

2. Parts of this discussion are from my book *Rest in Peace: A Cultural History of Death and the Funeral Home in Twentieth-Century America* (New York: Oxford University Press, 2003), 33–38.

3. Emily W. Leider, *Dark Lover: The Life and Death of Rudolph Valentino* (New York: Farrar, Straus, and Giroux, 2003), 315.

4. Ibid., 382–83.

5. Ibid., 390–91.

6. Ibid.

7. Quotes from Samantha Barbas, *Movie Crazy: Fans, Stars, and the Cult of Celebrity* (New York: Palgrave, 2001), 170–71.

8. Quoted in Leider, *Dark Lover*, 391. Broun was originally quoted in *Literary Digest*, September 11, 1926.

9. Irving Shulman, *Valentino* (New York: Trident, 1967). Much of this discussion is found in my book *Rest in Peace*, 35–38.

10. Shulman, *Valentino*, ix.

11. Lynn E. McCutcheon, John Maltby, James Houran, and Diane D. Ashe, *Celebrity Worshippers: Inside the Minds of Stargazers* (Baltimore: Publish America, 2004).

12. See Kate Douglas, "When You Wish Upon a Star," *New Scientist* 179, no. 2408 (August 8, 2003): 26–31. For a discussion of prestige, see Joseph Henrich and Francisco J. Gil-White, "The Evolution of Prestige: Freely Conferred Deference as a Mechanism for Enhancing the Benefits of Cultural Transmission," *Evolution and Human Behavior* 22, no. 3 (2001): 165–96.

13. Daniel Boorstin, *The Image: A Guide to Pseudo-Events in America* (New York: Harper & Row, 1961).

14. Richard Schickel, *Intimate Strangers: The Culture of Celebrity* (New York: Doubleday, 1985).

15. The authors discuss this odd mistake and their findings in Lynn E. McCutcheon, et al., *Celebrity Worshippers*.

16. Ibid., 45–46.

17. Ibid., 167–68.

18. Carlin Flora, "Seeing by Starlight: Celebrity Obsession," *Psychology Today*, July/August 2004, http://psychologytoday.com/articles/pto-20040715-000004.html (viewed January 16, 2006).

19. Eric Burns, "Celebrity Worship Turns Actors into Gods," FOX News.com, September 14, 2003, http://www.foxnews.com/story/0,2933,97215,00.html (viewed October 6, 2005).

20. M. Gail Hammer, "Cultural Saints," in *Religion and American Cultures: An Encyclopedia of Traditions, Diversity, and Popular Expressions*, vol. 3, ed. Gary Laderman and Luis Leon (Santa Barbara, CA: ABC-CLIO, 2003), 447.

21. LaTonya Taylor, "The Church of O," *Christianity Today*, http://www.christianitytoday.com/ct/2002/004/1.38.html (viewed February 3, 2006); for a more scholarly take on Oprah, see Kathryn Lofton's insightful "Practicing Oprah: or, The Prescriptive Compulsion of a Spiritual Capitalism," *Journal of Popular Culture* 39, no. 4 (2006): 599–621.

22. Elsie O'Shaughnessy, "The New Establishment," *Vanity Fair*, October, 1994, 209.

23. Marcia Z. Nelson, *The Gospel According to Oprah* (New York: John Knox Press, 2005).

24. Taylor, "The Church of O."

25. *All Things Considered*, National Public Radio, August 8, 2005; James Poniewozik, "The Year of Charitainment," *Time*, December 19, 2005.

26. Randal C. Archibold, "Where a Young Actor Died and a Legend Was Born," *New York Times*, October 2, 2005, B2.

27. Steve Hummer, "Following a Legend on the 'Dale Trail,'" *Atlanta Journal Constitution*, February 19, 2006, 1, 7.

5. Science

1. Ursula Goodenough, *The Sacred Depths of Nature* (New York: Oxford University Press, 1998).
2. Ibid., chap. 10 and 11, 131–152.
3. See the website that identifies the worldview of religious naturalism: http://www.religiousnaturalism.org/index.html (viewed February 27, 2006).
4. Daniel C. Dennett, *Darwin's Dangerous Idea: Evolution and the Meanings of Life* (New York: Touchstone, 1995), 521.
5. Ibid., 17–20.
6. Ibid., 85. Italics in original.
7. Ibid., 520.
8. Edward O. Wilson, *Consilience: The Unity of Knowledge* (New York: Vintage, 1998), 289.
9. *Science, Philosophy, and Religion: A Symposium* (New York: Conference on Science, Philosophy, and Religion in Their Relation to the Democratic Way of Life, 1941).
10. Albert Einstein to Hans Muehsam, March 30, 1954, Einstein Archive, 38–434. Found in Alice Calaprice, ed., *The Expanded Quotable Einstein* (Princeton, NJ: Princeton University Press, 2000), 18.
11. Marcelo Gleiser, *The Dancing Universe: From Creation Myths to the Big Bang* (New York: Plume, 1997), 235
12. Fritjof Capra, *The Tao of Physics: An Exploration of the Parallels Between Modern Physics and Eastern Mysticism* (Boulder, CO: Shambhala, 1975).
13. Ibid., 303.
14. Ibid., 242–45.
15. Renee Weber, *Dialogues with Scientists and Sages: The Search for Unity* (London: Routledge, 1986), 110–11.
16. See *What the Bleep* website, http://www.whatthebleep.com/groups/ (viewed September 26, 2008).
17. John Gorenfeld, " 'Bleep' of Faith," Salon.com, September 16, 2004, http://dir.salon.com/story/ent/feature/2004/09/16/bleep/ (viewed on March 17, 2006).
18. Portions of this section appeared as "Star Trek as Spiritual Quest," in *Emory Magazine*, Autumn 2006.

19. For one lively, entertaining example of this, see the documentary *Trekkies* by Roger Nygard (1996).

20. See the Doohan space launch website: http://www.spaceservicesinc .com/SpaceLaunch/doohan_message.asp (viewed April 12, 2006).

6. Medicine

1. Brian Skoloff (AP), "Rush Limbaugh Declares Victory in End to Prescription Fraud Case," *Newsday*, May 2, 2006, http://www.news day.com/entertainment/news/wire/sns-ap-limbaugh-painkillers,0 ,4133953.story (viewed May 8, 2006); Laura Crimaldi, "Kennedy Not Alone: Millions Need Rx for Addiction," *Boston Herald*, May 7, 2006, 8.

2. "Teen Pharmaceutical Abuse 'Entrenched,' " Nation in Brief, *Atlanta Journal Constitution*, May 16, 2006, A3.

3. Robert C. Fuller, *Stairways to Heaven: Drugs in American Religious History* (Boulder, CO: Westview, 2000) provides a nice introduction to drug use and religion.

4. See Richard Evans Schultes, Albert Hofmann, and Christian Ratsch, *Plants of the Gods: Their Sacred, Healing, and Hallucinogenic Powers* (Rochester, VT: Healing Arts Press, 2001). For broader discussion of "entheogens," or plant or chemical substances like peyote that are used for religious experiences, see Robert Forte, ed., *Entheogens and the Future of Religion* (San Francisco: Council on Spiritual Practice, 1997).

5. Charles Hudson, *The Southeastern Indians* (Knoxville, TN: University of Tennessee Press, 1976), 353.

6. Fuller, *Stairways to Heaven*, 35–39.

7. Ronald Siegel, *Intoxication: Life in Pursuit of Artificial Pleasure* (New York: E.P. Dutton, 1989); I.M. Lewis, *Ecstatic Religion* (Middlesex, England: Penguin, 1971); Fuller, *Stairways to Heaven*, 155–194.

8. For a comprehensive, well-informed study of drugs in modern society, see David Courtwright, *Forces of Habit: Drugs and the Making of the Modern World* (Cambridge, MA: Harvard University Press, 2002); and on America specifically, see Fuller, *Stairways to Heaven*.

9. William James, *The Varieties of Religious Experience* (New York: Macmillan, 1961), 306.

10. Albert Hofmann, *LSD: My Problem Child* (New York: McGraw-Hill, 1980).

11. Timothy Leary, *High Priest* (New York: World Publishing, 1968), 285.

12. Ray Moynihan and Alan Cassels, "A Disease for Every Pill," *The Nation*, October 12, 2005.

13. Many books have recently been published on the significance of direct-to-consumer advertising to pharmaceutical companies specifically and the dangers associated with their presence in American culture generally. See, for example, John Abramson, *Overdo$ed America: The Broken Promise of American Medicine* (New York: Harper-Collins, 2005); or Marcia Angell, *The Truth About Drug Companies: How They Deceive Us and What to Do About It* (New York: Random House, 2004).

14. For various discussions of this transition, see Paul Starr, *The Social Transformation of American Medicine: The Rise of a Sovereign Profession and the Making of a Vast Industry* (New York: Basic Books, 1982); Natalie Robins, *Copeland's Cure: Homeopathy and the War Between Conventional and Alternative Medicine* (New York: Knopf, 2005); John Duffy, *From Humors to Medical Science* (Urbana, IL: University of Illinois Press, 1993); Hans A. Baer, *Biomedicine and Alternative Healing Systems in America: Issues of Class, Race, Ethnicity, and Gender* (Madison, WI: University of Wisconsin Press, 2001).

15. The following is based on my article "The Cult of Doctors: Harvey Cushing and the Religious Culture of Modern Medicine," *Journal of Religion and Health* 45, no. 4 (December 6, 2007), 533–48.

16. From *Harvey Cushing's Seventieth Birthday Party, April 8, 1939: Speeches, Letters, and Tributes* (New York: Charles C. Thomas, 1939), 69–81.

17. Lori Arviso Alvord and Elizabeth Cohen Van Pelt, *The Scalpel and the Silver Bear: The First Navajo Woman Surgeon Combines Western Medicine and Traditional Healing* (New York: Bantam, 1999), 111.

18. Numerous articles and publications have appeared charting the dramatic rise in American interest in alternative medicine including a 2002 cover story, "The Science of Alternative Medicine," *Newsweek*, December 2, 2002; and even more recently, Benedict Carey, "When Trust in Doctors Erodes, Other Treatments Fill the Void," *New York Times*, February 3, 2006, A1.

19. This global perspective is provided, in part, in the edited collection *Religion and Healing in America*, ed. Linda L. Barnes and Susan S. Sered (New York: Oxford University Press, 2005).

20. Sarah M. Pike, *New Age and Neopagan Religions in America* (New York: Columbia University Press, 2004), 105–106; Robert C. Fuller, *Alternative Medicine and American Religious Life* (New York: Oxford University Press, 1989),113.

7. Violence

1. Much has been written on the evolutionary predisposition of males to be aggressive. See, for example, Michael P. Ghiglieri, *The Dark Side of Man: Tracing the Origins of Male Violence* (Reading, MA: Perseus Books, 1999); or Dale Peterson and Richard Wrangham, *Demonic Males: Apes and the Origins of Human Violence* (New York: Mariner Books, 1997).

2. William Broyles Jr., "Why Men Love War," in *The Vietnam Reader*, ed. Walter Capps (New York: Routledge, 1991), 71 and 78.

3. J. Glenn Gray, *The Warriors: Reflections on Men in Battle* (New York: Harper and Row, 1959), 38–39.

4. Quotation from Robert Jay Lifton and Nicholas Humphrey, eds., *In a Dark Time: Images for Survival* (Cambridge, MA: Harvard University Press, 1984), 64.

5. For one of the best discussions of sacrifice as primitive fact of life for the American nation, see Carolyn Marvin and David W. Ingle, *Blood Sacrifice and the Nation: Totem Rituals and the American Flag* (Cambridge: Cambridge University Press, 1999). Portions of this discussion appear in my article "Violence and Religious Life: Politics, Culture, and the Sacred in the United States," *Nanzan Review of American Studies* (Journal of the Center for American Studies) 29 (2007): 9–22.

6. Edward Tabor Linenthal, *Changing Images of the Warrior in America: A History of Popular Symbolism* (New York: Mellon, 1982).

7. Garry Wills, *John Wayne's America* (New York: Simon & Schuster, 1998).

8. Richard Slotkin's important series on this mythic theme is the most comprehensive exploration. See his *Regeneration Through Violence: The Mythology of the American Frontier, 1600–1800* (New York: Harper

Perennial, 1996 [1973]); *The Fatal Environment: The Myth of the Frontier in the Age of Industrialization* (New York: Atheneum, 1985); and *Gunfighter Nation: The Myth of the Frontier in Twentieth-Century America* (Norman, OK: University of Oklahoma Press, 1998).

9. Quote is from lobbyist Warren Cassidy in Osha Gray Davidson, *Under Fire: The NRA and the Battle for Gun Control* (New York: Henry Holt, 1993), 44.

10. Davidson himself conveys these mystical connections in *Under Fire*, 37–81.

11. Ted Nugent, "Nothing More American Than Our Own NRA Family Party," *Waco Tribune-Herald*, April 15, 2007, http://www.wacotrib.com/opin/content/news/opinion/stories/nugent/0415 2007_wac_nugent.html (viewed September 23, 2008).

12. Wayne LaPierre, 2005 Annual Meeting Speech, archived at www.nra.org/Speech.aspx?id=6023 (viewed June 20, 2006).

13. Dawn C. Chmielewski, "Converting Video Games into Instruments of God," *Los Angeles Times*, May 10, 2006, D1.

14. Ibid.

8. Sexuality

1. Julian M. Davidson and Richard J. Davidson, eds., *The Psychobiology of Consciousness* (New York: Plenum, 1982), 292–93. Also see more recently and more comprehensively, Barry R. Komisaruk, Carlos Beyer-Flores, and Beverly Whipple, *The Science of Orgasm* (Baltimore, MD: Johns Hopkins University Press, 2006).

2. Linda Lovelace and Mike McGrady, *Ordeal* (New York: Kensington, 2006 [1980]).

3. Julia Keller, " 'Deep Throat' Star's Unwitting Impact on American Life Was Huge," *Chicago Tribune*, April 30, 2002, C1.

4. Kenneth Turan, "After Deep Throat, G-Rated Life," *Los Angeles Times*, Calendar Live section, January 2, 2005, 1.

5. Pamela Paul, *Pornified: How Pornography Is Transforming Our Lives, Our Relationships, and Our Families* (New York: Times Books, 2005), 20; and also see recent work by Carmen Sarracino and Kevin M. Scott, *The Porning of America: The Rise of Porn Culture, What It Means, and Where We Go from Here* (Boston: Beacon, 2008).

6. David S. Reynolds, *Beneath the American Renaissance: The Subversive*

Imagination in the Age of Emerson and Melville (Cambridge, MA: Harvard University Press, 1989). Also see the informative British documentary *Pornography: The Secret History of Civilization*, 2002, which includes a section entitled "The Sacred and the Profane," for longer view, as well as Sarracino and Scott, *The Porning of America*.

7. This is described in painstaking detail on her website, http://www.anniesprinkle.org/html/writings/onstage.html, which is found at her popular and informative homepage, http://www.anniesprinkle.org (viewed July 10, 2006).

8. Found at http://www.anniesprinkle.org/html/workshops/ecstasy-breathing-workshop.html (viewed October 6, 2008). She is also co-author with Barbara Carrellas of *Urban Tantra: Sacred Sex for the Twenty-first Century* (New York: Celestial Arts, 2007).

9. Jenna Jameson, *How to Make Love Like a Porn Star: A Cautionary Tale* (New York: HarperEntertainment, 2004).

10. Richard Easton, "Guilt-Free Pleasures," Beliefnet.com, January 2, 2001, http://www.beliefnet.com/story/61/story_6115_1.html (viewed July 5, 2006).

11. Ramon A. Gutierrez, *When Jesus Came, the Corn Mothers Went Away: Marriage, Sexuality, and Power in New Mexico, 1500–1846* (Stanford: Stanford University Press, 1991), 16–17.

12. Much has been written on intersections of race, religion, and sexuality in the South, including Catherine Clinton and Michele Gillespie, eds., *The Devil's Lane: Sex and Race in the Early South* (New York: Oxford University Press, 1997).

13. Mark Jordan, *The Invention of Sodomy in Christian Theology* (Chicago: University of Chicago Press, 1998).

14. Guy Baldwin "Reclaiming the Exiled Self," in Mark Thomson, *Gay Soul: Finding the Heart of Gay Spirit and Nature with Sixteen Writers, Healers, Teachers, and Visionaries* (San Francisco: HarperCollins, 1994), 186.

15. Ibid., 187.

16. Robert H. Hopcke, "The Union of Sames," in Thomson, *Gay Soul*, 222–23.

17. The best overview of these two religious cultures is Sarah M. Pike, *New Age and Neopagan Religions in America* (New York: Columbia University Press, 2006).

18. Pike, *New Age*, 137.

19. Ibid., 137–43.
20. Deepak Chopra, "Sex and Spirituality" at Intentblog: http://www .intentblog.com/archives/2005/06/sex_and_spiritu.html   (viewed October 6, 2008).
21. For details and more comprehensive perspective on this topic, see the interview with Ogden at Oprah.com: http://www.oprah.com/ article/relationships/sex/sexy_spirit (viewed October 6, 2008).
22. Susan Bridle, "An Interview with Margot Anand," *What Is Enlightenment?* Spring/Summer 1998, 54.
23. Alex Comfort, *The Joy of Sex* (New York: Pocket Books, 2003).

9. Death

1. Alice Sebold, *The Lovely Bones* (New York: Little, Brown, 2002), 18.
2. My two previous books are devoted to these cultural efforts: *The Sacred Remains: American Attitudes Toward Death, 1799–1883* (New Haven, CT: Yale University Press, 1996) and *Rest in Peace: A Cultural History of Death and the Funeral Home in Twentieth-Century America* (New York: Oxford University Press, 2003); also relevant here is "Death," in *Religion and American Cultures: An Encyclopedia of Traditions, Diversity, and Popular Expressions*, vol. 2, ed. Gary Laderman and Luis Léon (Santa Barbara, CA: ABC-CLIO, 2003), 365–72.
3. Jessica Mitford, *The American Way of Death* (New York: Knopf, 1963; reissued 1996).
4. Gary Laderman, *A Cultural History of Death and the Funeral Home in Twentieth-Century America* (New York: Oxford University Press, 2003).
5. Jamal Joseph, *Tupac Shakur Legacy* (New York: Atria, 2006), 24.
6. See, for example, Michael Eric Dyson, *Holler if You Hear Me: Searching for Tupac Shakur* (New York: Basic Civitas Books, 2006).
7. Ibid., 97.
8. ThugLifeArmy.com, http://www.thuglifearmy.com/news/?id=8 (viewed September 26, 2006).
9. Jacquie Jones, "Time on the Cross," *Black Renaissance/Renaissance Noire* 1, no. 2 (October 31, 1997): 148–61.
10. For example, see David Menconi, "Larger Than Life: 10 Years after His Death, Tupac Shakur's Legacy Continues to Grow," *The News and Observer* (Raleigh, North Carolina), September 10, 2006, G1;

Nekesa Mumbi Moody, "Tupac Remains Hip-Hop's Most Complex and Compelling Character," Associated Press State and Local Wire, September 12, 2006; Andrew Gumbel, "Tupac: The Life. The Legend. The Legacy," *The Independent* (London), September 13, 2006, News: 24; and Mariel Concepcion and Hashim Warren, "Remembering Tupac, Ten Years Later," Vibe.com, September 13, 2006, http://www.vibe.com/news/online_exclusives/2006/09/remem bering_tupac_shakur_ten_years_later (viewed September 27, 2006).

11. ThugLifeArmy.com, http://www.thuglifearmy.com/news/?id=29 (viewed September 25, 2006).

12. See, for example, Greil Marcus, *Dead Elvis: A Chronicle of a Cultural Obsession* (Cambridge, MA: Harvard University Press, 1991).

13. See, for example, Erika Lee Doss, *Elvis Culture: Fans, Faith, and Image* (Lawrence, KS: University of Kansas Press, 2004); or Gilbert Rodman, *Elvis After Elvis: The Posthumous Career of a Living Legend* (New York: Routledge, 1996).

INDEX

Aaron, Henry, 49
Abdul-Jabbar, Kareem, 57
Adamson, Thomas, 7
addiction, 105–11
Adventures of Col. Daniel Boon, 131
African Americans
  the blues and, 28–33
  hip-hop and, 33–36
  Jordan and, 56
  rock and roll and, 36–38
  slavery and, 150
Ageless Body, Timeless Mind (Chopra),
  96
AIDS, 154
alcohol, 106
Alcott, Louisa May, 163
Ali, Muhammad, 58
All of Me, 164
All Things Considered, 82
altered states of consciousness, 27,
  105–11
Alvord, Lori, 119
Ambien, 105
American Idol, 72
The American Way of Death (Mitford),
  69, 166
Anand, Margot, 158
Ansco Companuy, 3
anthropology and religious life, xv
The Art of Sexual Ecstasy (Anand), 158
The Art of Sexual Magic (Anand), 158
Asimov, Isaac, 98
Associated Press, 35
AstraZeneca, 113–15
atomic bomb, 127
"At the Auction of the Ruby
  Slippers," 16
Auerbach, Red, 57

Baldwin, Guy, 153–54
Balinese cockfighting, 54
Baltimore Colts, 53
Bambi, 10
Banner, David, 35
baseball, 43, 48–51
Baseball Hall of Fame, 43, 48–51,
  62
  opening of, 50
  rededication ceremonies, 49
  "Reverence," 48–49
  "Sacred Ground," 43, 48–49
  as a shrine, 50–51
basketball, 56–62
Baum, L. Frank, 13
Beatles, 93–94
Beetlejuice, 164
"Be Like Mike?: Michael Jordan and
  the Pedagogy of Desire,"
  58–59
Beloved (Morrison), 163
Bhagavad Gita, 9, 87
Bible
  film and, 1–5
  idol worship and, 63–64
  rituals and, 2–3
Big D Jamboree, 37
biomedical dominance, 116–20
Bird, Larry, 56, 57
Black Elk Speaks, 9
"Black Jesus," 173, 174–75
Black Renaissance, 177
Blood and Sand, 65
blues music, 28–33
  crossroads myth and, 28–29
  as the devil's music, 29–30
  everyday realities and, 31–32
  as godless, 30

blues music (*cont.*)
  revitalized black communities and,
    30–31
  sexuality and, 29, 30
  transformative power of, 31–33
Boggs, Wade, 49
Bohm, David, 95
Bohr, Niels, 92–93
Boorstin, Daniel, 73–74
Boston Celtics, 56
Boston Red Sox, 51
Brady, Erik, 55
brain surgery, 118–19
Broun, Heywood, 69
Brown, Jim, 58
Broyles, William, Jr., 126
Bryant, Professor M. Darrol, 7–8
Buddhism, xiii, 28, 59, 87, 93
Burns, Eric, 76–77
Burns, Ken, 51

Caffey, Jason, 60
Campbell, Joseph, 18–19
Capra, Fritjof, 94–95
Carolina Panthers, 51
Castaneda, Carlos, 94
Catholicism, 3, 171
celebrity, 63–84
  critics of culture surrounding,
    74–77
  death and, 82–83, 99, 101, 171–80
  group pathology and, 65–71, 75
  idol worship, 63–65, 71, 77
  Jordan, 56–62
  as media-created, 73–77
  Oprah, 77–82
  as pervasive and powerful force,
    71–72
  product endorsements and, 103–4
  psychological profiles and, 74–77
  shrines to, 70
  twentieth century, 64–65, 71
  Valentino, 65–71
Celebrity Worshippers (Houran), 76
"Celebrity Worship Scale," 74–75
"Celebrity Worship Turns Actors
    into Gods," 76–77

Chamberlain, Wilt, 57
Chappelle, Dave, 173
Cheever, John, 163
Chesterton Wizard of Oz Festival, 16
Chicago Bulls, 56–57, 60
Chicago Tribune, 56
childhood, journey out of, 11–12,
    18–19
Chopra, Deepak, 156
Christ, Jesus, 56–57, 81
Christianity, 2–3, 28
  film industry and, 4
  sexuality and, 144–45, 148–50
  video games and, 139–40
Christianity Today, 81
Christian Wisdom of the Jedi Masters,
    19
Chuck D, 36
"The Church of O," 81
Cinderella, 10
"Cinema, Religion, and Popular
    Culture," 7–8
Clinton, Hillary, 134
Cobain, Kurt, 82, 178
coffee, 106
The College Dropout (West), 34–35
"Colors," 35
Coltrane, John, 94
Columbia University, 97
Comfort, Alex, 159–60
Comiskey Park, 43
complementarity, 92–93
Cone, James, 30
Congress, 26
consciousness, 96
Cooper, James Fenimore, 131
copying behavior, 72–73
cosmic soup, 28
cowboys, Hollywood, 129–32
creationism, 89
Cronenberg, David, 119
Crowe, Russell, 73
Crunk Juice, 35
crunk music, 35
crystals, 121–22
cults, 15, 46, 71, 98
  medical, 117–20

"cultural saints," 41
Cushing, Harvey, 118–19

Dances with Wolves, 130–31
The Dancing Wu Li Masters (Zukav),
    95
Darwin, Charles, 89, 90
Darwin's Dangerous Idea (Dennett), 90
Davis, Harry, 5
Dead Ringers, 119
Dean, James, 82, 83
death, 161–80
    ancestors, 171
    celebrity and, 82–83, 99, 101,
        171–80
    cultural responses to, 166–69
    films about, 164–65
    funeral homes, 67–68, 168–71
    ghosts, 161–66
    Hollywood and, 65–71
    literature about, 163–64, 166
    music culture and, 38, 41
    relations between living and,
        163–66
    sacred, 171
    science and, 87–88
    sex and, 159–60
    triumph over, 10–11, 46
    in war, 127–30, 171
Deep Inside Annie Sprinkle, 146
Deep Throat, 144–45
DeGeneres, Ellen, 151–52
The Deluge, 4
DeMille, Cecil B., 4
Dennett, Daniel, 90–91
Depp, Johnny, 82
"devil's music," 29–30, 33
The Dharma of Star Wars, 19
Diana, Princess, 73, 82, 178
DiMaggio, Joe, 58
Disney, Walt, 9–12
DMX, 34
doctors, 116–20
Doohan, James, 101
Doom, 136
Do the Right Thing, 36
Doubleday, Abner, 51

Doyle, Charles, 50
Dr. 90210, 118
drug abuse, 26, 104–11
Dylan, Bob, 82
Dyson, Michael Eric, 58–59

Eakins, Thomas, 119
Earnhardt, Dale, 82, 83
Eastern philosophies, 92–98, 156,
    157–58
Eastman, George, 1, 3–4
Easton, Richard, 148
East Side Boyz, 35
Edison, Thomas, 3–4
The Ed Sullivan Show, 37
Einstein, Albert, 91–92
Eisenstein, Sergei, 11
Eliot, Charles, 69
The Entombment 2004, 83
Erdrich, Louise, 163
erectile dysfunction, 115
ESPN, 57–58
ET: The Extraterrestrial, 5
Evil Dead, 136
evolution, 85
    celebrity and, 72–73
    music and, 24–25
    science and, 85–91
experimental science, 116
"The Eyes," 163

Farrar, Jay, 39
Farrell, Thomas, 127
fetishism, 113–15
Field of Dreams, 48
"Fight the Power," 36
film, 1–22
    beginnings of the industry, 1, 3–4
    Biblical stories and, 4–5
    celebrity and, 65–71
    children and, 9–12
    as competing with the Bible, 1–3
    death and, 164–65
    Disney, 9–12
    family and, 12
    theater architecture, 6–7
    values and, 8–12

film (*cont.*)
  viewing, as a ritual activity, 5–8
  see also Star Wars saga; *The Wizard
    of Oz*
Filson, John, 131
Food and Drug Administration, 113
football, 44, 51–56
Forbes Field, 43
The Four Horsemen of the Apocalypse,
  65
FOXNews, 76–77
Frank E. Campbell Funeral Home,
  67–68
Franks, Jerome, 7
Freud, Sigmund, 90
From the Manger to the Cross, 4
"Fun with Ecstasy Breathing and
  Energy Orgasms," 147

Garcia, Jerry, 40, 41
Garland, Judy, 13, 15, 82, 83
gastroesophageal reflux disease,
  113–15
Gaye, Marvin, 158–59
Geertz, Clifford, 54
Ghost, 164
The Ghost and Mrs. Muir, 164
Ghost Recon, 137
ghosts, 161–66
Ghost Town, 165
Gibson, Mel, 4–5, 139
Glass, Brent, 15
God
  American belief in, xiii
  death and, 162
  drugs and, 111
  films and, 13, 16–21
  Jordan as, 56–57
  music and, 30
  religious life without, xvii–xviii
  science and, 85–92
  war and, 124
Goodenough, Ursula, 85–89, 91
good over evil, 11–12, 18
Goodwin, Reverend Hannibal W., 1,
  3, 4, 18
Gorenfeld, John, 97, 98

The Gospel According to Oprah, 80
gospel music, 34–35
Gottlieb, Meyer, 98
Graham, Billy, 80
Grand Theft Auto, 137
Grandview Theater, 7
Grateful Dead, 39–42
Gray, J. Glenn, 126
The Great Train Robbery, 5, 130
The Gross Clinic, 119
Gun, 137
guns, 127, 132–35

hallucinogens, 105–11
Halo, 137
Hammer, M. Gail, 77
Hancock, Butch, 37–38
Hanks, Tom, 77
Hawthorne, Nathaniel, 163
Heart and Souls, 164
Heaven Can Wait, 164
Heisenberg, Werner, 94
Hendrix, Jimi, 82, 178
Herbert, Frank, 98
The Hero with a Thousand Faces
  (Campbell), 19
Heston, Charlton, 73, 134
High Priest (Leary), 111
Hinduism, xiii, 28, 93, 94, 95, 135
hip-hop, 33–36
  as expression of black culture,
    33–34
  reality of the streets and, 35
  religion and, 34–36
Hofmann, Albert, 110
Homo Ludens (Huizinga), 45
homosexuality, 151–54
Hondo, 129–30
Hopcke, Robert H., 154
hospitals, 116–20
Houran, James, 76
House of Prayer Episcopal Church, 1
House of the Seven Gables
  (Hawthorne), 163
How the West Was Won, 129–30
How to Make Love Like a Porn Star
  (Jameson), 147–48

Hudson, Rock, 154
Huizinga, Johan, 45
I Can't Accept Not Trying (Jordan), 61
Ice T, 35
imitation, 72–73
Immigration Act of 1965, 94
The Innocents, 164
Inside the Actors Studio, 76–77
Internet Movie Database, 14
Ironweed (Kennedy), 163
Irving, Washington, 163
Islam, 2, 35
It's Dark and Hell Is Hot, 34

Jackson, Janet, 51–53, 55
Jackson, Phil, 57, 59
Jackson, Stonewall, 129
James, William, 109
Jameson, Jenna, 147–48
Jefferson, Blind Lemon, 29
Jefferson, Thomas, 150
"Jesus Walks," 34
John Paul II, Pope, xiii
Johnson, Robert, 28
Johnson, Walter, 50
Jolie, Angelina, 82
Jones, Jacquie, 177
Jordan, Michael, 56–62, 82
Journal of Nervous and Mental Disease,
    74
Journal of Psychology, 74
The Joy of Sex (Comfort), 159–60
The Joy of Sports (Novak), 46–47
Judaism, 2, 3, 28, 31, 34, 63–64, 135

Kama Sutra, 157
Kennedy, John F., 60–61, 166
Kennedy, Patrick, 105
Kennedy, William, 163
Kerry, John, 134
KiMo Theater, 6
King, Martin Luther, Jr., 34
King of Crunk, 35
Knight, Judy, 97–98
Knight, Suge, 172
Kodak, 1, 3–4

Koran, 2, 35
Kournikova, Anna, 82
Krishnamurti, Jiddu, 94, 95

LaFeber, Walter, 58
Landis, Kennesaw Mountain, 50
Lang, Fritz, 98
LaPierre, Wayne, 134–35
Larsen, Deborah, 7
"Latin Lover," 65–71
Leary, Timothy, 110–11
Leatherstocking Tales (Cooper), 131
Lee, Spike, 36
Left Behind series video games,
    139
"The Legend of Sleepy Hollow,"
    163
"The Legend of the Ancient Sacred
    Prostitute," 147
Lennon, John, 82
The Life of Moses, 4
Lil John, 35
Limbaugh, Rush, 105
Lincoln, Abraham, 128, 169
Lion King, 11
Lipitor, 112
Lipton, James, 76–77
"live your best life," 80–81
Loews 72nd Street Theater, 6
Lombardi, Vince, 53
*The Lord of the Rings: The Return of the
    King,* 5
love, 88
Lovelace, Linda, 144, 145
The Lovely Bones (Sebold), 163–64
LSD, 110–11
Lucas, George, 17, 18
Lunesta, 112

Madonna, 82
Malcolm X, 34
Mandelbaum, Michael, 47
Manning, Tom, 50
Matisyahu, 34
Mayer, Louis B., 12
The Meaning of Sports (Mandelbaum),
    47

medicine, 103–22
    alternative, 120–22
    biomedical dominance, 116–20
    celebrity endorsements, 103–4
    drug abuse, 104–11
    "good health" and, 104, 111–12
    healing and, 116–22
    prescription, 111–15
Michael Jordan and the New Global
    Capitalism (LaFeber), 58
Mitford, Jessica, 69, 166
Mohammed, 34
Monroe, Marilyn, 82, 178
morality
    Hollywood, 66, 68–69
    sports and, 51–53, 56, 58, 61
Morrison, Toni, 163
Moses, 39, 63–64
Munchkin Convention, 16
music, 23–42
    binding communities, 23–28
    concerts, 39–42
    early American, 25–26
    impact of, 24
    raves, 23, 26–28
    see also blues music; hip-hop; rock
        and roll
Music and the Mind (Storr), 24
myths, 13–14

Namath, Joe, 53
National Institutes of Health, 120
National Public Radio, 82
National Rifle Association (NRA),
    133–35
Native Americans, 31, 107–8
    sexuality and, 149–50
natural selection, 90
Nature, 85–89
New England Patriots, 51
New Testament, 2, 53, 63
New York Jets, 53
New York Times, 60, 147
New York Yankees, 51
Nexium, 113–15
Nietzsche, Friedrich, 90
Nike, 56–57, 60

Nimoy, Leonard, 103–4, 112
nitrous acid, 109
No Depression, 39
Notre Dame, 44
Novak, Michael, 46–47
Nugent, Ted, 134

Ogden, Gina, 157
"Oh Father, Father Why Have You
    Come Back?", 163
Old Testament, 2, 9, 39, 141, 142–43
Oliver, Paul, 29–30
Olympic Games, 45, 46, 47, 51–52,
    56
Onassis, Jackie, 83
"Only God Can Judge Me," 174
The Oprah Winfrey Show, 15
Orbison, Roy, 37
Ordeal, 144
Orwell, George, 45–46
OxyContin, 105
Ozmopolitan Convention, 16

The Passion of the Christ, 4–5, 96, 139
Patton, Charlie, 29
Paxil, 112
Personality and Individual Differences, 74
Petroskey, Dale, 48
Peyote Church, 31, 105–6
The Phantom Menace, 20
pharmaceutical companies, 112–15
physics, 92–98
pilgrims, 50, 100
Pinocchio, 10, 11
Pippin, Scottie, 60–61
Pitt, Brad, 82
plastic surgery, 118
playing games, 44–46, 62
PLUR (peace, love, unity, respect), 26
PMDD (premenstrual dysphoric
    disorder), 113
Polo Grounds, 43
pornography, 141, 143–48
power and empowerment, 55–56
Presley, Elvis, 36–38, 58, 82, 169, 172,
    178–80
Prilosec, 112, 113

Progressive Baptist Church, 78
Protestantism, 2–3, 64
　music and, 25–26
Prozac, 112, 113
Psychology Today, 75–76
Public Enemy, 36

Quantum Healing (Chopra), 96
quantum theory, 92–98
questions, enduring human, xiv

racism, 29, 36
Rajneesh, Bhagwan, 158
Ramtha's School of Enlightenment,
　98
rap music, 33–36, 41, 172–78
rave culture, 23, 26–28, 109
"Rave New World," 26
Reems, Harry, 144–45
religious naturalism, 85–89
Return of the Jedi, 18
rituals
　Bible inspired, 2–3
　celebrity and, 79
　drugs and, 115–16
　funerary, 161–62
　going to the movies, 5–8
　sports and, 45–48, 62
Robinson, Brooks, 49
rock and roll, 36–42
　dancing and, 37–38
　Elvis and, 36–38
　Grateful Dead and, 39–42
　live concerts and, 39–42
　religion and, 38–39
　roots of, 36
Rock and Roll Hall of Fame, 41
Roddenberry, Gene, 99, 101
Rodman, Dennis, 60–61
Ross, A. Larry, 139
Roxy Theater, 6–7
Rushdie, Salman, 16–17
Ruth, Babe, 49, 50, 51, 58

The Sacred Depths of Nature
　(Goodenough), 85–89
sacred texts, xiii, 1–3, 9, 16

Sandburg, Ryne, 49
Sanford, Tom, 83
Santino, Jack, 55–56
The Scalpel and the Silver Bear
　(Alvord), 119
science, 85–102
　death and, 87–88
　debates about religion and,
　　85–92
　Eastern philosophies and, 93–98
　evolution and, 85–91
　God and, 85–92
　medicine and, 116–20
　physics and, 92–98
　sex and, 87–88
　surgery, 119
science fiction, 98–102
The Searchers, 129–30
Sebold, Alice, 163–64
Second Amendment, 132–34
"The Second Coming," 59
secular humanism, 89–90, 99
secular sources of religious
　experience, xv–xviii
　see also specific sources
"Seeing by Starlight: Celebrity
　Obsession," 75–76
September 11th, xiii, 55, 80, 123–24
"Sexual Healing," 158–59
sexuality, 141–60
　battles and conflicts over, 150–51
　the blues and, 29, 30
　Christianity and, 144–45, 148–50
　death and, 159–60
　drugs and, 111
　Eastern, 156, 157–58
　homosexuality, 151–54
　neo-paganism, 155–56
　New Age, 155
　nonreproductive sex, 155–56
　orgasm and, 142, 158, 159–60
　pornography, 14, 143–48
　rock and roll and, 37
　sadomasochism, 153–54
　science and, 87–88
Shakur, Afeni, 173, 174
Shakur, Tupac, 41, 82, 83, 172–78

Shane, 130
Shatner, William, 102
"A Short Text about Magic," 16
Shulman, Irving, 69–70
Shyamalan, M. Night, 165
Simpson, O.J., 59
Sinatra, Frank, 82
The Sixth Sense, 165
"slash fiction," 20, 21
slavery, 150
Sleeping Beauty, 10
Smith, Mamie, 29
Smithsonian Institution, 15
Snoop Dog, 177–78
Snow White and the Seven Dwarfs,
    10–11
Son of a Sheik, 65
South End Grounds, 49
The Spiral Dance (Starhawk), 156
"The Spirit," 60
spiritual anchors, xv
Splinter Cell, 137
sports, 43–62
    baseball, 43, 48–51
    basketball, 56–62
    books about, 46–47
    criticism of, 45–46
    fans and ballparks, 48–49, 55
    football, 51–56
    high stakes in, 48, 51, 55
    morality and, 51–53, 56, 58, 61
    nudity, 51–52
    organized play, 44–46, 62
    pilgrims, 50
    religion and, 43–55, 58–62
Sprinkle, Annie, 146–47
The Square Trap (Shulman), 70
Stagecoach, 130
Starhawk, 156
Star Trek, 99–104
Star Wars Battlefield, 136
Star Wars Chicks, 21
Star Wars Roleplaying Game, 20
Star Wars saga, 5, 17–22
    communities of feeling and, 20
    as godless, 17–18, 19–20, 21
    impact of, 18, 19–22

journey of the hero and, 18–19
    religion and, 17–18, 19–22
Stellar Awards, 34–35
Storr, Anthony, 24
Strike Force, 137
Sunshine, 23, 26
Super Bowl, 51–56, 62, 103

"Take Me Out to the Ball Game," 49
Taoism, 28, 93
The Tao of Physics (Capra), 94–95
The Tao of Star Wars, 19
Taylor, LaTonya, 81
Ten Commandments, 39, 63–64
The Ten Commandments, 134
Teresa of Avila, Saint, 73
"Theologians," 161
thuglifearmy.com, 175–77
Tibetan Book of the Dead, xiii
Ticket to Paradise, 7
Tiger Stadium, 48, 49
Time, 26, 57, 82
tobacco, 107–8
Topper, 164
Tracks (Erdrich), 163
transcendence, 30–33, 79, 80
transformation, 32–33, 79, 80, 115,
    121, 124–25, 153–54
True Grit, 129–30
Truly Madly Deeply, 164
Twain, Mark, 98
Tweedy, Jeff, 161, 162

Uncle Tupelo, 39
Upanishads, xiii
USA Today, 27, 55
U2, 55

Valentino, Rudolph, 65–71, 83, 169
values
    cowboy, 129–32
    film and, 8–12
    sports and, 61
Vandenberg Air Force Base, 101
Vanity Fair, 79–80
The Varieties of Religious Experience
    (James), 109

"A Variety of Religious Experience,"
47
Ventura, Michael, 37–38
Verne, Jules, 98
Veterans Stadium, 49
Viagra, 112, 115
Vicodin, 105
video games, 135–40
Vietnam War, 126
violence, 123–40
    cinematic cowboys, 129–32
    God and, 124
    guns, 127, 132–35
    video games, 135–40
    war, 123–29
Vioxx, 113

Waco Tribune Herald, 134
war, 123–29, 171
Washington, George, 129
wave function, 95
Wayne, John, 129–30
Wells, H.G., 98
West, Kanye, 34–35
western films, 129–32
West Theater, 7
Wharton, Edith, 163
What the Bleep?! . . . , 96–98
"Whiskey Bottle," 39

"A Whisper in the Dark," 163
"Why Men Love War," 126
Williams, Raymond, 20
Wilson, Edward O., 91
Winfrey, Oprah, 15, 74–77, 157
Winkie Convention, 16
The Wizard of Oz, 12–17
    attraction of, 14–15
    fans of, 15–16
    as indictment of religion, 13, 16
    power of myth and, 13–14
    religious cultures and, 16–17
    ruby slippers, 15, 16, 83
Women Who Love Sex (Ogden),
157
The Wonderful Wizard of Oz (Baum),
13
World of Warcraft, 139
World Trade Center, 55
Wrigley Field, 49

X-tastyle, 23, 26

Yankee Stadium, 43
"The Year of Charitainment," 82
Young, Cy, 50
Young Doctor Kildare, 119

Zukav, Gary, 95